RIDE THE HORSE
IN THE DIRECTION
IT'S GOING

A TRUE TALE OF TRAVEL, CULTURES, AND SPIRITUAL HAPPENINGS

D1827198

To Megan and John

Remembering our
Tibetan adventures

Joyce

JOYCE RASBACH

Outskirts Press, Inc.
Denver, Colorado

Outskirts Press, Inc.
http://www.outskirtspress.com

ISBN: 978-1-4327-3656-9

Library of Congress Control Number: 2009920235

Outskirts Press and the "OP" logo are trademarks belonging to Outskirts Press, Inc.

PRINTED IN THE UNITED STATES OF AMERICA

Contents

The Author

J oyce was a stay-at-home mother and wife, real estate and fine art sales person until her long-wished-for trip to Mongolia in 1995 finally happened, ending by traveling the Trans-Siberian Railway to Moscow. It was a trip that changed her view of the world and its people.

Some twenty trips later she has learned that:

* Traveling alone, or with a single partner, allows one to get close to the local people, their families, their customs, and their beliefs.
* Stickers on the backs of childrens' hands are always a success.
* One can put up with a lot: countless decrepit vehicles always breaking down, filthy cold hotels, pillow covers stuffed with dried beans and forever unwashed, being interrogated and kicked out of a country, guides that have you lost at midnight, horrible roads, and marooned at a military checkpoint for hours while your guide and driver search for a solution to being declared illegal.
* There are rewards like drinking goat milk tea with a poor

woman in a shack on a remote hillside in Sikkim; living with nomadic Mongolians; trekking with a Nepalese guide who knows all of the Eagles' songs and explains about the mountain spirits that protect his village; walking with a monk who unexpectedly recounts his life story; shamanic cleansings in Ecuador; spiritual meditations at ancient stone circles on the barren moors in Cornwall; discovering mystical wall designs of the centuries-old Bon religion; living with an Afghan family and teaching at girls' schools in Kabul in 2002; kind ministries of women everywhere.

This is a book of Joyce's insights gained through travel:

* People everywhere are kind, caring and sharing.
* People are basically the same the world over.
* People espouse countless religious beliefs which, at their core, follow Buddha's suggestion that, "All paths lead to the top of the mountain".

For those of you who have already ventured to these remote spots, I think you will find yourself laughing and nodding at her adventures. And for those who will never physically visit these places, I hope that reading each chapter will bring to life the wonderful people and incredible cultures around the world. Peek into their lives and homes, and maybe, just maybe, you will find yourself contemplating such a journey.

Joyce and I live in Evergreen, Colorado. From inside our house, part way up a mountain and surrounded by evergreens, one can look out and see several long prayer flags wafting gently in the breeze. This is indeed the home of a "traveler".

Jim Rasbach
November 2008

To Jim, my husband,

without whom this

effort would never

have reached fruition

THE TRAVELER

As a traveler rather than a tourist
What have I learned?

To speak English slowly and expressively
And to use my hands to communicate.
To smile and offer "hello" to everyone.
To admire every woman's and child's apparel
And put stickers on every child's hand.
To ask before taking pictures
And to always send copies of photos as promised.

To accept graciously whatever food is put before me
Knowing full well dishes have not been truly washed,
That flies have had a part in the preparation.
Never to refuse the hospitality drink.
To watch and imitate my host's behavior.
To happily sit on or lie on whatever is offered.
To gratefully take a child's grimy hand while walking.
To immediately fit into each situation as best I can
Regardless of how little time I have to assess it.
Never to stand back reluctantly.
Always to accept the friendly offer
And most importantly, to offer in return
My friendship without reserve.

This is how I make the "people connection"
If there is one waiting for me.
This is what encourages others to tell me
Their personal inner thoughts.
This is what makes us friends for life.

You never know what is out there --
Waiting for you, the traveler.

Joyce Rasbach

Mongolia and the
Trans-Siberian Railroad

Beijing - Disaster on My First Solo Trip

I t is July 1995 and I am on my first trip alone -- to Mongolia - to be followed by riding the Trans-Siberian Railroad to Moscow. It is 1:30 a.m., Beijing time as I land at the Beijing airport. Retrieving my backpack from the carousel, I walk outside to find a taxi. The first cab in line is driven by a very young man, about 18 years old. I get in. He can't speak English, naturally. I tell him the name of the hotel I want, but he knows nothing about what I am saying. I show him a map of Beijing in the Lonely Planet Guide book and indicate that we should go to the southwest area of the city. So off we go on one freeway and then another. I completely lose my sense of direction and leave it all to the cabbie. Forty minutes later we reach the southwest sector of the city. I tell him the hotel name and address again but it means nothing to him. I indicate that he should ask another taxi driver and finally he stops one. I tell the other driver the name of the hotel, and he gives directions to my driver who then proceeds in one direction, then turns around and goes in another. It is obvious he has never been in this section of the city, which is certainly not a tourist area. After a few minutes of this casting about for the correct street to no avail, I motion that he should again ask another cabbie whom he then pulls over. Again I tell the name of the hotel and the road. More directions are forth coming. After another ten minutes of hit or miss driving, my driver pulls into a very short driveway off the road, stops the vehicle and motions that here "it" is.

I indicate that he should go to make sure. He locks me in the cab and disappears for about five minutes. I am beginning to feel extremely uneasy. After all it is 2:30 a.m. I am exhausted, having left that morning in Denver for Los Angeles and eventually boarded my plane for China which took twelve hours to reach Beijing. Now, at least an hour into our "drive" about the city, I can't wait to see the hotel. My driver returns, unlocks the door, climbs in, turns around and makes a sign of crossing his hand across his throat. He is indicating that either there is no hotel or that it is closed! I can't believe it -- it's not possible. He must have made some mistake. I motion him to go back and look again. He soon returns and makes the same motion across his throat! I stare at him. Then he indicates that I should get out and accompany him. I am reluctant to get out in this strange city, in an area that not even the driver knows, in the pitch black of night. He encourages me and I open the door and get out. He locks the cab which makes me feel even more uncomfortable. We walk ahead about fifty yards to a wall with a small printed sign pasted on it. I peer at it in the semidarkness of street lights and realize that it is written in English and says, "This hotel has been closed by the department of health for reasons of unsanitary problems!" This cannot be happening! I have the paper from the tour company with the hotel name and address on it. There is no WAY it can be closed!

The young man signals we should return to the car. Probably he is not any more at ease in this area than me. He unlocks the door and I get in. I just sit here considering what my options are, if any. I feel so vulnerable. The driver turns around in the seat and makes a

2

sign with his two palms together and resting on the side of his tilted head. I realize he is asking me if I want him to find me a hotel and I nod yes. We drive around for a couple minutes and draw up to a small hotel. I indicate that he should go in to see if there is a room. He returns and shakes his head "no". So I urge him to go on. Soon we stop at another hotel. There are many small hotels for Chinese travelers where no one speaks English. He checks again, but returns with another negative shake of the head.

I urge him on; once more he stops at another hotel, this one with two doormen (or are they security men?). He asks them about a room and they tell him that the hotel is full. So I ask them with sign language to call other hotels which makes more sense than driving around until morning to no avail. Surprisingly they understand my request and one man dials on his cell phone. After several attempts, he indicates that there is a hotel with a vacancy and off we drive to find it.

The driver pulls up in front and indicates that here we are! I motion that I need help with my backpack and to fill out the necessary paperwork. He has finally realized what a pathetic creature I am and how much I am depending on him. So he accompanies me inside. After I register, I pay him what he indicates plus a good tip (I think, but I still don't know the value of the money) and say farewell to my first and only "friend" in Beijing, knowing that I can't communicate with anyone in this hotel.

The deskman leads me upstairs to my room, opens the door, lays down my backpack and leaves. I look around and note that the furniture looks as if someone threw it out the window, retrieved the pieces and brought them back in. There are holes in the furniture, and handles are missing. A bare light bulb hangs down on a wire from the ceiling providing the only light. Locking the door, I prepare to make this place a temporary "home".

It is unbearably hot and humid. But I realize I must close the window since I am on just the second floor. I pull the tattered curtain across the window and sit down wearily on the bed. Taking off all my clothes but leaving my money belt around my waist I lie down at last.

As totally exhausted as I am, thoughts start to swirl around in my head. What am I going to do in the morning? My information from the tour company in Hong Kong gives the name of my destination hotel and also a phone number to call (to the hotel which is now closed). Tomorrow is Sunday but I note that the office of the liaison group in Beijing will be open from noon to 5 p.m. on Sunday. The office in Hong Kong, through which I made all my arrangements and sent all my payments, is closed on Sunday. The permit to visit Mongolia will take two days to process and, if I manage to connect with some local person, cannot be undertaken until Monday. The tour group will fly off Tuesday to Ulaan Baatar (capital of Mongolia). Of course, there is no guarantee that I can manage to reach either the Beijing or Hong Kong office. So it looks doubtful that I will be able to catch up with the tour.

Then what happens? I begin to have visions of taking a taxi to a "tourist" hotel in the morning where someone can help me to change my return flight to tomorrow. I will return to Evergreen with my head drooping and my husband and friends all saying "We told you so; you couldn't do this alone!" What a disappointing finale to this ill-starred attempt at solo travel. Exhaustion is finally claiming my mind and I stop conjecturing and give in to closing my eyes.

Morning comes all too soon. I'm awake by 8 a.m., dress and go out into the halls, wandering up and down looking for a live person. Finally, I spot a man carrying a load of towels which he is presumably about to deliver. I ask him if he speaks English and he says, "a little". I tell him I need him to make a phone call for me at 1 p.m. and we agree to meet right at this exact spot and he will do it for me. On the way back to my room, I see a woman in business attire walking toward a room labeled Business Office. I ask her if she speaks English and she says, "Yes"! She agrees to make a phone call for me at 1:00 p.m. because that is the moment that the office of Moonsky Star (alias Monkey Business in Beijing) opens on Sunday. We will try the number I have in my information pack.

I return to my room, alternately trying to rest and trying to figure out my next moves if I get nowhere with the phone call at 1 p.m. I truly am a nervous wreck.

Somehow the minutes and hours tick away until it is almost 1 p.m. I walk to the Business Center, the woman is there waiting for me. I give her the phone number and she dials, listens briefly and passes the phone to me. It is a recording in ENGLISH explaining that the current phone number of Monkey Business has changed! I absolutely cannot believe I am hearing an English voice! I ask the woman to dial the new number for me, which she does and hands the phone to me. A voice answers. I tell him who I am and where I am staying. He says rudely, "What are you doing there? We sent out 200 notices to our customers telling them that we had changed our office location." I tell him that I never received a notice and he really doesn't believe me until I repeat it several times. Finally he tells me the new address and I tell him that I will be there as soon as I pay my bill and get a cab.

I just cannot grasp that I have made contact with the English-speaking world and will enter it very shortly. It seems impossible. However, I am thrilled beyond words.

Within half an hour my cab pulls up in front of a hotel where the Reception person speaks English! He directs me to the Monkey Business Office. I reach it, open the door and feel a rush of air conditioning! As I walk in I see that both sides of a small narrow room are lined with chairs filled with people. One says, "Hi!" Yes, this IS the English world at last. My ordeal is over.

The person behind the desk tells me that he needs at least one day (tomorrow) to process my application for a visa for Mongolia. So although the rest of the people in the room will depart tomorrow for Ulaan Baatar as planned, I will have to go a day later. It sounds just great to me!

I check in and get a room (also miraculously air conditioned) which is a far cry from the one I had last night.

I eat at the restaurant next to the hotel. Obviously I am ahead of the crowd. There is only one other person here who looks at me as I pass and says, "Hi". How nice to hear English even here. I order chicken in peanuts and peppers (very hot), and rice and spinach. Also two bottles of beer.

When I finish and am walking out, the man who was there eating when I arrived invites me to sit down and have a beer! Well, why not? I discover Carl fought in Vietnam and then returned home. But he felt quite unsettled. He contacted his military buddies and found they had been fighting as "soldiers of fortune" in various parts of the world since they left Vietnam. They invited him to join them, which he did. Who would think I would meet a mercenary soldier here in Beijing. I have always regarded them as despicable, but here is a nice guy telling me that he had fought as one. Finally he tired of the job which entailed moving to new locations constantly. He moved to Africa where he started his own safari company which he has owned for twenty-five years. Now I am beginning to see the advantage of traveling alone where I can chat with anyone and meet fabulously interesting people.

I am in bed by 8:30 after a glorious bath.

In the morning I meet a girl named Mia in the lobby and we have breakfast together. She is not planning to visit Mongolia but will take the Trans-Siberian railroad to Moscow when her friend arrives in a couple days. Monkey Business is securing her visa.

Since we have a day to kill, we decide to rent bicycles at the hotel and pedal off into the streets of Beijing. The city streets have a bicycle lane so the venture proves safe enough and loads of fun. We ride on many side streets where water melon is for sale everywhere.

Late in the afternoon I return to Monkey Business to get my visa. I find a bank to obtain more one-dollar bills in return for larger currency American money. They will only give me twenty of them after much insistence on my part. I recognize the man, Carl, from the restaurant last night at the bank and he agrees to ask for single dollar bills for me. But he can only procure ten of them. He says he has several rolls of quarters and sells me one, although I can't imagine what good they will do me in Mongolia.

Mia and I have dinner together. I am in bed very early since I have to be up by 5:00 a.m. to get my taxi for the airport. In the morning I have time to eat at an outside restaurant where Chinese riding their bikes buy "fast food" on their way to work. I finally go up to the order kiosk and point at what looks like rice in hot water (rice porridge) and the nice woman points to the sugar to which I nod in agreement.

I am in the lobby waiting for a pre-arranged and prepaid taxi at 7:30. The driver doesn't show until 8:45. In the meantime I am quite nervous about missing my plane. However, I don't have enough yuan left to hire another taxi since Monkey Business exchanged most of my yuan late yesterday for one-dollar bills.

Finally the driver arrives in the filthiest vehicle I have ever been in. He has a glass of tea in the front cup holder with a piece of glass on it to keep it warm. Eventually we arrive at the entrance of the road leading into the airport. He stops and looks at me holding out his hand. I have no idea what he wants. Finally after he repeats this a number of times, I get the picture that he wants me to pay the toll for the road. I tell him no, I don't have any Chinese money left. But he sits there stubbornly, waiting for me to hand something across. Finally I give him a few dollar bills which makes him very angry, but he realizes I have nothing else and proceeds to the airport.

After standing in many confusing and time-wasting lines in the airport building, I finally go successfully through security and soon am in the air on my way to my long-dreamed of destination.

*   *   *

Mongolia

For many years the idea of visiting the wide open steppes and the horsemen of Mongolia has made me want to see this far-away country. One night at a dinner party in Evergreen, a woman suggests that we go around the table and tell the country that we most want to visit. When it is my turn, I say I want to go to Mongolia, but don't know how to go about it. Another woman at the table says that there was a big article in the travel section of the Sunday paper a week ago. She thinks she can find it and will send it to me. The article describes a road trip called Mongolian Adventure Tour offered by a tour company in Hong Kong called Moonsky Star. There is an address to contact them (this was before the days of e-mail communication).

I receive a detailed itinerary which sounds fascinating. I sign up immediately for the trip and wire my money to them. In return, I receive confirmation of my space and information about where to find the office in Beijing where they will obtain my Mongolian visa for me and my railroad tickets for the Trans-Siberian Railway which I will ride to Moscow following the Mongolian tour.

*   *   *

As I fly over the Gobi desert, I look down and see tiny white spots

8

which I take to be the homes of nomads and narrow dirt tracks ambling around. How exciting! It is really happening!

When the plane lands on a stretch of grass outside Ulaan Bataar, a nice Mongolian man meets me. He speaks passable English. He explains we will go first to my guest house in the city where I can shower and change my clothes. Then we will drive back out near the "airport" to watch the childrens' horse race which is in progress. Once we are there, he shows me where the end of the race will be, where I can wander (all around the huge flat area with thousands of people who are tourists and Mongolians), and where I should plan to find the bus at the end of the race to take me to the city. So I am on my own watching Mongolians on horseback with others who are also there to watch the race.

This event is one of three major sport competitions at the annual festival, Naadam, which is held each July. Mongolians travel from all over the country to take part as competitors or spectators. They bring their gers (round canvas tents) with them and set them up here near the horse-race venue.

I try to move closer to the line that will be followed by the horse racers. The riders are all children aged four to twelve, girls and boys. Earlier they rode to a pole with their fathers to chant Mongolian "long songs" about valor and courage. Then they rode out onto the steppes thirty-five kilometers to the starting point. Each child wears a brightly-colored coverlet with his number on it. The riding clothes are multicolored. Some ride bareback, others on Mongolian saddles. Sometimes children fall off and are hurt; horses often fall and are trampled which necessitates a tractor to go on the track and drag them off.

The racers left for the starting point probably an hour and a half ago and are already racing. While I am watching eagerly for them to appear, a Mongolian man on a horse next to me invites me to ride his horse. I mount the animal which seems of small stature compared to horses I have ridden in the States. My legs bend almost in two so my feet can get in the stirrups. I feel top-heavy and much too large for the animal. The saddle is small and made of wood with painted designs and with front and rear solid pieces rising about five inches high. The man leads me around for a while as his family look on with pleased smiles. My first impression of Mongolians is very favorable.

Participants in horse race

As I look around at the people, I realize they are usually short. Men seem to have short legs but average-sized torsos. This is why they appear so comfortable on their horses.

Now the crowd starts to roar and I realize the arrival of the racers is imminent. I see a huge cloud of dust in the distance and soon distinguish forms of children and horses running for all they're worth toward the finish line. Many are in the first group. As they come closer I can see the children frantically whipping their horses, urging them on for one final push. At last amid a huge roar, one horse crosses the line accompanied less than a second later by several others. As they begin to slow down, I can see how tiny these little riders are, especially the four-year-olds. What a great experience to see this feat of riding by children who often know how to ride before they learn to walk. They are literally "born in the saddle"!

Now I look for my bus and see it a short distance away. As I board it, I say "Hello" to the seated people. Some of them acknowledge my greeting, but some never say a word. These are my travel companions?

The bus drops me off at my guest house. I am beginning to realize that most of the others are staying some place outside of the city proper. Another girl gets off the bus who proves to be my roommate. The tour leader on the bus tells us to be ready at 8:00 a.m. in the morning when the bus will pick us up for the day's activities. My roommate is Amy, a twenty-five year old American who has been teaching English in Japan for a couple years and will return to the States after this Mongolian tour.

We have a small cooked-to-order meal in the tiny dining room, then go upstairs. I take my shower, but have to be diligent indeed that the water does not run over the low lip of the shower. Then it is Amy's turn. Before I know it, I see thick heavy soap suds running under the door into the room. I warn her there is a real problem, but she ignores me. I think she is washing her clothes in the shower. When she finally steps into the room, she is as dismayed as I. We grab the paper-thin towels and start soaking up the water. This is a huge project since the towels are flimsy and hold little water. Finally we pronounce the job done as well as we can do it. We leave the windows open wide, and are careful not to have any of our belongings on the floor.

Our group bus takes us in the morning to a small stadium to watch men's and women's archery which is one of the three sports which are celebrated at Naadam. The participants are in national costume. I can't believe the accuracy of the shooting.

Archery contest

Out to the horse racing venue once more. This time we are early enough to watch children gathering in groups of thirty or forty to ride slowly around the flag pole singing "long songs" - traditional Mongolian songs which seem to go forever. The fathers ride part way out to the start of the race with their children and then return to the crowd. While we are watching and waiting for the beginning, three little children make friends with us and we meet their father and older brother. The father asks me in sign language if I would like to ride one of his extra horses which he brought with him and I answer "yes". He takes me into the circle with him and his horse. He whistles the "long song" as we ride round and round the pole with the others before the children ride out to the starting point of the race. During this race a horse dies near the finish -- I'm so glad I don't see that.

Our tour gave us box lunches for the day. One of the delicacies is a mutton burger! Cold! We walk through the ger camp of the Mongolian spectators which is interesting, then on up the hill to where the forest starts. Birch and aspen trees. Now we reach the alpine tundra with thousands of miniature flowering plants growing everywhere.

Amy and I eat in our room tonight: soup and bread sticks. The carpet is still soaked as are the clothes Amy washed last night.

Buya, our 22 year-old guide, picks us up an hour early in the morning. We aren't even dressed yet. He says we are to move into the hotel with the others, so we have to pack up all our wet laundry. At the new building outside the city we climb up four flights of steps and find our room has absolutely no wall hooks to hang anything. But thankfully there is a clothes line out on our tiny balcony. We name this new place, "The Tenement", because it is on the top floor of a very dilapidated, ancient apartment building.

The entire group goes out to the same area as yesterday, this time to watch wrestling, the third national sport. One man is so tall and his opponent so short that they look like David and Goliath. David does manage to hang in there for about five minutes. What an act of prowess.

Our bus brings us back to the "guest house" for lunch where we have a great meal of mutton and vegetable soup, then cooked mutton patty and vegetables and rice. I opt not to return to the venue, but instead take a trolley back to the city to explore. In the main square, I watch many families in holiday dress having their children's photos taken by professional photographers who wait around the square for customers. Mongolians from the hinterland don't own cameras because they will never be close enough to a place to get the film developed. Using a photographer provides them with the photos of their children to put on their Buddhist altars in their gers back home.

The next day I again return by trolley to the city. I visit the Ulaan Baator Hotel -- very high class. I fax Jim, then visit an art museum. An artist is having his show there. He is present and also his lady interpreter. They both spend an hour with me explaining Mongolian art. Much of their art depicts a scene where many characters are doing different jobs. All of the art is pastoral, showing daily life in the countryside.

As I walk along the sidewalks of the city, I notice Mongolians in their dells (long work robes) riding horses down the middle of the streets. Cows lie chewing their cuds on the tree lawn in front of a building. Quite a different urban scene from any I have seen before.

Later in the afternoon I visit the office of Jurgin Selchim. He is a friend of a person I contacted in Denver who has been to Mongolia many times and does business here. Jurgin was Vice President of Juulchen Tours, but left and formed his own tour company. We talk at length and he tells me his concerns about hunger and poverty in the world. He is the Vice President of the local Lions' Club chapter. His wife works for a Japanese company. They have a ten-year-old daughter whom they will educate in the US. He says changes are occurring in Mongolia at such a rapid rate that guide books can't keep up with them. Mongolia has one of the highest literacy rates in the world because schools are a legacy of the Soviet system that was in place until 1991, even though Mongolia was not legally a part of Russia. Russia also installed universal health care and provided an endless market for the Mongolian sheep. He and his employees work until 11:00 p,m, each night because one must work long and hard to get ahead. I'm so pleased that I have had the opportunity to visit with him.

Marilyn and a German girl, both in our group, invite me to go with them to a folklore show tonight in a huge outdoor stadium. It starts so late -- 10 p.m, and will end at 1:00 a.m. It seems to be a show for Mongolians, very beautiful costumes, symphony orchestra, excellent choreography. It is done mostly in vignette style with no talking, more a representation of ideas rather than totally authentic.

Since public transportation ceases for the evening at 11:00 p.m., we hitch a ride back to the guesthouse. A private driver stops and we negotiate how much to pay him. Now I know how to hold out my right arm with the hand flapping down to attract a ride.

Breakfast in the morning of fried fritters with jam -- good. All the travelers who have been staying in the guest house with us and who are not going on the Adventure Tour leave this morning for the airport and Beijing. This leaves Marilyn, Amy, Vaughan and myself. Buya now moves us to the only luxury hotel in the city, the Ulaan Bataar Hotel. Each of us receives our own private room. We are living like rich travelers now that the Tour has "officially started". We sort out items we will leave in the storage room of the UB hotel and those we will take with us to the Gobi Desert on the plane tomorrow which allows each passenger ten kilograms each.

Morning arrives and we are still in UB! So Buya takes us to the Gandan Monastery -- a Buddist school and temple. We watch monks "chanting the scriptures", copied from Tibetan "books" (flat loose pages). They alternate chanting with playing bells and gongs. We return to the hotel for lunch and languish in our rooms for the rest of the day. Buya is not very informative on what exactly the program is. We finally figure out that the commercial plane which flies to the Gobi Desert is not flying today. It didn't fly yesterday either, which is when we were to have departed. There seems to be some problem with MIAT, the Mongolian Airline. So now we won't leave until "tomorrow".

The next morning Buya informs us that the plane won't go today either. Now we are really upset. We tell him that we are losing out on what we would have accomplished in the desert. But he says he has no control over the situation. He speaks of a woman who perhaps is the head of the tourist company. We tell him to tell her that we WILL fly tomorrow no matter what the problem is. He finally admits that the problem is fuel for the plane. When Mongolia was under the wing of the Russians, there was no problem obtaining fuel. But now there is a big problem.

We continue to hang out in UB where we have a delicious lunch at the hotel followed by a city tour. Buya is trying to stretch out the "entertainment". The tour turns out to be a trip to a viewpoint over the city, a stop at the post office, and a drive around town. Afterward I visit the "department store", which is sadly lacking in a selection of everything.

In the late afternoon we attend an excellent cultural performance which is very authentic.

Buya tells us that Ulaan Bataar voted in the elections in1992 for reform against the state of things when the Russians were in control calling themselves the Big Brother. Out in the countryside, however, the people voted for continued communist government, because they wanted to continue to receive free government education, health care, and help with marketing their goats and sheep as they had been receiving for years and years. The reform group won. Now everything is changing quickly, which makes for a difficult situation for the ordinary person.

Morning comes and it is obvious that we will be here yet one more day. We visit the Natural History Museum to see the flora and fauna of the Gobi, the steppes, the mountains. There are numerous, wonderful dinosaur skeletons. Afternoon at the Winter Palace of the last Bogd Khan (out of eight). We see glorious silk thankas, clothes of the Khan and his wife, their beds and banquet dishes. His ger (yurt) is set up covered with 158 leopard skins and elaborate and expensive trappings inside. The Khan had his own private collection of stuffed animals. The first Bodg Khan went to Tibet to learn about Buddhism and brought the religion back to Mongolia.

At the Fine Art Museum we see paintings and thankas created by the first Bodg Khan. He was a great artist, in addition to being a sculptor, metal craftsman, and a monk. Two famous pictures out of a set of four called "One Day In Mongolia" by a recent artist are displayed. Presumably the other two are lost. These pictures started the recent phase of this type of painting. We also see ancient rock art and stone stele with deer motifs.

I take a cab to a watch repair place. The driver greatly overcharges me, but does walk me to the shop where a worker puts on a new buckle in five minutes for no charge! I win -- and lose.

Reportedly this is our last night in UB. The four of us (Marilyn, Amy, Vaughan and I) who are going on the Adventure Tour decide to have a room party after dinner to celebrate our imminent departure.

We're up at 5:45 to get the plane for Dalanzadgad in the desert at 7:30. Our luggage is weighed, and we hand it up to a door in the tail of the plane where it is secured with a net so it won't roll forward to the seating area. The interior of the cabin is strange. There are seat belts that don't work. The backs of the seats fold down forward on the seats themselves. When a passenger sits down on a seat, the whole seat rolls up toward the ceiling. This is a Russian plane, but more importantly, it is used to transport cargo to the desert! Well, this plane is full of passengers with just a few huge boxes strapped to the seats. Off we go on our one-hour flight. Just like when I flew to UB from Beijing, we can look down and see white round gers here and there and dirt tracks leading everywhere.

We land on grass and gravel. The "airport" is a tiny building with a few chairs. Actually the building houses a radio station for communicating with incoming and outgoing planes. We wait two hours for our vehicles to arrive. It seems there is always a question of which of two "airports" a plane will use; it turns out that our vehicles were waiting at the other one two hours away by road!

We have a Dutch couple in our party now, so the entourage consists of one Russian van or "personnel carrier", one jeep, two drivers, one mechanic, one cook, and one guide. Chukka is the driver of the bigger vehicle. Enka, our mechanic, sits in front with him. Nara is the jeep driver and Biemba, our cook, sits in front with him. Buya sits in our vehicle on the seat behind the driver facing backward. Marilyn and I switch off between a left window seat and the middle seat, with Vaughan having laid permanent claim to the right window seat. The front windows are supposed to open but don't. So that leaves the two wing windows in the back to ventilate this large space. It is sweltering inside. The "tenders" of the windows stick jackets in the open windows to keep them from blowing shut. Amy is in the jeep with the Dutch couple.

Off we go in tandem across the desert on any old track the driver feels like taking. We are heading for the Yol Valley which is at much higher altitude than the surrounding desert. Once there we walk along the valley floor, seeing mountain wild flowers and, amazingly, a Yol eagle nest high up on the cliffs.

We see piles of rocks sometimes that have broken glass and pieces of metal added with a piece of a prayer flag at the top. They are "ovoos". We must always stop when we see one, walk around it three times clockwise, adding one stone each time to the pile for good luck, happiness, and God and touching our forehead at the end. You can leave money for the gods if you wish.

18

We arrive at the end of the valley, where some ice actually remains blocking the stream here in the middle of July. When we get back to our vehicles, we enjoy a great shish kabob meal that our cook roasted on a wood fire while we were gone.

We drive along through the desert again, seeing an occasional ger here and there and many goats and sheep which children are herding. Every couple of hours we stop for a "cigarette break". The entire crew smoke as do Marilyn and Vaughan. Vaughan obtained some "pot" back in UB from the owner of Monkey Business who came with his daughter and her friend to Naadam. On our last cigarette break of the day, Vaughan rolls a joint on his lap on the back seat which he shares with all the guys. They are pretty happy with that.

Finally we arrive at our ger camp: four sleeping gers, another for a dining room, one for a kitchen, and an outdoor shower and toilet. The Dutch couple are very unfriendly, but the four of us climb up the high rocky hills to the top. We meet in the dining ger for a beer. Buya teaches us the Mongolian toast: you dip your ring finger in the drink and flick into the air four times, saying, "To good luck, to happiness, to Mongolia, and to me". You touch your forehead at the last word. A really beautiful toast.

We learn interesting things from Buya: Mongolian babies are all born with a blue spot on their bottoms, which disappears by three years of age. "Sambano" is the word for hello.

I sleep poorly in the narrow wooden bed which creaks all night. There is a loose heavy quilt on top.

Breakfast is rice porridge with goat's milk on top and something like a fried twisty donut. Good.

We start out on a 200-kilometer drive at 9:00 west across the desert, stopping once to photograph a group of wandering camels and some gazelles racing across the road. Where camels live, there is sparse, coarse grass, even low cedar bushes.

We stop for lunch. Our cook puts together her take-apart stove and fixes chicken broth with bread followed by fried beef steak and stir-fry vegetables. We carry a fold-up table and stools with us that she sets up. It is quite interesting sitting on the desert eating our lunch at table and chairs! I spot a huge barrel in the back of one of our vehicles and see that all the meat we will have on the trip is submerged in a sort of gel, which we think might be MSG to preserve it from the time of leaving UB throughout the trip!

As we drive along we see many animals: antelope with white rumps, gazelles looking just like them, but with white tails. Both types leap into the air intermittently. There are saiga deer which are very rare, endangered, and appear in the World Red book which lists all the endangered animals on the planet. The deer head resembles a moose head but much smaller. There are also camels; these are not really wild. They belong to nomads.

As we approach our ger camp, a sand storm engulfs the vehicles. Sand seeps in through the edges of the windows, through everything and gets in all our gear and our teeth and eyes. We have to stop temporarily.

This ger camp is not nearly as picturesquely situated as last night's.

In the morning we visit sand dunes, some of which are 1200 feet high and always shifting in the wind. We climb up as far as we wish but the sand is really hot on our bare feet. I am sitting halfway up a huge dune looking out at the desert expanse spreading out forever below me. This is a place I have forever known I must visit and here I am at last. An idea gradually comes over me like a flower slowly unfurling. I realize that my life is changing forever. I completed my work of bringing up children and now am ready to go on to a new phase of "being". The spiritual side of life is now to be vitally important and I am, at this moment, embarking on a spiritual journey which might take me all over the globe for years to come. I will let my instincts lead me onward and I will "ride the horse in the direction it's going".

A short distance further along we encounter a small area of red exposed sandstone about 30 to 50 feet high where many dinosaur bones were found in the 1950's and again in the 1980's. We think our ugly ger camp is a remnant of what housed the groups that came to excavate, since it contains some very old vacant buildings.

Visiting a family

After lunch and siesta back at camp we leave to visit a nomad family at their ger near the dunes and along a small stream running right through the desert! The family owns 100 camels, 50 horses and 500 goats and sheep. The grandma and grandpa had 11 children, five boys and six girls. There are four or five grandchildren. One of the sons, his wife, and children live in a second ger very close by. They are all there to greet us in the main ger which contains two narrow beds, a painted cupboard, a Buddhist shrine, and a table and stools in the middle, all painted with the Mongolian style folk painting. There is even a treadle sewing machine!

As we enter the ger and find places to sit, the grandmother serves airag, fermented mare's milk. One must accept anything offered with one's right hand with the left hand touching the right arm above the wrist. The bowl is passed on to the next person with the right hand. Several kinds of hard goat cheeses are passed around plus a kind of cake, more like a cookie but not sweet.

After the airag makes several rounds of everyone, the grandmother serves a distilled drink called arik made from the airag. This is very strong and we gingerly sip tiny amounts. We present the family with gifts Buya had told us to purchase at the market in UB:

toothbrushes, thick needles, shampoo, pencils, candles and socks for little kids. The smallest child, perhaps about one and a half years old, is naked from the waist down. We put a pair of small socks on him and thereafter refer to him as "Socks". We take a lot of photos of the family in their traditional dress or in rag tag dirty garments in which they live and work. We promise to send them copies of the photos via Buya on another expedition he will make later in the summer.

Boy we named "Socks"

The father of the children sings a beautiful song about sun, wind, and blue Mongolian sky in a loud strong voice. Three teenage girls sing a lovely song. Now we are to reciprocate, but we can't think of a suitable offering and settle for "Home on the Range" and "Happy Birthday" which they learn easily. It is a warm and friendly get-together.

We go outside to watch a daughter milking a mare which she has to do every four hours. Then we take turns riding a camel which works fine until the animal starts to lope, at which point one feels very precariously perched.

Our cook prepares a nice picnic for us near the vehicles. Two of the nomad boys follow us out, and we offer them a slice of tomato and cucumber on bread. They eat it and immediately throw up. Their systems aren't used to vegetables or fruit, since their diet consists exclusively of milk and meat products.

As we drive back to our ger, it looks like another sandstorm is approaching and we run inside quickly after closing the canvas over the opening at the top. It is breathless inside.

The next day we drive 200 kilometers through the desert, stopping in an area of unusual green-colored slate to watch a horseman bringing his horses and camels to a well in the middle of nowhere. He pulls up a bucket of water from underground and pours the water in a wooden trough. First the horses drink and finally the camels.

We drive through a "forest": short evergreen trees like bushes, called saxual trees. They disappear as fast as they appear. We drive and drive endlessly out to the middle of nowhere! There is no ger camp to be seen. By evening we stop at an isolated ger plus a kitchen ger. This is our "home away from home" for tonight. It belongs to an old man whose wife died recently and his grown daughter with a teenage boy and girl. The daughter acts as the hostess. The patriarch looks ancient, but he is only 65. He looks wonderful in his traditional dell with his knives in a case sticking out of his boot. The family has 30 camels, 30 horses, 50 cows, and 300 sheep and goats.

Watering horses and camels in the desert

The hostess does the airaq tradition again, plus yogurt and finally vodka: we are pros at using the proper hands and positions to accept and pass. We give our gifts to her, and she plays a guitar and sings for us.

The four of us walk out quite a way to the low rock formations. I caution the others that we mustn't walk too far or we might lose our bearings and get lost. Everyone in the family walks way out way to the rocks to go to the bathroom and we will, too.
.

The family and our crew will all sleep in the kitchen ger, a very tight fit. The four of us plus the Dutch couple will sleep in the main ger. Buya tried to erect a tent for the Dutch couple at their behest, but the wind kept blowing it down, so the unhappy Dutch are relegated to the floor. Our cook brings dinner to us, which we eat at the tiny table and stools.

Airaq and hard goat cheese

Amy, Marilyn and I settle down to sleep on the three beds with quilts. Vaughan and the Dutch use sleeping bags provided by Buya. The woman repeatedly returns to our ger on several pretences. Finally Buya returns and explains that she is very upset because the Dutch man's (Bob's) feet are pointing at the altar -- definitely a "No No". Bob moves them temporarily, and, when Buya leaves, moves them back. Vaughan gives him a huge thump to show our disapproval, and Bob finally decides to abide by the rules. Such disrespect seems really disgraceful. In the morning we leave our family. The woman tosses airaq into the air with a ladle three times to wish us well on our journey. As we ride north, the Gobi slowly changes to green steppe. We stop briefly in the "capital" town of the aimag (province). It is market day. There is wool for sale and buyers for it. Also grain, milk in huge milk cans, spices, meat, pickled vegetables, candy, and cheese. There are many people in a different kind of traditional costume -- Kazakhs from the western provinces. I think the main reason we stop here is so our cook can buy new bread, which is definitely a good idea, since the bread we have been eating since UB has been tasting a bit moldy the last day or so.

To the north we see huge collective wheat and corn farms with Russian-made equipment. We pick up some hitchhikers and our men all help a man whose motorcycle won't start by pushing him downhill.

This is a really fun day, cruising, shoes off resting our feet on the seat in front of us, joking and laughing the whole time. Vaughan rolls a joint and passes it to Buya sitting in the seat across from him. Buya passes it to Enca in the front seat, who passes it to the driver. I know what is coming next, so I have to figure out what my decision will be. The driver passes it to Marilyn. She takes a drag and passes it to me. I take a drag and pass it on to Vaughan. The two of them are astonished, but on we go with our round-robin. The guys in the front pull out a half drunk bottle of vodka from under their seat and pass this around. What a mellow time this turns out to be!

We stop at a beautiful old small monastery, Shant Hiid, built by the first Bodh Khan. We enter the chanting hall where many monks in bright habits are holding a "string of Buddha beads" in their hand and praying silently during "recess". There are women on benches behind the entrance door also praying. What a lovely surprise.

Eventually we reach Harhorin which is really Karakorum, the ancient capital of Mongolia. The ger camp is really nice, but there is no electricity till dinner time. Therefore there is no water until then because an electric pump brings it up from a well. We haven't been able to wash even our hands for two days since there was no water last night at the "family ger". But finally we have a shower, wash our hair and our clothes we haven't changed in five days. But at least we have been using deodorant, which is more than the Dutch have done, and they haven't changed their clothes since at least two days before we left UB.

We learn a new game from Buya, Ankle Bones. As you look at a goat's ankle bone, you can see four different appearances of it as you turn it over four times. They are called: "sheep, goat, camel, horse". The player throws four bones into the air at one time like we would "jacks". The winner is the one who throws all four shapes at one time.

For three days now I have been eating all the raw salad and vegetables that our cook has fixed. I have been drinking the well water after treating it with iodine pills in my water bottle. No problems. Of course I drink the boiled tea with each meal that our cook prepares.

This is Buya's third trip this season for the Mongolian Adventure Tour. The first was in May, for two Swedish girls when he was the guide and also the cook. He also had a driver, of course, and a mechanic. Then he did another trip in June with six people and now ours in July. In August he will have twelve people and then another trip in September. He says he now knows the way on the dirt trails in the Gobi better than the drivers! To us it is impossible to tell which is the main trail and when to turn and cross the grass to find another track a quarter or an eighth of a mile away. We have had to backtrack a few times and make another attempt. But for us it is this feeling of uncertainty that makes it so much fun.

This morning we visit Erdene zu, the famous monastery complex that the grandfather of the first Bogh Khan built in 1586 when Karakhorum was the capital of Mongolia. Originally, on these monastery grounds, stood the largest ger in the world (the Bogh

27

Khan's) and an artificial lake with a big fountain. All of this is gone now, because the Russian Communists destroyed all but three temples here during the Cultural Revolution. When the five-year-old Dalai Lama was brought here, he was placed in a special house which is still standing.

This afternoon we arrive at a large grassy area near a river where several gers are spaced out. We are greeted in one ger with airaq, yogurt and a bowl of three kinds of yak cheeses. We ride their horses. The saddles are wooden with an upright of wood at the front and the back. It really hurts the inside of one's thighs -- we are told that you should push your knees out and not hug the horse as we do with our kind of saddle. You must sit the saddle while trotting and stand up while cantering. Such fun. People are shearing their sheep. There are dung piles beside each ger to use for fuel. Nomads live "outside the economy" and are self-sufficient.

Steppe Horses

We have a party tonight with our entire "crew"(minus the uninvited Dutch) in the "bar"ger at our camp with Mongolian music playing on their boom box. When we arrive, the barman tells us he has no more cheap Mongolian vodka, only Russian vodka which costs $14 a bottle. So we settle for only Kirsch until Buya arrives, at which point Mongolian vodka mysteriously "appears". We mix Kirsch with the vodka. Not bad. After a few drinks, we all get crazy. We stand in a circle and various of the men make "horse" dashes across the circle. They play some Zhivago music (waltzes) and Enka and I waltz together around our circle and then we polka. Some of the waitresses join the group and we have 15 people at one point! Great fun! We finally fall in bed at 12:15.

In the morning we are on our way 70 kilometers north to Ogii Lake, minus the Dutch (thank heavens). Along the way we see some ruins, stones, and sculptures. Some are from the sixth century A.D. when a Turkic king had his palace here while he was trying to invade China! There are Turkic hieroglyphics on one side of a tall stele and then on another side Chinese characters telling of his conquests. As we stop at each fenced-in site, a horseman (a caretaker) arrives riding from one site to another to tell us about the writing and make sure that no one defaces the ruins.

As we near the lake our driver starts to cross a rather large deep stream. Half way across the stream, the radiator, which is located between the driver and passenger seat, starts to steam and smoke. So we sit in the water which is up to our doors for twenty minutes letting the radiator cool off in the water!

At the lake our cook fixes Mongolian barbecue of pork kabobs. One of our "team" catches a large fish and cleans it, but is not planning to cook it because he doesn't know how with the skewers. So I cut the fish into strips and thread them on the skewers and cook them for ten minutes. Delicious!

There are many types of biting flies and insects which drive the many horses standing in groups just crazy.

On the way back to our ger camp, the Mongolians sing folk songs all the way. They know so many, maybe fifty at least, and sing, sing all the time. They have truly beautiful voices.

Today is a long day of driving back to UB. We stop at an old monastery in a rocky area reminiscent of Greece. Our cook prepares our lunch. I begin to feel queasy. Diarrhea strikes. It is so hot in the van. It seems like the trip will never end. We arrive at 8:30 p.m. I decide not to join the others for dinner and am sent on a mission to buy more film for everyone. The photographers are out in the square as usual. I am loathe to buy their film because they keep it in metal boxes right in the sun! How can it be good? But there is no choice so I buy about 20 rolls for the four of us and hope for the best. When I arrive in the dining room to tell them of my triumph, I see they are eating fried chicken! Buya gives me his since the kitchen claims there is no more. It is just delicious. This is the last night with the Dutch! We have driven a total of 1000 kilometers on the trip.

In the morning four of us are leaving for the north of Mongolia by helicopter! Marilyn has decided to buy in for this part of the trip instead of flying back to Beijing. The helicopter is an old Russian military one with an open hole in the floor for parachuting out! It is covered now with a small Persian rug! The huge fuel tank is in the cabin with us over on one side. Our new cook, who is with us on this part of the trip, sits leaning her elbow on the fuel tank while smoking a cigarette! Is this crazy or what?

After an hour we drop down to Bayongol, a tourist ger camp in the northeastern forested part of the country. As we descend from the plane, we are astounded to see myriad wildflowers all around us: cinquefoil, Icelandic poppies, calendula, dark reddish -brown bistort, yellow yarrow, pinks, huge edelweiss at least two inches across, a light lavender flower, light purple vetch, larkspur, king's crown, tall yellow flowers with multiple small flowers, and thistle with a head about one inch wide. What a wonderful surprise!

When we reach the ger area, I meet a woman who is visiting the camp as a guest of her girl friend who is in charge of the camp. This visitor is a cardiologist in UB and wants to practice English. Buya tells us that he will arrange five horses so we can all go riding in the afternoon. The horses don't materialize until about 4 p.m. and then only three show up. They apparently were grazing free and are not happy about the situation. Vaughan and Amy go out with Buya first; Marilyn and I hike up the hills through the flowers and all the flies and insects which constantly land on us. The ride doesn't last long because of uncooperative horses. There is only one manageable one, which Marilyn and I take turns riding around the camp.

Dinner is late. Outside it is rainy, damp. We write in our journals and eventually settle down to a game of cards and vodka until midnight. We teach Buya an American card game, and he wins eventually, which is amazing because Mongolians all play a game where cards have different values than ours.

In the morning we ride again in the helicopter. The "crew" of the camp also go along including their children! No seat belts of course, just a bench all around the cabin.

We stop first at some large rocks which the people of the area claim is the fireplace of one of Chingis Khan's habitations! There are carved words on the rocks, but, of course, we have to take the people's word for what they say. We fly on to Beldan Bereven Lama Monastery, most of which the Communists tore down in the 30's. The parts of the buildings that remain are really charming. Many natural rock formations surround the area. Shamanism is still alive and well in this area where there are many ovoos. A tall man in shirt and pants approaches us and tells us in sign language with Buya's help to climb between two rocks without touching one's feet to the ground -- this will cause one to be "born again"! Then we sit in a chair-like rock which concentrates all our ills from the waist down and cures them.

This area was traditionally a place where Russians, Chinese and Mongolians gathered for trading. We walk around the rocks here clockwise and pray for peace, prosperity, and trade. Peasants are rebuilding temples and a new small structure to house a huge rock with carving, part of one of the destroyed temples. Buya and Vaughan are enlisted to help carry it to a new location. They place two huge tree trunks underneath the rock and carry it sedan-chair style.

We climb back in the helicopter for a short run to a small lake (Lake Hangol). Some of the camp crew and children swim. Some "locals" show up out of nowhere on horses. The crew serves everyone rose hip tea and cookies. Then we get back in the helicopter but it won't start. The tool box comes out and some repairs are made. Then we take off for camp. What a nice day this has been.
Rain arrives for all the rest of the afternoon and evening. A nice, young man, seventeen years old, comes to our ger to make a fire in our stove because it is so cold and damp. Amy and I invite him to stay and play cards. We play the Mongolian card game first and then teach him "Oh Hell". He is very bright and clever with cards as I am sure all Mongolians must be.

Dinner at 8 p.m. and then we teach Buya to play charades. We pick simple words and phrases. He catches on immediately and does exceptionally well guessing and acting out. Because we are also drinking vodka, Buya gets a little rambunctious, falls backward onto one of the wooden beds. The slats fall out and he lands on the floor!

At 11:30 we go to the dining room bar ger in our "grubbies. Little do we dream that locals from miles around would show up on their horses. There are 30 people in all and some rode 10 kilometers!

32

They are dressed in their traditional dress. The battery from the helicopter is removed and brought inside to run the boombox. The guests play beautiful waltzes and do these people (herdsman by day) know how to dance! Precision-perfect. Where do these people learn to dance? It really is like a "Zhivago" scene with many candles on the tables.

Our guests ask us to dance with them many times. They dress us in traditional costumes and hats and dance with us some more. It is one man's 21st birthday. We buy two bottles of vodka from the bar and present it to him. He shares it with everyone. We pass the bowl from one person to the next.

It is extremely difficult to extract ourselves from the party since we are obviously the guests of honor, and it is increasingly clear that the others plan to party all night long. Finally we go to bed about 3 a.m. What a perfectly delightful and enchanting evening. Really make-believe! Has my impression of Mongolians changed today!

We are up at 6:30. Only three hours sleep! The pilot of the helicopter replaces the battery in its proper position. After breakfast, we pack and are back on the helicopter. It does not want to start but some fiddling with wrenches seems to fix it. Now we see that the pilot has his small boy sitting on his lap in the cockpit and is ready to take off in that position. We call out "No"! Earlier this spring a Russian plane crashed somewhere in Russia and killed all people on board; the pilot of that plane had been flying with a child on his lap!

The men of the local "ger crew" bring us extraordinarily beautiful bouquets of wild flowers! It is sad to leave them, because after the "dance", we can see these men at their workday jobs. What a surprise to see a superb dancer cleaning up the area after the party. They wave and wave as we take off. Then we swing around and they are still waving their jackets way down below.

33

In 50 minutes more we arrive at Terelj -- a much more touristy camp connected with a hotel, unisex showers and unisex toilets. Buya tells us to ride horses today and hike tomorrow, because another large group of tourists will arrive and want horses. The rest of the day is taken up with lunch and haggling over the "horse price" which goes like this: the other part of our group at the Naadam Festival in UB told us that they rode here at Terelj before the festival for $1.75 an hour. The "asking price" is $3.00. We expect Buya to bargain for us. A guide we remember from Naadam is here and he says he got a horse for $2.00. So we don't want to pay more, although this is a ridiculously low price. But the horse owners now know they had made a big mistake to come down in price for the other previous group because the groups tell each other what they paid. So the owners hold fast to $3.00. As we bargain, one of the owners "breaks" and says $2.00; but as he goes for horses, other owners browbeat him, and pull him back in the ranks and he reneges. So any time we "strike" a bargain of any sort, they break the bargain. We have been haggling since 3:00. Now a large French group arrives to ride at 4:00. We tell them to only pay $2.00. They are soon disillusioned with the haggling and leave for a hike. Now we hang in there once again, and at 5:00 we depart by horse at last for $2.00! We ride through glorious scenery -- beautiful rock formations and, of course, the green meadows and flowers.

When we finish riding, we make a deal with the owner to ride in the morning for $2.00 an hour. When morning comes, he has only three horses! He says the French are going to ride and there are not enough horses. Vaughan decides he will go hiking instead. We have a lovely ride with the owner running on foot behind us because there is no horse for him! This is "the land of two million horses" but there are never enough for us all to ride together!

After lunch the rain starts; it rains all afternoon and evening. We nap, write in our journals, read, play card games. It is cold and damp. We try to start a fire in the stove. There is no paper so we end up using toilet paper. The fire goes out after five minutes repeatedly because all the wood we have is a few sticks. Terelj is quite a disappointment after the other ger camp. The food is very mediocre; there is never paper or wood for our stoves. Dinner consists of pasties once again (meat pies).

Chukka from our original crew arrives in the pouring rain in the morning to take us back to UB. Amy and I share a two-room suite which is a bedroom and a living room in the Ulaan Bataar Hotel. After showers in HOT water at last, we wash our clothes. We hang the wet items over a chandelier in the living room plus over lamps, chairs and then the drapery rods at the windows.

In the lobby a young Brit is trying to figure out how to get to the hinterland on a shoestring. He's really hung up because all he can purchase are chlorine pills, and he wants iodine to combat hepatitis. I give him one of my bottles of iodine pills.

Our farewell dinner really fizzles: people are preoccupied with packing, getting visas (Amy's visa for Vietnam never materialized in the three weeks we were gone). I decide to buy Mongolian hats, and the lady in the shop in the hotel finds a box for mailing. Amazing in a land where paper is almost non-existent.

Amy flies off with Marilyn in the morning without her Vietnamese visa. I mail my hats at the post office. It takes over half an hour. What a system! You have to arrive with the package still open. The postal people inspect the package and tape it shut. It costs me $18, but I won't have to worry about the hats the rest of the trip. I buy some typical Mongolian earrings; Buya comes and helps Vaughan and me buy film, Chinghis Khan match boxes, and then a Mongolian cassette for me. We are trying to waste time till we can go to our hotel which turns out to be, of course, the old tenement building where we stayed at the start of the trip.

Vaughan and I have a good lunch here and relax until 7 p.m. when we have dinner. I think Buya is sad to see us go. He gets on the train with us and settles us in a compartment for four with two other guys. Then he leaves us and waves as the train pulls away at 9. We are on our way to Moscow!

* * *

The Trans-Siberian Railroad

Our compartment mates are a Japanese guy, Kenji, about 20, who is attending Shanghai University to study Mandarin because "China is the last great market" and an American, Steve, who is 28 and taught English in Japan for two years. We are provided with a blanket, a pillow, two sheets and a pillowcase. Vaughan and I share dried soup (which I brought on the trip) reconstituted with boiling water from the samovar at the end of our car. And we have Vaughan's bread and jam.

Our compartment has four bunks, two on each side. I take the one below Vaughan's since the two guys are already ensconced on the other side. There is a tiny table by the window which we can drop down when we don't want it. It's about large enough for three bottles of water and maybe some other small incidental item. Vaughan has a large opening in the wall above his bunk, where he can store a lot of stuff like all our food supplies. Kenji brought a mammoth suitcase a la Orientals which doesn't fit in the bins under the lower seats. That means we'll have to put up with it in the middle of the floor for the whole trip!

At dusk the train stops at a small station. A group of young people in beautiful Mongolian costumes stand outside. We open our window. They are delighted to have their pictures taken and they give us their address. We think they are learning Mongolian folk dances, perhaps.

The train stops repeatedly throughout the night to let other trains pass. We are on the part of the railroad called the Trans-Mongolian railroad which goes from Beijing to the Russian border. At 5:30 a.m. we stop at Erde Bataar, the Mongolian border town. Police enter the train and conduct searches and passport checks. They tell the four of us to come out in the corridor and stand four abreast. Vaughan and I don't look enough like our passport pictures. We are scrutinized a long time and our passports carried away for about ten minutes; the four of us continue to stand in the corridor. During this time the compartment next door is searched repeatedly. One Mongolian came along earlier in the evening and tried to hang a leather jacket in our compartment; we squelched that luckily.

Finally our passports are returned. The train starts up again, goes a couple miles and stops at the Russian border town for seven hours! During this time we do get off the train and change dollars to rubles. There is a pitiful street market with practically nothing for sale. We want beer, but there are only "fruit-looking" drinks in liter bottles, probably made with untreated water. Steve comes back from a short walk with some fruit. He gives us a pear and an orange to share. It's the first fresh fruit we have eaten in a month. Yum!

About 3 p.m. when we are sure we are going to die in the heat of our car, the train starts up. We think it was waiting all this time for some cars coming south from the first station north of the border. But I really can't see the logic in that because we are heading north to within six kilometers of the city of Ulan Ude and then turning west finally on the Trans-Siberian Railroad.

It's now 7 p.m. and we have made about six stops and never exceeded 30 kilometers per hour. How will we get to Irkutsk by 8:45 a.m.? We pass villages with lovely wooden houses and windows decorated with colorful designs on the shutters and lentils. At first we see only blue decorations with the rest of the houses unpainted, but in one town the houses have green decorations.

We stop at Goose Lake (5771 kilometers from Moscow according a mile post at the town). People are selling smoked and fresh trout, a lot of it. But I can't imagine what the people on the train would do with them.

I am getting a sore throat. Vaughn has been sick for three weeks. He caught it from Amy who got bronchitis in Beijing. Steve has a bad cold and Kenji is catching one.

I think that, at the rate we are moving, we are going to lose precious time in Irkutsk -- we will only have one and a half days there under the best conditions. But this trip has taught me that much time in the East is spent waiting and there is no rushing anywhere. Therefore, this has been the most relaxing trip I've ever been on.

We leave the steppes behind. Now we have many kinds of hardwood trees, big rivers, people making hay (cutting the grass with a scythe and raking it into big stacks). There are low mountains in the distance covered with evergreens.

We are up at 7 a.m. to eat breakfast; my dried oatmeal and Vaughn's bread and jam. We pack up and the train pulls into Urkutsk right on schedule! So all those stops and delays were built into the schedule!

Our guide, Alexander, meets us at the station with a car and driver. They take us to our guest houses. I will be alone at one, Kenji and Steve will be at another one and Vaughn will be driven to a little town near Lake Baikal. My place is a fifth-floor walk up flat. The hostess, Sanya, meets me at the car. She speaks a few words of English. She takes me into her bathroom and tells me to undress and step into the bathtub. She brings hot water in a large bucket which she puts on a board across the tub. It is wonderful to have a bath! When I finish, she prepares a huge frittata for breakfast (and lunch).

Sanya and her husband Sergei are in their 40's. They have a beautiful, sweet nine-year-old girl named Sveta. There is also an eight-year-old boy who is staying at his grandmother's. They have two white cats with blue eyes. The flat consists of a tiny front room with a couch, coffee table, fireplace, an eat-in kitchen with a small refrigerator and apartment-size stove and oven, a tiny sink, very limited cupboard space but a nice size round table and four chairs. A piece of oilcloth serves as the tablecloth. The rest of the flat consists of a small room with a couch, coffee table and fireplace, plus a large bedroom with a big round table which Sanya uses for sewing. Finally there is Sveta's room (which I use) with a twin bed, an armoire, chair and piano. The flat is ancient with ugly pipes everywhere. All the furnishings are very old and worn out.

Sanya asks Sveta to play the piano for me. She stands and plays beautifully while singing an accompaniment. She has long hair in a braid. Then she runs out to play.

At noon I walk out into the city with Sanya's map to meet Kenji and Steve and our tour guide Larissa for a walking tour of the old city which is charming and quiet with lovely old buildings. We visit an excellent history museum with beautifully-arranged displays of the stone and bronze ages. There are models of people like the Mongolian Reindeer People with their costumes, tepees and their shaman's accoutrements. A display of soldier costumes and weapons from the time of "War and Peace" completes the offering. A wonderful gift shop offers lacquer ware, birch bark carved boxes and carved wooden and amber earrings, plus dolls with clothes made of bark.

When I return to Sanya's, Sergei is having a nap in the bedroom. A friend of theirs sits in a chair in the kitchen. He is a translator for a company which has a French joint venture. The three of us discuss art films at length. The friend asks me why I have come to Russia. I say that it is because of "Zhivago" and he nods his head in understanding.

Sergei joins us. He met Sanya at university where they obtained architectural degrees which are worthless at this point since, because of high inflation, no new buildings are being built. He can't find a decent job and now works at a gas station - 24-hour shifts.

We have a rice dish with beef and onions after a salad of cucumbers and tomatoes with oil and soy dressing. I ask the three of them to sing folk songs. They sing beautiful, plaintive slow songs to me as it gets dark while we sit around the table. What a lovely moment in time. Amazingly, the men belong to a professional musicians' group that seeks out old almost-forgotten folk songs, preparing to produce and sell a recording.

About 10 p.m. a woman arrives who teaches English to Sanya and Russian to foreigners. The phone rings constantly. Sanya says she will go to a meeting with the woman. A meeting that starts at 10 p.m.? Also Sergei announces that he will go out. I am glad to go to bed because my throat is unbelievably sore and I feel I am going to be very sick.

Some Russian words I have learned: Previat - hello familiar; nostovovien - cheers; pagalz - please or you're welcome; spasiba - thankyou; zdrazdviytye - hello formal. I wake feeling worse than the night before. But cheese blintzes with cream and jam on top make me feel like I might get through the day. Sanya and I enjoy coffee together. At 10 a.m. our new guide, Helen, picks me up with the driver and Steve and Kenji to go to Lystoi Viance and Lake Baikol. We visit the limnological (lake) museum which is fairly well done and includes a video. Then to the house where Vaughan is staying, but he is out on a hike. We have lunch here-- an entire fish curled around itself with the scales still on and homemade apple juice. This is another very poor abode.

Then we're off to St. Nicholas Church. St. Nicholas is the patron saint of sailors. It is very old and simple and each wall is covered with icons. The church is wooden as are all the buildings in this tiny town. They have the decorative lintels and shutters like we saw from the train. But nothing is painted, a symbol of how poor this village is.

We go to the beach at Lake Baikol which is stony and littered with broken glass! It is a beautiful, hot sunny day. Townspeople are sunbathing and a few children are playing in the freezing water. A legend says one must submerge oneself in the lake to add 25 years to one's life. We force ourselves to do this while Helen watches. Another legend, which she then tells us, is that one must drink vodka after the "dip". There are no shops in the vicinity, but Steve goes off down the street hunting for a bottle of vodka. When he returns successfully from his mission we all join in, including Helen, in drinking up the bottle. Helen must love this job. She probably convinces tourists each day to buy vodka of which she can partake.

Toasting on the beach at Lake Baikol

We leave by car at 4:30 p.m., stopping a short way out of town at an open air museum. There are many old buildings which had to be moved when a dam was built on the Ankara River near by. There are some large octagonal, wooden yurts which rich people lived in long ago. The yurts even have a kitchen area inside.

We are back on the road and immediately have a flat tire. Our driver has an incomplete set of socket wrenches, unfortunately, and can't remove the fourth lug. We stand there, constantly stopping drivers of cars identical to ours hoping to borrow one that will work. Time goes on and on. Finally Steve, Kenji, Helen and I hitch a ride back to the city for the equivalent of $5. I wonder when the driver finally solved the problem.

At Sanya's and Sergei's I eat a warmed-up dinner because it is now after 8 p.m. I have a quick bath and pack. Then Sanya and I take off walking across town for one and one-half miles to visit a couple who are friends of theirs. They live in an ancient wooden house which is a very poor place indeed. They show me at least 200 photos of Irkutsk and Baikol which they took during autumn. Then we look at photos of their paintings which are of Baikol. What is this agenda?

Finally, about 11 p.m., I say I am tired and have a bad sore throat. So off we walk, this time to the post office about a mile away, to have Sanya make a phone call to a woman, Alla, in Moscow whom I arranged to visit before the trip. Sanya shouts into the phone over and over and reports that all is arranged; the people are expecting me in Moscow.

Now we walk about another two miles back to Sanya's house. It is midnight. She had left a key outside the door when we left. Now we knock. A man unlocks the door and immediately turns his face from mine and does not respond to my introducing myself. So the clandestine operation which seemed to be operating when Sanya mysteriously went to her meeting last night goes on. As we walk in, three people stand in the hallway. They immediately turn their faces from mine. One person is dressed warmly with a large back-pack on. Before we left the house earlier, there were many very brief phone conversations in English. Also the grandfather arrived to take Sveta to his house for the night.

All the people walk into Sanya's bedroom. I try not to act curious. They start talking in Russian. I just get ready for bed as quickly as possible. Sanya sleeps on the sofa in the tiny living room while all the others sleep in her room.

I consider all the possible scenarios I can conceive of: An "under-ground railroad" for Chechneyans (the Mafia); moving Bosnians or Serbs from Yugoslavia; dealing in weapon sales.

Finally I go to sleep.

I am up at 5 a.m. for breakfast. Then I say goodbye to Sanya and walk down the five flights with my backpack to wait for the van to go to the train station.

There are 21 people on one group ticket to Moscow on the Baikol Express. They seem to come out of the woodwork at the station. They are all really young, many are British. All the people speak some English. Kenji, Steve, Vaughan and I share a compartment once again. It is about 40% better than the train from UB which was so filthy.

We leave the station at 7:45 a.m. and are pleased to see that we are moving right along at about 50 miles per hour. It doesn't stop every ten minutes like the other train. I fall asleep exhausted with the bad cold and cough and sleep most of the day while everyone else in the car is partying around in all the compartments.

The trip to Moscow takes four days. Every time the train does stop, everyone in the car piles outside for a cigarette; I am the self-appointed guardian of our compartment. We have been warned not to leave the compartment unattended. Passengers rush around out-side trying to buy beer, vodka, fruit, bread, cucumbers. Kenji re-turns with two newspaper cones of blueberries and raspberries. I am amazed and tell him to watch our things while I jump off to buy berries from a babouska-scarved woman. Oh, how wonderful these berries taste. I can't get enough of them. At this point I will eat all fresh produce and throw all caution to the winds.

One of the girls on the train, Sheri, from New Zealand, is very New Age. She's into mystical and feminist books and is reading a book I have read, "Women Who Run With the Wolves". I find her fascinating and extremely intelligent. She does Tarot for Vaughan and me.

During the day, I read my Lonely Planet Book about the Trans-Siberian Railroad and a guide book about Russia but principally about Moscow. The railroad book lists every town we pass, how many kilometers it is from Moscow and interesting history about the town. Vaughan works on his journal from another trip. An Australian girl from another compartment spends much time with us. We play cards, teaching Kenji American games such as "Oh Hell", and "Hearts" which the Kiwis call "Black Bitch"! At lunch Vaughan and I share sandwiches made from the cans of tuna and chicken that he brought along. He also has something like salad dressing to substitute for mayonnaise.

"Babuska" lady at train stop selling tomatoes

I continue to marvel at this group of 20 to 30-somethings: so well read, so intelligent, so well traveled with so much time to do what they want. "All this" has been "out here" in space and I never dreamed it. It all adds to the Magic Carpet Arabian Nights scenario of the whole trip. Vodka starts to flow by noon. Some "victims" from the night before abstain for a while but then start in again.

Once Steve gets really sick in the middle of the night. He is throwing up in bed. Vaughan helps him down from his bunk to the bathroom. He is the only one who has gone to the dining car which was attached to the train in Irkutsk. We all think he is sick from something he ate there.

The next day we pass the obelisk demarking the end of East Asia and the beginning of the west (Europe). Naturally the train never slows down so we can get a photo! Our food bag is holding up nicely. For lunch today we have chicken with slaw dressing,

45

chopped fresh tomatoes, and cucumbers on bread. Delicious! We drink the last of the vodka and orange juice and set our watches back two hours before bed.

In the morning we "divvy" up any of our left-over food since we are arriving today in Moscow. Kenji is delighted with the "possibilities."

We arrive in Moscow at 3:40 p.m. and are met by a person named Alexander. He has no ID. Monkey Business warned us not to go with a person without ID because the Mafia might be trying to kidnap us all. But really, there is no alternative. We shoulder our back packs and follow Alexander. It is as though we have been in a sort of "prison" for four days and don't know how to accept our new freedom and operate responsibly!

We reach an ancient building with an even more decrepit elevator and ride it to the sixth floor, the Travelers' Guest House. I receive a room with five other beds which turn out to belong to unpleasant Chinese women. After a welcome shower, the four of us are off to try to change money and find a place to eat. I have the only Russian money and lend money to Kenji and Vaughan because it is too late to find a "change" place open. But we discover a kind of fast-food chicken place. It is a lot more expensive than we expected: chicken sandwich $4, fries $4, cokes $4, coleslaw, $4. Outrageous! It takes the last bits of money we have. I tell them we have to "make do" with four sandwiches and three fries. Kenji manages to spill the tray with the fries on the filthy floor, but he and I scoop them all up in our hands and put them back on the tray! It's so exciting to have "western" food that we don't want to lose any of it. I don't know, however, how the Moscovites can afford it. But they are out buying, buying!

We finally change money at a tourist hotel and then come upon a "westerners' super market". We buy wine, cheese, beer, water and chips and have a party back at the "guest house". I try to call the

Russian lady I am to visit, but people answer the phone who cannot speak English! I am also trying to reconfirm my air tickets, but can't get through to Air France.

In the morning we are up early to begin sightseeing by 8:15. Before leaving I finally reach someone at the Russian lady's house who perhaps speaks some English. I say I am not coming to visit - it sounds as though it could be a disaster!

Sherie, Vaughan and I take the Metro to visit the Kremlin and Red Square, We have a picnic lunch in a park. The Pushkin Art Museum is a total surprise. I can't believe the number of European impressionists represented. Absolutely wonderful. Down to the Moscow River in the late afternoon to a Mexican eatery for dinner.

Today is the last day of the Magic Carpet. Since it is impossible to get through by phone to Air France, the three of us take the Metro to the lone air office which turns out to be close to a park. So we explore that, too, and have another picnic, then a ride on a huge ferris wheel in an amusement park. On to the Tretnikov Art Gallery which just reopened. Amazing! What a museum! All the Russian artists up to 1919 are represented. The colors in the paintings are brilliant, gorgeous. A fabulous experience. We buy beers to drink on the way to the guesthouse as we race through the city and many Metro stops.

We get back just in time for Sherie to catch a ride to the train station where she will take a train to St. Petersburg. Vaughan's train leaves an hour later. I settle into my room with three new guys from Eastern Europe who are dismayed to learn I will be up at 4 a.m. They want to know if I will let my alarm clock ring! Wimps!

The Magic Carpet Has Landed!

Vietnam

Goddess Quan Am / Cham Towers /
Bad Effects from Larium

I n November 1996 I find myself in Ho Chi Minh City (Saigon) in southern Vietnam. I arrived yesterday, a day before meeting my tour, hopefully to have time to overcome my jet lag.

*   *   *

At home, just before leaving for the trip, I began a course on the world's goddesses. The first one we studied was a goddess from the Far East, Quan Am (Vietnamese) or Quanyin (Chinese). When she appears as a statue or in a painting, she is always white. She is the Buddhist equivalent of the Christian Virgin Mary. She is the Goddess of Mercy, Fertility and Love, also the protective goddess of sailors. She usually stands or sits on a lotus blossom, symbol of purity.

I am walking in Ho Chi Minh the morning of my rest day. I just happen to look across the street and up four stories to an apartment balcony of a French-era building. There she is, Quan Am, about four feet high, pure white! So amazing to see her on my first day here! It is as though she were here just for me to start out right on this odyssey!

Ambling along slowly I visit the central square where children sell half coconuts with straws pushed down in to suck out the milk. I walk on to the Muslim mosque and enter the Hindu temple dedicated to a goddess, Mariammen, certainly another correlation to Christianity's Virgin Mary.

I hire a ciclo (bicycle rickshaw) driver to show me the downtown sights. As we drive along, I am amused to see a row of barber chairs outside facing a wall. There is a mirror on the wall in front of each chair and a customer in practically every chair getting a haircut or shave.

In the afternoon I bargain with a group of ciclo drivers to find one who will take me eight kilometers northwest first to the Giac Lam Pagoda, the oldest pagoda in Ho Chi Minh City, dating from 1754. My young driver takes me to the monastery first. Dusk is already falling. I walk into what appears to be the dining room for the monks. There are no lights but I can see light coming from down a long corridor. I continue down and turn the corner. The light is shining from a bare light bulb hanging from the ceiling in a very small room. Three monks are chanting and playing instruments (a gong, cymbals, and a horn made from a conch shell) in an offering of Buddist prayer. I stand silently leaning against the wall and slowly slide down till I am sitting on the floor. I don't know if the monks know I am here, so caught up are they in their prayer-making. What a privilege to experience this beautiful moment. I am the only onlooker – it is as though it were happening just for me.

Back outside my driver takes me a short distance to the pagoda proper. A huge white statue of Quan Am, rising perhaps forty feet, stands in front of the pagoda. Just breathtaking. I enter the pagoda followed by my driver who has never been here before. A care-taker guides us up the seven levels of the tower. There is only one object in the center of each level, a statue of Buddha, one of them with a halo of colored lights.

The four others from my tour have arrived and we go with our leader to the Majestic Hotel for dinner. This building is the former U.S. embassy during the Vietnam war; the roof is where the U.S. evacuation helicopters picked up the last remaining American ci-vilians and ex-pats during the fall of Saigon while the Vietcong were shelling the city from all sides. I remember the newspaper photos and newsreels from these tragic moments when some peo-ple were left behind because the helicopters were filled to the brim.

In the morning we visit an old house where a famous Vietnamese war photographer lives. It was his private home during the war. After the fall of Saigon, he was sent to a "re-education" camp in the countryside. Several years later he was allowed back in the city and now lives in his old house. He is a pauper, having lost every-thing except his old furniture and huge private collection of his war-time photos which were the most famous of the war. He never received any recognition for his work. We look through the hun-dreds of photos; I choose a small size print of perhaps the most famous of the evacuation from the embassy rooftop. It depicts a very small Vietnamese child hanging on with her two small hands to the rear of the helicopter as it takes off. What a pathetic sight as one realizes the tragic finality of this moment.

A couple days later our small group leaves the city. We drive about 20 kilometers north. Suddenly there "she" is again! Another tower-ing Quan Am statue at road level protects a winding path leading up to an equally huge Buddha at the top of the hill. She certainly seems to be everywhere!

As we drive along we see coffee beans and rice drying on the road.

When vehicle tires roll over them, it amounts to threshing them. We stop a couple times to watch boys playing jacks and girls with an oblong game board using stones for markers. Small children wear knitted winter hats even though the temperatures are always in the nineties and humid. Our guide, Viet, says that mothers feel they have to protect the child's head and the developing brain until he is at least five years old.

All along the way people have set bottles of all sizes filled with petrol on small tables by the road. It seems to work on the honor system. If you need the petrol, you take a bottle and leave some money.

About a week later we are in the area of the Cham towers. These are small, brick offering-temples built on hilltops by the Cham people (originally from China) between the seventh and twelfth centuries. The inside walls are brick but the outside brick is covered with stucco with beautiful intricate carvings. The shape of the temples is most unusual with the roof rising high like a pointed cone above the temple proper. The temples are used today by ethnic Chinese and Vietnamese Hindus to pray and make offerings of food to various Hindu gods and godesses depicted by statues inside. There is an altar in the center of each tiny temple where the offering is placed. The brick walls are cantilevered up, up, up on the inside till they form a small hole at the top for smoke from the incense to escape. There are four towers in the first complex. A small statue of Quan Am is inside the largest tower. Nanda, the sacred Hindu bull, lies outside.

We visit two temple complexes. Approaching the second one, the visitor walks up a sacred stairway to the top of the hill. As I slowly ascend the steps to enter the first temple, I am overcome by a certainty that I have been here before in a prior lifetime. I can just feel myself walking up the stairs with my offering of rice and fruit, laying it on the altar, lighting the incense and making prayers to the deities. It is a very mystical moment.

Cham Towers

Viet, our guide, is Confucian. He explains his religion, which is basically ancestor worship. I wonder if all people of his faith are as kind, gentle, and helpful as he is. As we drive along the roads we repeatedly see tiny "houses" like bird feeders on poles in the peoples' yards. These are called "spirit houses". Viet explains that families use these "houses" to pray to the spirits of their ancestors. They place food gifts and light incense there each day.

Spirit Houses

People standing along the road and outside their houses all chew "beetle nuts", a mild narcotic. Their teeth and lips are permanently stained bright red.

I am realizing again that in Asia, and perhaps all around the world, no religion is pure. People practice at least two religions simultaneously. But they are unaware that these practices do not all belong to the one religion they say they are following. I find this mixture of ideas stimulating. I think it makes their religion very personal, crafted especially for their own clan.

Our group visits some remote tribal villages. None of the main world religions play a part in these locations. Each village has its own religious practices.

At a Mnong village we eat lunch in the tribal longhouse; many kinds of nuts, seeds, fruits, and baguette bread (a holdover from the days of French influence). Some village men take us out on a quiet tranquil lake in dugout canoes. Lotus plants line the shore. A very peaceful spiritual interlude.

We drive through a second village where women and girls stand on the porches of their stilted houses, smoking pipes.

We arrive at a third village which is well known to Viet. He likes to come here for days at a time to meditate and knows the local men well. The "long house" is a beautiful building of thatch and bamboo. Gongs of all sizes hang on the wall of the single room where men play them for sacred occasions.

We walk through the village to the cemetery. The custom here is to bury deceased people in the ground with tiny tunnels down to the face of person in the grave. A miniature house is constructed over the grave. Women come with food three times a day, prepare a meal for the deceased, and pour it down the tunnel. In this manner, they feed the dead person for four years while his soul is gradually moving to a spirit world. This practice is every bit as important to the religious life of this community as praying in temples is to Buddhists and Hindus.

When we walk back, darkness falls quickly as it always does in the tropics. Viet leads us back to the long house. We stumble inside and sit on woven mats in the total darkness. After a silent interlude, a mysterious thundering sound fills the room. A half-hour gong concert ensues. While we were gone, the men hung the sacred gongs from the ceiling at one end of the room. The gongs sound like a xylophone as the men strike them. It is truly amazing to hear these tones in the pitch black of the room. I think this is only the second time that these men have ever played the gongs for visitors. They do it as a favor to Viet and we benefit from it. This kind of experience teaches tolerance to the traveler who truly wishes to understand people he encounters all over the world.

Another day we go to see a beautiful waterfall. It has been raining a great deal. The dirt road is extremely muddy and our driver is afraid to go further. So we hike about three miles to the falls. Along the way we pass a woman frying sweet potato slices dipped in batter. On the way back, heavy rain starts to fall again. We are soaking wet. The driver of a truck filled with spinach agrees to transport us to our vehicle. I sit in the front with the father and his daughter. But the rest of our group certainly tramples the spinach in the back which is on its way to market. Our tour leader gives the farmer enough money to cover the loss of the spinach and we reach our vehicle much sooner than we would have if we had had to hike all the way in the downpour.

The trip ends eventually in Hanoi in the northern part of the country where we visit the Fine Art Museum. I am intrigued with a very small boy painting pictures on the tile floor. He does not know we are watching him. His mother evidently works at the museum. A girl about five years old has a handful of long red flower petals and is creating various designs with them on the seat of a wooden chair. She is so creative in her own little "art world". Watching children everywhere is an enchanting experience for me.

*   *   *

During the trip in Vietnam I have an extremely distressing experience with symptoms that stay with me during the remainder of the trip through Cambodia and Thailand. In some way it seems integrated with my spiritual experiences and that is why I am including it here.

I have been taking an anti-malarial drug called Larium. No one told me of the possible side effects and, since I took it two years ago in China without a problem, I never dreamed that at this point, it could have terrible results. I am sitting in a restaurant about a week and a half into the trip when I suddenly feel extremely disoriented, rather sick and weak. Viet, my guide, walks me back to the hotel which is a good thing because I could not have walked here without his help. My coordination ability has seemingly dropped to a distressingly low level. A doctor in our group tells me at the restaurant he thinks the problem is Larium and I should stop taking it at once. I took a pill one week before departure, another on the first day of the trip and one a week later. He says people can experience bad side effects on a second trip even though there were no effects on a prior trip.

I stop taking the drug, but the unpleasant symptoms grow worse with each day. I am unable to eat. I find it difficult to make decisions, and my memory is fast deteriorating as well as my coordination. Combined with all this is the sense of not being really sure what the problem is. It is quite frightening because I am going on from Vietnam to Cambodia alone; it will be an optional extension of my Vietnamese trip. At one point I consider going home. But my husband (Jim) is to meet me in Thailand once I leave Cambodia, so I force myself to keep going.

The last night in Hanoi (and the last night of the Vietnam part of the trip), my tour leader telephones a doctor who professes to speak some English. She explains my symptoms. He says that he is at this moment dealing with a double emergency resulting from the head-on crash of two motorcycles, so he cannot come to check me. But he is absolutely certain my problem stems from Larium and I will begin to see improvement with each passing day. Accordingly, I decide to go onward with the trip.

Cambodia

Angkor Wat / Meditations /
A Cambodian Wedding Feast in Jeans

I fly alone from Hanoi to Phnom Penh, the capital of Cambodia. The tour of Vietnam ended with Hanoi and I had booked a six-day extension in Cambodia. In my hotel room in Phnom Penh I feel so distressed that I call "Reception" to send me a doctor who speaks English. The Philippino doctor arrives an hour later and decides that my malady is not due to Larium but to a deficiency of vitamin B! She gives me several packets of the vitamins and I am off the next morning on a small plane to Siem Reap and the famous Angkor Wat temple complex.

Bunan, my young local guide meets my plane. I explain my problems to him. He says we will do alright together since he is taking pills for a relapse of malaria and is feeling sick. We are both quite weak, but we embark on our walking tour of the largest temple, Angkor Wat. Every few minutes I have to sit down and rest. Not the best way to see this magnificent building with its hundreds of bas-reliefs on the outside walls. There is a story to go with each relief. Bunan tells me all of them, but my memory is so messed up, I can't repeat one of them a minute later. We just keep going, climbing up one set of steps and down another. In the meantime we hear frequent explosions somewhere in the general area. This really alarms me because I know the Khmer soldiers are still a threat. Bunan says there are many, many unexploded landmines in the vicinity. Officials are detonating some of those today. It is very disconcerting in this religious environment, to say the least.

I told Bunan when we met that I wish to meditate three times while I am visiting Angkor. He takes this very seriously and provides me with three wonderful opportunities. At the very top of the temple, there is a room with a large Buddha statue and nothing else. I feel compelled to stop here. Bunan waits for me out in the corridor. I have the place to myself and enjoy a meaningful meditation.

Finally it is time to go back to the hotel for lunch. Once we are in the car, Bunan and the driver in the front seat and I in the back, Bunan shows me an invitation to a Cambodian wedding feast and invites me to go with him and the driver. It is happening at this very moment about fifteen kilometers away on very, slow dirt roads. If I had all my senses about me, I would, of course, answer "No". Stories abound of American tourists being kidnapped if they get off the beaten track. And there are also hidden landmines being detonated everywhere!

Instead I ask him first where the feast is. Then I say, "I can't go because I'm dressed improperly. I am wearing jeans." He said there is no problem.

I say, "I don't speak the language". He says he will translate.

I say, "I don't know the proper behavior". But he assures me he will tell me what to do. I consider for a moment, then incredibly say I will go. After all, here is an opportunity not offered to the usual visitor!

Off we go on deeply rutted roads. We pass sentries standing in front of tiny guard houses. When I ask why they are there, Bunan tells me they are protecting farmers from the Khmer who sweep down at night and kidnap the farmers. This is the essence of great adventure it seems in my muddled state of mind. And it helps to take my mind off my physical distress with my "illness".

At last we arrive at the site of the wedding festivities. We are in the middle of rice fields stretching in every direction. Two large houses stand close together. A huge plastic tarpaulin hangs between them protecting an area of perhaps twenty tables from possible showers and also hot sun. As we approach the area we see a large new car decorated for a wedding – probably rented and waiting to take the bridal couple to a distant village where they will honeymoon.

My lucidity returns temporarily. We find a table where a couple of women in national dress are sitting, leaving three chairs for us. Bunan instructs me how to go to meet the wedding party and what to say. He escorts me to them. They are so welcoming. It's not every day that an American woman visits a wedding reception dressed in jeans in rural Cambodia! They want me to be in some wedding photos. There is a video man and a still photo man. They stand us in a long row in front of the flag of Cambodia. All women in the wedding party and guests are wearing the national costume. I am a full head taller than any of the other people. I am told how to stand and how to place my arm and hand. All the other guests watch this episode intently. It is a successful endeavor.

We sit down again. There are a few hors d'oeuvres such as peanuts and dried shrimp on our table. Everything is covered with flies. Bunan wipes the rim of our glasses with a tiny napkin and pours some Sprite. Gradually more food arrives accompanied by more flies. The boom box plays at top decibel.

Posing with wedding party at feast

Finally it is time to leave. The bride distributes small envelopes to all the guests. We place our money gifts in the envelopes, then hand them to the bride as we walk by a table holding an urn. She drops the gifts in the urn. The groom lights a cigarette for every male guest and hands it to him on the way out.

What an opportunity for me to experience a traditional Cambodian wedding party! Why did Bunan extend the invitation? I think because he saw that I am a traveler seeking to approach Buddha in a meditative and devout manner. Would the invitation have been forthcoming if I had not been in a state of confusion? Perhaps. I feel sure that my guide took pity on me and decided to include me. A temporary silver lining had shown itself.

In the afternoon we visit the Bayon, another huge temple complex. My muddled mind, lack of coordination, and other maladies return, but I am learning to rise above them for short periods of time.

As we leave the Bayon, we drive by Angkor Wat once again, its reflection in the lovely lake in front of it. Bunan suggests that we go inside once more, climb the steps to the top, and wait for the sunset which is due to occur momentarily. There are about thirty people awaiting this event. Probably they are mostly British or Australian, for these travelers feel it is imperative to watch sunsets from all the important sites in the world. However, the French and Germans are not far behind in this aspect. I learn at this moment that a sunset is a significant spiritual event in the day. Now I must make sure I never miss one at an important destination. This one is gorgeous and long lasting, perhaps because we are into October.

Reflection of Ankgor Wat

I had told Bunan that I want to go early in the morning to the back side of Angkor Wat to see the sunrise. The driver and Bunan pick me up at 7:00 a.m. and we drive to the temple area. A narrow dirt road leads behind the temple where we eventually arrive at a military check point. Our documents are checked; we are allowed to drive through only after Bunan passes the guards two cigarettes. At a tiny dirt parking area Bunan tells me to get out of the car and approach the back side of the temple where I will see a beautiful Buddha statue. I find it -- a rather modernistic rendition. I meditate there in front of the statue.

We then visit Ta Prohm, the temple complex which was allowed to return to the rainforest. Trees and roots and vines have broken many buildings and encompassed others. There is a mysterious, mystical air about it all. Quite spectacular!

We head back to the town and the hotel for siesta. I have felt so sick and uncomfortable the entire time I have been in Siem Riep that I have not been able to eat anything even though the hotel boasts a four-star French restaurant. I do manage to eat some bananas from the market. The distressing feelings intensify during siesta. I become more worried about my problem because it certainly has not diminished in the two weeks since I stopped taking the Larium pills. Maybe the problem is due to something else entirely. I call down to "Reception" and tell them I need to see a doctor who speaks English. They say my guide will take me there when he comes after siesta.

Bunan and the driver arrive and drive me out of town to a rural area where there is a single small thatched hut. Bunan and I go inside. A narrow cot with a hot pink satin pillow case stands in the middle of the tiny room. The single person in the hut motions for me to lie down on the cot. It is immediately evident that this person neither speaks nor understands any English. So Bunan translates for both of us!

This very kind man listens and then explains that my problem is indeed entirely a result of taking the Larium! But because it has been two weeks since I stopped the pills, I certainly will begin to feel better. It is comforting just to be with him. I have no idea how he even knows about Larium or its effects, but he really does seem

64

to understand the whole phenomenon. He has no remedies to be seen. I feel sure I am in the presence of a shaman, and feel very loved while I am with him.

My spirits seem buoyed a bit when we leave. This malady is so strange because I can feel better for a short while and then am encompassed by the symptoms once again. This alternation seems to go on and on. And every time I ask for help, I am told the opposite of what the last person told me.

We visit more and yet more of the wonderful temples, lakes, and statues all afternoon. On our way back to the hotel, we stop at a nunnery. Numerous shaven-headed nuns live here and show us their tiny rooms with nothing but straw mats. The nuns are kind and friendly. Next door is a monastery where just a few monks live. Between both buildings stands a monument dedicated to the millions of Cambodians who were killed by the armies of Pol Pot. Inside the monument is a pit filled to the top with human skulls of the victims. Now Bunan tells me how his father was killed by soldiers who came to the family house when Bunan was about seven years old. They made Bunan stand with his mother and brother on one side of the room and watch while they stood his father against a wall and gunned him down. Stories like these bring the atrocities to life. I begin to understand the terrible circumstances under which ordinary people lived for so many years.

The next morning Bunan takes me back to Angkor, over the bridge through the first set of stone gates, into the first of many inner courtyards. He sits me down on a low stone wall in a corner so I can meditate in peace once more before I leave.

What a phenomenal, spiritual experience this has been -- the hours I have spent with Bunan at the temples and attending the wedding.

I leave on a small plane to return to Phnom Penh and stay at the same luxury hotel as when I arrived the first time and eat about as much – nothing.

Thailand

"Farewell Letter" to Jim / Hospital / Jim At Last

As I climb aboard the plane in Phnom Penh bound for Bangkok, I have two day packs plus the checked bag. Knowing that I am in trouble with my memory slipping, slipping away, I put both packs between my legs rather than on the shelves because I am afraid I will leave them behind. A woman beside me explains nicely that I can put them up above; but I tell her that I have some strange malady and need to have them right at my finger tips.

We start sharing information about ourselves, and I enjoy about one hour of lucidity. When this happens, it feels so good, so normal. Sandy works for CDC (Center for Disease Control) in Atlanta. She just completed a mission in Cambodia trying to help teenage prostitutes with venereal disease problems. She has really dedicated herself to all those who live in poverty. Her husband works for the same organization and was very involved in the SARS epidemic of 2003 in China.

I am met at the airport by an affiliated group of the travel company in Cambodia. I had requested that they meet me and take me to my hotel, knowing that I would not be able to handle the logistics in my condition. It is the hotel where my husband, Jim, will arrive at midnight tonight with a tour group which I will be joining.

It is Sunday. Waves of the dreadful, mysterious feelings come and go. I call "Reception" to send me a doctor who can speak English. An hour later a Chinese man who has no expertise whatever in English arrives. He declares that my problem isn't due to Larium, but he doesn't know what it is. So he gives me pills to take every four hours and leaves after I pay him $150! I take one pill and imagine that I feel worse!

I write a "farewell letter" to Jim, thinking that I could be dead by the time he arrives. Since my coordination is so bad, I write extremely illegibly and on a 45% slant up the page. I lay it on the floor just inside the door so Jim will see it when he arrives. Then I call the American Embassy, tell them I need to go to a hospital, and ask them for some names of facilities that Americans use.

I call a hospital and ask for someone who can speak English. People pick up the phone, and when I ask if they speak English, they hang up. This goes on and on. I am really despairing of ever reaching someone who can communicate with me. After about ten minutes, a man picks up the phone and says he can speak some English. When I tell him my symptoms, he says it sounds like a neurological problem (which was what I had deduced). He wants me to come immediately before the neurological specialist leaves for the day. I dress quickly, grab my money belt and am waiting for a taxi in five minutes.

An hour later I arrive at the hospital. I am so weak they put me in the emergency room. The specialist finds me, asks all manner of questions, discovers that my memory is fast disappearing, my coordination is in very bad shape and I am a wreck emotionally. He tells me to stay overnight and in the morning I will receive a CAT-scan of the brain and all other tests to determine the true condition of my nervous system. The doctor starts immediately with blood tests to see if I have some strange disease. He says it appears to him that I may have had a stroke. He knows about Larium but isn't aware that it might cause all these symptoms.

I worry about Jim who will arrive at midnight. But the doctor leaves my phone number in the key box at the hotel Reception. Naturally Jim is upset and mystified when he sees my letter on the floor. He calls the number the doctor left for him and reaches me in my private room. I try to allay his concerns and tell him to come the next morning.

In the morning an ambulance takes me an hour away to the one and only CAT-scan machine in the entire city! When they bring me back, there are Jim and the doctor. I am to stay overnight again so that we will have the results of all the tests the next morning before I leave on the trip.

The results turn out all negative. The doctor gives me anti-anxiety pills to calm me down and I am released into the great unknown of Bangkok. However, I continue to have bona fide mental problems which include an acute lack of memory. I am sitting in the cab which is taking me back to the hotel. I hold the fare in my hand to give the driver. But I decide he is really hurrying to the hotel so Jim and I will be able to catch up with the tour. I want to give him an additional tip. I take out more money from my money belt. Then I have all the money in one hand that I want to give the driver. But the money bag with all the rest of my money falls to the floor unbeknownst to me. I get out of the cab, give the man his money, walk inside the hotel leaving $400 in the money bag on the floor! Of course there is also a credit card which entails calling our daughter, Amy, in St. Louis asking her to cancel it immediately.

Jim and I are soon off with the manager of the local tour company. He is going to help us catch up with our tour. But today nothing goes right. The electricity begins to fail in his Mercedes and pretty soon we are at a dead stop waiting for another vehicle to come and take us the rest of the way!

We arrive at the hotel about three hours later and quickly join the group for dinner on a boat to watch the Sound and Light Show on the River Quai. A tour member named Allen, sitting right behind me on the bus, leans over and asks what my malady is. I tell him it remains a mystery. He asks me if I have been taking Larium. I tell him yes, but that I took it two years ago with no problems. He says that is the usual scenario -- the first time, no problem, the second time, huge problems. When he took it a second time, he had horrible hallucinations for his entire trip and other people had other mental and physical problems.

It is good to hear this concrete explanation. The anti-anxiety pills are working and we are beginning to have a good time.

During our trip we see many gorgeous Buddhist temples. And here are those "spirit houses" again on poles so each family can have their very own altar to which they can bring daily offerings.

We visited Sukhothai, Thailand's first capital which flourished in the thirteenth and fourteenth centuries. The Sukhothai kingdom was the Golden Age of Thai civilization with the most classic of Thai styles. We explore the huge area during the day and again at night with orange floodlights on the buildings and all the Buddhist figures. There are so many temples, moats, pools, lotus plants, steps, Buddhas. Truly a spiritually over-whelming experience for me. It seems again as though I have been here before in another life.

The next evening our local guide and I find a quiet place in a corner of the lobby. I explain the spiritual events that have happened to me on the trip: The Cham towers in Vietnam, Quan Am everywhere, spirit houses, my Vietnamese guide who taught me about

Confuscianism, my experiences at Angkor Wat. I wonder what they all mean. He tells me that I am on "the right track". I don't need to change anything. If a time comes when I feel that I must convert to Buddhism, I will know it then and can do it. In the meantime, just continue on "my path". It is a great comfort to talk to him. He is like a kind monk helping me though my spiritual confusion.

Buddha of Sukhothai - ancient capital of Thailand

As we continue north in Thailand to the area of the indigenous tribes, I find them more than just an oddity. I begin to feel at one with all these people and to feel gratitude that I have had a chance to connect with them. I can see that their lifestyle is very meaningful to them -- more "paths to the top of the mountain".

Southeast Asia is an incredibly fascinating place with many religions and customs. But it is the people everywhere that are leading me onward. I "am riding in the direction my horse is taking me".

When I return to the States after this three-week trip with its tumultuous ups and downs, I visit my doctor to get his idea on the cause of all this. He researches Larium and finds to his surprise that a number of people who take Larium have severe side effects. Also that people who have the neurological problems can have them for several months afterward and find them returning during the stress of each subsequent trip, making it very difficult to remember all necessary details of traveling, even to the point of not remembering what they had seen and where and when. So the mystery is at last solved!

My pharmacist tells me of a customer, a man who recently returned from Indonesia. He had such problems with Larium that he was hospitalized and treated for heart attack. Another woman was treated in a distant country for extremely severe breathing disorders. Two more examples of what Larium can do to people.

Every trip has great plusses and a few minuses especially if one is traveling without a previously-known roommate in third-world countries where there are adjustments to be made in lifestyle and comfort. Larium just made it a whole lot harder to deal with these. I wouldn't, however, have forfeited those remarkable experiences I had, even though it required enduring days and days of discomfort.

Ecuador

Shamanic Healings

I read an astonishing book in 1997, "The World is as You Dream It" by John Perkins. John worked for the Peace Corps in Ecuador years before. He became acquainted with the Shuar Indians of the rain forest plus members of other tribes. He observed many shamans at work since every tribe had a shaman. He described what he had learned from these indigenous people concerning their ideas of the earth and the universe, their ability to meditate to reach other worlds, and how some of them could transmutate into birds and fly to other "realities". John also wrote about the shamans' healing techniques.

When he completed his Peace Corps mission, John returned to the States, got a business degree, married, entered the business world and started his own business. The business did very well. But always John was thinking of the people he had met in Ecuador and wishing he were back there. Finally he decided that his life had to intertwine with those of his old friends.

He sold his business and began organizing trips in which the participants would meet with, and have healings by, at least four shamans, visit a Shuar home and family, and do a marvelous walk in the rainforest to a sacred waterfall. Group members would learn about the life and world concepts of the Indians and their mysticism and religion. Of course I had to have this experience!

* * *

Before long I am flying to Quito, the capital of Ecuador. I'm here a day before the rest of the tour members arrive. So once I am settled in the loveliest tiny guest house I have ever seen (with murals on all the walls), I hire a taxi driver (Tomas) for the day to show me the city. I could have joined an English-speaking bus tour at a hotel. However, I prefer to explore alone or at least not in a large group setting. Tomas speaks only Spanish, but I boned up a bit before coming to Ecuador. I tell him I have to sit in the passenger seat so I can see his lips as he speaks. We do just fine together. I learn about his life and his concerns, one of which is the roaming of stray dogs most of which are rabid. He feels unsafe taking his dogs out on a leash for a walk.

The U.S State Department had said not to visit the Old City because of political unrest. Tomas says everything is safe, and, of course, it is. We see the New City and the Old City, with lovely cathedrals. We make a pilgrimage to the monument of the equator where one can stand with one foot in the southern hemisphere and the other foot in the north. We look down into volcano calderas.

Late the next day our small bus arrives with the rest of the thirteen participants and our tour leader, Mary Tendall, plus Juan, our Ecuadorian tour guide. We start out driving through beautiful landscapes and on twisty roads close to many lofty volcanoes. The volcanoes all have names given to them by the Indians. Their name for the "Earth Mother" is Pachamama. It is to Her that the people pray. On the bus, each of us sips a mouthful of the national fiery drink called trago. We leave a bit in the glass to pour on the floor of the bus or the ground, saying "To Pachamama".

We eventually arrive at an ancient hacienda which now serves as an inn. There are beautiful gardens and trees, Amazingly, John Perkins happens to be here with his daughter, so we have the opportunity to meet them!

In the morning our group forms a circle on the lawn. A famous and mysterious volcano, Cotopaxi, rises high just above us. Mary and Juan tell us their reasons for being here. Of course, it is because of the close associations they forged with John Perkins and their resultant commitment to preserving the rainforest and helping the indigenous peoples to develop sustainable methods of agriculture and make creative handicrafts to sell.

We play a get-acquainted game with a ball of twine. The first person with the ball tells about himself, why he is here. Then he throws the ball to someone across the circle. Soon everyone has a chance to say something about himself.

There are only two men in our group. One of them is Sunee. During the "circle", Sunee mentions that he has just read a mystical novel about indigenous people and the rainforest. The title is "Spiritwalker" by Hank Wesselman. I, too, just finished the book. So when we take seats on the bus for the day's drive, I sit next to Sunee and tell him that I just read the same book. He says he liked it so much, that once he finished it, he read it a second time. Interestingly, I did the same thing. So it is obvious that we are on the same wavelength. He turns out to be my favorite person on the trip.

By late morning we arrive at the complex of the first shaman we will visit, Don Alberto Taksas. It is a wood and thatch building built in a circle with narrow bedrooms in triangular shapes. Attached to the building is an open air kitchen where Indian girls prepare lunch: squash soup and a variety of vegetarian food from the garden.

After lunch we meet with Don Alberto. He is wearing a long white shirt and long white pants. He looks like a saint, most specifically Jesus of Nazareth. Such a beautiful person. I can feel love emanating from him.

Don Alberto on fire circle edge with healing herbs

We enter a large circular room with a fire pit in the middle, Don Alberto's ceremonial round house. We sit on the edge of the wall rimming the pit. Don Alberto begins to build a fire in the center. The shadows produced on the walls by the flames create an atmosphere of mysticism and expectation. Those who don't want a healing are not coerced in any way. They can simply observe. But I believe that everyone decides to have one.

When it is a person's turn, she discards most of her clothes except for underwear. Then she steps onto the skin of a jaguar by the fire.

Jaguars are spiritual animals and bring good fortune to "seekers". Once she is standing on the skin, Don Alberto gathers herbs with long stems into a bundle. He shakes them around her head for a long time always chanting in Quechua, the native language. Sometimes he "camays" her, taking a mouthful of water, spraying it out between his teeth all over her to cleanse her.

The chanting, the "camay-ing", and shaking of herbs continues for a long time. It is rather hypnotic. At times Don Alberto touches the person with the herbs in areas where he divines she has a problem that needs curing. There is a loving, protective atmosphere in the room, easily felt by all of us,

When all the healings are completed, it is about time for our evening meal which, being vegetarian, resembles lunch. People who want special help with problems have an opportunity tonight to meet individually with Don Alberto.

In the morning before we leave, each of us takes a moment to personally thank Don Alberto and give him a gift of money for the healing. I tell him in Spanish that I feel he held me in the palm of his hand while experiencing his strong love. His smile is beautiful. The whole experience has been so mystical. Certainly my whole body and mind were cleansed. It was an incredible opportunity for me.

*   *   *

Four months after I took my trip to Ecuador, our daughter Amy, who was about thirty-five years old at the time, took this same trip. She also had a healing with Don Alberto on the jaguar skin. She had been having problems with depression at home which stemmed from her six-year-old daughter, Megan's, severe childhood depression problems over the past year. Megan's behavior was very upsetting to Amy. She felt alienated from Megan. Both Megan and Amy were on antidepressants and in therapy with no results.

Amy had a healing like everyone else in her group, but then asked for an additional healing for her daughter. The rest of the group left to eat dinner, leaving Amy, Juan, and Don Alberto alone. Don Alberto asked Amy if he could burn Megan's picture. He gently placed it in the fire. Then he began to chant. Suddenly across the room Megan "appeared", complete with blond ponytail. This spirit form ran across the room straight to Amy and leaped into her arms. Amy was overcome with emotion as Megan's spirit meshed into hers. It was an amazingly, beautiful experience. Amy threw her antidepressants away that night and never needed them again. She was able at last to deal with the difficulties at home with good results.

Our daughter's experience shows that not everyone is aware of receiving help from a healing, but there are those who obtain amazing results.

* * *

When we leave Don Alberto, we drive for hours toward the edge of the rainforest on a very narrow, slow, twisty road far above a river. There is road construction and no room for two vehicles to pass. An interesting adventure! Finally we arrive at a small village called Shell, named for the oil company. There is oil in the rain forest and Shell is endeavoring to get it out. Here each of us buys our high rubber boots for the rainforest expedition.

We fly on an old small four passenger plane deep into the jungle to be guests of the Shuar Indians, a tribe who were head hunters only a generation ago!

We fly and fly over the forest seeing only the trees and here and there small rivers which are the headwaters of the Amazon, landing finally on a grass runway right next to one of the rivers. Indian women and children meet our plane. Men with dug-out canoes load our gear for a short poling trip down the river. We disembark and hike for a mile to our destination, the Indians bringing along our gear.

Our "compound" consists of wooden buildings and thatched roofs. There are small double bedrooms with windows (but no screens and amazingly no insects), shared sinks, showers and toilets. Nearby are an outdoor kitchen and dining room. Monkeys walk along the top of the walls. The Indian workers live in small, round thatched houses with their families.

In the morning Indian guides take us on an educational hike telling us about plants and insects and their medicinal properties. We also visit the primary school in an area with a very interesting church built years ago. Many stools in the shape of turtles provide the seats inside the church. A painting of the Virgin Mary and the infant Jesus depicted as Shuars hangs on a wall. Even though this was originally built as a Catholic church, it is filled with a variety of Indian religious artifacts and symbols. Another painting shows shamans mixing up "creation" in a jaguar pot, and yet another of God creating man and woman "equal" and giving one the hoe and the other the blow gun. Birds, monkeys and musical instruments abound in the pictures. It is fascinating. Children often have to walk ten miles through the forest to get to school. For those who live farther away, there are small boarding school buildings.

In the evening we have a fire in the central pit in the common area of the compound. The Indian men play Indian-style instruments and sing for us in Quechua.

The next day we hike to a sacred waterfall. It takes four hours. Amazing vines, trees, and myriad varieties of orchids and other flowers line the path. It is necessary to walk very close to the edge of the river and only about eight feet above it, to climb over huge boulders and sometimes cross the raging river with slippery moss on the rocks hidden under the surface. At one point I slip and fall into the river on tops of rocks and boulders injuring my back. I really don't know if I can continue to the waterfall. But I walk slowly, and eventually get there.

What a beautiful spot. Huge flat rocks lie in the middle of the river. Two narrow, wispy falls, five feet apart, stream down to the rocks. The strange thing is that one of the falls is very hot and the other very cold! The Indians have always considered this a spiritual place. We do a "sauna" thing: sitting under the hot water for awhile and then the cold. It is a nice relaxing time under the falls and lying on the rocks.

When it is time to return to our compound, one of our Indian guides stays behind the others and, using Spanish, Quechua and sign language, explains that he will accompany me very slowly. Juan tells me that these Indians and their shamans use a method of sucking the pain out of the place where it hurts. The man is very young. At one point he indicates that I should lie down in the path; I feel somewhat alarmed because I don't know what he plans to do. He asks me where my back hurts. I show him. He pulls up my shirt and begins sucking on that place! Such a strange experience! Here I am with an Indian man I know nothing about who is conducting unconventional healing practices on me. Gradually I relax as I realize there is love in his healing techniques.

We slowly walk ahead awhile. Then he tells me to lie down again and he repeats the process. We do it one more time before we reach the compound.

By the time we finish eating, a Shuar shaman and his daughter arrive. They have been hiking through the forest for six hours because he is to do healings for us tonight. He brought ayahuasca, a hallucinagen, with him from his home and needs to mix it up with other ingredients. He will perform the ceremony for those of our group who wish to try it. I have read about it for years and want to try it, but because I have high blood pressure, Mary, our leader, cautions me not to do it. About half the group take the drug and the other half of us are "caretakers". The participants have abstained from food for twenty-four hours; how they did the hike today without nourishment seems impossible. In addition to sometimes causing frightening hallucinations, the drug usually induces vomiting and diarrhea. This creates the cleansing of the body and soul and, in effect, produces the healing.

What a strange, magical environment. The flames of the fire provide the only light, alternately shooting up high and then dropping down low. Shadows created by the flames are almost supernatural.

Once those who want to participate with the ayahuasca are involved in the various steps of their cleansing, the shaman turns to the rest of us to do healings without the drug. Of course, he chants and shakes dried plant leaves above and around each of us (one at a time). He "camays" us many times, not with water this time, but with trago, the local alcoholic drink. He asks the person having the healing where his problem is. And then the shaman commences a prolonged sucking activity at the site of the problem.

At first this seems unspeakably weird, but each of us is there with friends in a mystical situation. And each of us came on the trip to learn as much as possible about shamanic healings. Participation is how one learns. So it is only right that I "ride the horse in the direction it is going"!

It takes hours to get to healings for all the people who did not participate in the ayahuasca healing. The people who took ayahuasca are still having amazing hallucinations at two a.m. They are also vomiting and having diarrhea. So it proves not to be a quiet night for anyone!

We all head out on a two-hour hike in the morning to the home of a Shuar family. Again we are delighted with all the beautiful flowering plants. Finally we come to a large clearing with two buildings of wood and thatch. When anyone enters the house, he must remove his wet, muddy boots and dry them upside down on sticks standing outside. We then enter one of the buildings which is divided in half with a doorway through to the back section. The front section is for entertaining guests and for men. The back section is a small kitchen where the wife and all the children and babies spend their time.

The wife is busy making chicha, the national Indian drink made from manioc. The woman chews the manioc, mixing her saliva with it. Then she spits all of it into a bucket. It ferments and in a couple days is ready to drink. It seems, however, that fermentation is not always necessary if time does not permit. Or possibly, there is always some fermented chicha left over in the bucket from another time which adds the necessary "kick".

Indian woman preparing chi-cha

We sit on rough wooden benches along the wall. The children look out at us from the doorway to the kitchen. The wife dips a small bowl into some chicha and hands one of us the bowl. We take it with the right hand. After drinking it, we hand the bowl back to her with our left hand. Traditions must be followed. Proper etiquette demands we each drink several bowls of chicha. A daughter who looks to be about six years old, and is allowed in the room, drinks chicha each time it comes around!

The wife busies herself in the kitchen once more. She brings a large palm leaf for each of us which we place on the hard dirt floor in front of us to use as a plate. She serves each of us half a baked fish with the head or tail and scales still on it, plus cooked plantains and manioc. The "plates" can then be thrown into the jungle; no dishes to wash.

Once we finish our meal, the husband takes us outside to teach us how to use a blowgun. It's not as easy as it looks, especially if we try to reach a target, a squash standing up on the ground, a short distance away. The Indians still use the blowguns for hunting.

Before we leave, all members of the family's children and the neighbor children pose in a group for us.

Dugouts take us back down the river from where we walk to our compound. On the way we stop many times to see interesting and unusual water birds.

That night our Shuar cook places a birthday cake in front of me! He made it from scratch and used jelly for the frosting! There is a candle in the center. And someone made a birthday card which all members of the group have signed. What a nice surprise here in the jungle!

Our hosts have prepared a cultural show for us. It begins with two women chewing manioc to make chicha. So we all participate in another chicha ceremony. There are several dances accompanied by Indian instruments. Some dances are performed by the men and others by the women. A loose theme or story is woven between them. Eventually the dances become more animated, the men and women dancing all together. And finally all of us join the circle to do the dances. Such great fun.

The Shuar men carry our baggage in the morning while we walk to the airstrip. The whole village gathers to say goodbye. The women have several jewelry items to sell, but actually they give them to us free in exchange for our boots. A good exchange for everyone.

We fly out of the forest by a different route than when we came in. Soon after we land high up in the highlands of the Andes. Our bus delivers us to a lovely, modern, hotel that has natural hot springs just outside the building. Soaking in the springs is a delightful way to spend the afternoon.

In the morning we drive up to an area of cloud forest where we hike over slippery vines and roots. On our way again, we continue past rushing rivers, horses, llamas, and volcanoes and come at last to a region of farms where we find the house and barn of our next shaman, Don Esteban, and his sons. Don Esteban is an ancient man said to be over one hundred years old. His sons appear to be in their eighties or even perhaps their nineties. They all belong to the "bird people" who "fly to other realms" when they meditate. These bird people live solely in a valley between two sacred volcanoes. The sons appear to be "shamans-in-training".

The inner courtyard opens to many rooms one of which serves as a cow barn. We walk through a door to a "sacred room" where healing ceremonies are performed. Women and girls sit around the walls on benches wearing typical highland dress. Some knit. Some nurse babies. Don Esteban's sons are preparing a rectangular table, the altar, for the ceremony. They wear wide-legged trousers and wide-brimmed hats. One son grinds up geranium petals which will be used for the healings. Any light in the room comes from lighted candles stuck on the altar, creating strange, provocative shadows on the walls.

Don Esteban enters wearing a "bird person's" hat made entirely of exquisitely colored feathers of the sacred Quetzal bird. Now the three men begin chain smoking which continues throughout the entire ceremony because tobacco is a part of their ritual. Don Esteban reads our palms after we scratch our name on our own candle.

Don Esteban of the Bird People tribe; hat of quetzal feathers

Next we undress to our underwear and four people at a time stand in a row in front of him. He and his sons "camay" each group with a tremendous amount of trago until all are dripping wet and the alcohol fumes just hang in the air. The sons move their lighted cigarettes close to the group. The cigarette fire and alcohol explode which continues the cleansing. Sometimes the trago is exploded with cigarette lighters just behind the group's legs. Quite frightening. During the explosions, Don Esteban chants in Quechua while shaking herbs over our heads. Finally he gives each person an egg-shaped Inca rock and an ancient spear to hold while the frenzied chanting continues. At last the participants rub geranium petals all over our bodies followed by cologne.

This is a very magical, mystical and apparently powerful cere-mony. When it is my turn to be healed, I feel very much in the power of these men. You can imagine the awe experienced by the local people when they receive healings.

Does it work? As with all ceremonies, the people need to believe in their shaman and his powers. And they need to believe in the rituals. They can become mesmerized. Lo and behold, some are healed, I think a good deal of the time. Also the shamans know the medicinal powers of their herbs, just as American Indians do, and can effect healings with those.

An incredible thing happens to me about an hour later. I develop a powerful case of diarrhea which lasts a day and a half. I ate the same food for the past two days as the other people in the group, but no one else is afflicted. We conclude it is a symptom of clean-sing, similar to the ayahuasca.

A beautifully restored hacienda, chapel and gardens are the setting for tonight's hotel. I am having so many abdominal problems I can't really appreciate this place until the next day.

After visiting the Otavalo Market in the morning, we drive on to another farm area and our final shaman, Maria Juana. Her farm house has the traditional courtyard in the middle from which we enter the ceremonial room. As one might expect, Maria Juana's ceremony is peaceful and rather tranquil compared to that of Don Esteban. She gives us necklaces made from geranium flowers which we are to wear until they fall off. Her husband cleanses all of us together "camay-ing" us with water. Then one by one each person who wishes a healing steps forward and Maria Juana shakes the dried herbs and chants over him.

* * *

The trip to Ecuador was designed to give us as much information and experience as possible. Thirteen spiritually-inclined people shared this education about shamanic healing. It would have been difficult not to have been spiritually affected. "Riding my horse in the direction it was going" was proving to me a most amazing adventure.

* * *

Sunee's Story

There is a beautiful sequel to this story. It happened about a year after the trip was over. We had a round-robin letter going around to let others know what we were doing and thinking so we wouldn't lose touch with each other. One day, Mary, our leader, called to tell me that Sunee was diagnosed with pancreatic cancer, and had only six weeks to live. He was in terrible pain and was moving from California to his mother's house in Pennsylvania so she could care for him.

Within the week I called him at his mother's and we had a good conversation. I asked him "if he was ready for his next great adventure" and he said "yes, it couldn't happen too soon because of the horrendous pain". I called him every week in the late afternoon when he seemed to be somewhat aware of what was going on in spite of the morphine. One week I bought a very small mosaic box made in India. There was a tiny scroll attached which said to open the box and leave it open at your bedside and you would have beautiful dreams. The box contained pot pourri. I sent it off to Sunee and then had to go to Florida to visit the my mother and mother-in-law. When I returned there was a message from Mary saying Sunee had died. I was unable to attend the ceremony in California when Sunee's friends and relatives gathered to spread his ashes in a river near where he lived.

About three months later I attended a Body and Soul conference here in Denver. Particularly I wanted to see Brian Weiss, a psychiatrist and author of several books about past-life regression. Brian's books are fascinating. A friend and his son who were both very interested in Brian's work went with me. Brian presented the morning session.

The afternoon program was conducted by James von Prague, a man renowned for his ability to connect with people in the afterworld and help relatives to receive information about them. About four hundred people were in the room. James would gradually begin to get a message from a spirit and speak it aloud. People who would think the information concerned their loved one would stand up. But as more information came through and James conveyed it, some of the people would sit down when they realized the new information did not pertain to their loved one. Finally there would be only one person left standing. Then James would give him a lot of information about the person spoken from the spirit world by their loved one.

James' remarkable ability amazed us all. During this session he had connected with about four spirits who wished to "talk" through him to their loved one. At one moment he was involved with the woman sitting directly in front of me whose son had recently died in a motorcycle accident. James gave more and more information until the woman could not doubt that she was hearing from her son.

Unexpectedly James mentioned that her son had a friend named Sunee. Of course her son didn't, but I did, and raised my hand. James said he would tell Sunee to wait and he would get back to the two of us shortly. When James did start giving me information from Sunee, he mentioned that Sunee was gay and was very happy to have arrived at the place where he was. He was beside a beautiful sparkling blue lake. James asked me if I did crafts, because Sunee said something about a box. I don't do crafts but knew

88

immediately what he was referring to – the little box I had sent him. Sunee was thanking me for it and said he had always had it by his bedside. Then he thanked me for spiritual books and tapes that I knew others of our group must have sent him, that he had read and listened to. That was the end of the message.

You can imagine my astonishment at this occurrence. My friend and his son said I would never have to try to tell someone about it and not have them believe me because they themselves had witnessed it and knew it was true. That evening I called Sunee's mother to say I had something I wanted to tell her; but if that would possibly upset her, she should just tell me. She urged me to go on and was so happy to hear the message. She said Sunee had received so many books and tapes from people in our group. Particularly he liked the little box. In fact she had left it on his bed table after he died.

How amazing it was to receive Sunee's message. I had never been present at any event where similar things were happening, so it was even more incredible. And it gave me complete closure as it did his mother.

Nepal and Tibet

Fall of 1997

In the fall of l997 I arrive in Kathmandu late in the afternoon from Bangkok. My tour group will not arrive from London for a day and a half. I am hopeful of dispersing some of my jet lag symptoms before the others get here.

It is a great chance to explore this ancient Hindu city on my own. A taxi delivers me to the center. I wander through narrow alleys that serve as streets in Kathmandu, and I repeatedly consult my Lonely Planet guide book. People and hand-drawn and pushed vehicles crowd around me, constantly blocking my path. In the center of each square is a statue of a Hindu deity, covered in part with red henna. People believe that by rubbing the henna they will obtain good fortune from the god.

Woman with prayer wheel

I happen into the main square, stand and absorb the sights in this hectic place. There are a number of very small temples with a sheep or goat tethered on the steps. The Festival of Durga, the Black Goddess, begins in the next day or so. At that time these animals will be sacrificed to the goddess. Across the tiny square under a small open canopy a holy man, a sadhu, sits on the floor. This is the first sadhu I have ever seen and I stare curiously at him. His hair is long, scraggly, and filthy. He is wearing a dirty loin cloth and is barefoot. Suddenly he lunges out of his seat, jumps to the ground and rushes full tilt at me. I am frightened, but he is so quick there isn't time to move. When he reaches me, he rubs his finger on my forehead and then rushes back to his seat. I don't realize at the time that he has henna on his finger. He has made a holy mark on me. It is obvious I am not Hindu since I am wearing western clothes. Is it a way to "baptize" me into the Hindu beliefs? Is it punishing me for blatantly staring at him? I am simply astonished and quickly leave the square to find a taxi to return to my hotel and pull myself together.

The next morning I walk 45 minutes to Patan, a small village about two miles away. Durbar Square in the center is spectacular. It is packed with gorgeous multi-storied Hindu temples and palaces built very close together, leaving no room really to walk between them. Ambling around the perimeter, however, I am just fascinated by the sight. The roof of each tier of a building is decorated with intricate wooden figures, many of them erotic in honor of Tantric ideas of Hinduism. There is a stupa at each of the four corners of the city erected by the great Buddhist emperor, Ashoka, in 250 B.C. But the building boom in Durbar Square came in the sixteenth century A.D. when the focus had shifted to Hinduism. All around the square are many other temples, several multi-storied, some with copper or gilt on the roofs.

This city is simply a feast for the eyes. There is a very spiritual aura. I am on a fast-track course in Hinduism.

As I walk about, I come upon two "watering" places - faucets lining walls in a sunken square where villagers come to get water and also wash themselves. Sacred cows wander the streets. Children play dice, marbles, hopscotch, ping pong, and a sort of billiard game with a miniature table. Kites fly everywhere above the buildings. Bright red house decorations for the festival are for sale in many booths.

In the Patan Museum next to Durbar Square the differences between Hinduism and Buddhism are well documented, using exquisite examples of art. The town is renowned for its cast bronzes and gilt copper repousee; there are explanations and many examples of the art forms in the museum.

I am learning that I can explore anywhere on my own and not worry for my safety. I find when I am alone I can savor the sights completely and feel totally a part of this strange new world.

*   *   *

The Tour Group –
Meeting Roger, Anne, and Sue

Tonight the tour group arrives in time to go to dinner. My new roommate, Sue, is in the room when I return from Patan. She spent a week with a Nepalese family up in the hills and is looking forward to a quiet night and decides not to go to dinner.

Since the group members are all British, they naturally vote for an Indian restaurant. I worry that the food will be too spicy for me, but I have no choice. I sit next to a man who looks at me skeptically and asks, "What are YOU doing here"?

I think swiftly, knowing my answer will determine my relationship with these people for the next two weeks. I answer, "Trying to escape from my fellow countrymen, I believe".

Roger remarks approvingly, "Not a bad idea".

The next morning during a walking tour of Kathmandu we visit the House of the Living Goddess. The beautiful young girl, selected to be the Goddess until she reaches puberty, shows herself to the public while we are there. She is indeed lovely as a goddess should be.

I find myself accidentally separated from the group at one point, so I decide to explore alone once more with my Lonely Planet book which describes several possible walks in the old city. One is the textile market area with an abundance of bright colorful bolts of fabric everywhere I look.. A dazzling sight. A second walk winds through back alleys in a quiet section. I see men combing cotton that was removed from quilts and that will again be placed in new quilts when the lumps are satisfactorily removed. Another man is making gorgeous kites. A large stone phallic symbol stands in the center of a miniscule square. Rats run here and there.

Happening upon a small square with a wooden temple I am amazed to see brightly colored, intricately-painted carvings under the roof gables all the way around. They depict an astonishing number of sexual positions, for this temple belongs to the cult of tantric Hinduism. There are Buddhist temples elsewhere which are Buddhist tantric. Devotees of both religions believe that the moment of sexual orgasm is the identical feeling one attains when reaching Nirvana. Hence this experience is sought by many, in the hope of reaching a higher consciousness.

Tonight Sue and I get better acquainted. I realize that this is a truly amazing woman. She is afflicted with lupus, but it doesn't slow her down and it certainly does not affect her appreciation for everything she sees or does. I am indeed fortunate to have her for a roommate because we are certainly on the same wave length when it comes to appreciating new cultures and religions. When you and your roommate are in sync, it makes for a very enjoyable trip.

*   *   *

Tibet
Nomad Women / Sue's Poem "Little Boy"

The next morning we fly over the Himalayas to Lhasa, passing Mt. Everest at about the same altitude as its summit. The clouds part so we can see the summit! Extraordinary!

95

Our Chinese guide, Gast-en, a driver, and 12-passenger bus are waiting for us at the airport many miles distant from Lhasa. As we drive toward the capitol, the scenery occupies us completely. Tall, grey stone mountains, golden fields of ripe barley, the Brahmaputra River lined by golden-leaved trees, perfect reflections of the trees in the water. Truly a different landscape than any of us have ever seen.

We request a "rest' stop. The guide has the driver pull into our first Tibetan monastery which isn't even on the itinerary, usually a "no-no". The two "toilets" or holes in the ground are out in the open at the top of a flight of steps cut into the side of a hill. Sue and I are used to Asian toilets from previous traveling. It is a bit different, however, to perch like statues on the top of the hill. But, of course, it is do-able, as are all strange customs in a new culture. We provide courage for the other women who have been thinking this is impossible.

We wander about the temple. I see one of the men in our group, Steve, climbing a very steep ladder, holding onto a rope hanging down for balance. I follow him. At the top we find a room with a tiny, wizened old monk sitting on a bed, his thermos of tea on a small table beside him. Many banknotes lie haphazardly on the table. I believe they were left in payment to him when he consented to pray on a person's behalf. Since we don't know for sure, we add some money to the pile. The monk seems kind and friendly. This is our initiation into Tibetan Buddhist structures and monks. And Steve and I are the only ones to experience it. It always pays to wander away from your group and explore what else is out there.

Our hotel in Lhasa is typical of hotels all over Asia, although of course, far below five-star edifices which I always avoid. Everything in expensive hotels may work, but the guests are totally isolated from the local people. They might as well be in New York City!

Our hotel has problems which are common to three star or less hotels in third world countries: sometimes there is no water, sometimes there is only cold water, only infrequently is there any warm
water. Since we have no water in our assigned room, Sue and I request a different room. Upon entering the second room, we find the
water doesn't work here either. In frustration the staff gives us a
room in a part of the building that has never been redecorated. The
water works. But in payment for this, we have to stare at never-
replaced carpet with almost every square inch covered with brown
spots – the result of hundreds of Chinese guests spitting on it, an
ingrained part of their culture.

We spend three days in Lhasa to allow us to acclimatize to the altitude of 12,000 feet. Altitude sickness is a common problem, especially for people who live at low elevation. The first night Anne
(Roger's wife) begins to feel really sick. I have a prescription with
me for altitude sickness and finally several hours later convince her
to take the pill. She begins to feel better immediately. The pills
really save her trip; she had begun to think she would have to return home immediately.

Hotels in Tibet usually can provide their guests with "rubber pillows" filled with oxygen. There is a tube at one corner. The afflicted person breathes in the oxygen from the end of the tube a bit
at a time. My roommate, Sue, really needs this breathing aid.

Lhasa is the holiest city of Tibetan Buddhism. Hundreds of pilgrims daily circumambulate the holy quarter of the city and the perimeter of the Jokhang, the holiest temple of Tibet. Dressed in their
finery with coral and turquoise jewelry, the pilgrims amble along
twirling their prayer wheels. They prostate themselves repeatedly
before the temple. Juniper branches burn in large ovens. The
smoke wafts the prayers to heaven. A giant bazaar (the Barkhor)
completely surrounds the temple. The walk through the inside of
the temple divulges thousands of magnificent art pieces, thankas,
butter sculptures, and hundreds of lighted butter lamps throwing
shadows all over the walls. It's a marvelous mystical place in spite

97

of the fact that so many people are crowded into every small room. The pilgrims exude a rather unpleasant odor because they smear their skin with rancid lanolin from sheep, as we would use an emollient face cream.

The Barkhor is a fascinating place to wander for a couple hours. Merchants, many of them women, speak no English but can understand basic bargaining. The women are stunning in their Tibetan dresses and silver, turquoise, and coral jewelry which is even wound into the hair. I move slowly in the market as it curves around the outside of the temple and come eventually to prosaic merchandise such as horse bridles. These are also decorated with silver and turquoise stones. Next are stalls full of dishes and pots and pans. Everywhere I see colorful scenes of Tibetans, monks and lay people, browsing and buying.

There are so many areas to visit in Lhasa. The Dalai Lama's Potala Palace, the Tibetan medicine hospital, a large nunnery, the Dalai Lama's summer palace. The list goes on and on. On the outskirts of the city are two marvelous monasteries with monks performing their appointed jobs. One is the Dreprung. The other is the Sera. At the Dreprung, one monk block-prints pages of scripture, while four others cut wood for cooking. Some cook as others make barley beer or prepare butter tea on solar-powered burners. There are gardens to be tended and decorative motifs to be constructed to complete a stupa in the courtyard. This is almost a Buddhist Williamsburg surrounded by high grey granite mountains.

The best part of a monastery visit is being present during one of the chanting sessions. The whole group of residents gathers together several times a day in the Chanting Hall. Chanting is beautiful to listen to, and, even more impressive, if the session happens to include music from gongs, cymbals, conch shell horns, and long horns. This is the essence of Buddhism for me -- definitely a spiritual experience.

On the fourth day we leave Lhasa, driving on the Friendship Highway which traverses the central part of Tibet, always on the high plateau. We cross a high pass, the Kamba La at 14,382 feet. At the summit we look back down to the Yarlung Tsangpo which is the Tibetan name for the Brahmaputra River. We walk among poles from which fly hundreds of faded, wind-torn prayer flags. Freezing wind nearly rips our clothes off. Before reboarding our small bus, we peer over the far side of the pass to see a magnificent emerald-blue lake -- the Yamdrok-tso. Once down the pass, the dirt road follows the north end of the lake where we stop for a picnic lunch. When we step out of the bus there is no one in sight, but a minute later children run toward us from all directions to stop and stare at us. They wear ragged, dirty, nondescript clothes and winter jackets. We give them what we have left of lunch and our empty water bottles which the families will use to bottle their barley beer.

Prayer flags at the summit of a pass

A hanging glacier is high above the road as we cross another pass, the Karo La, at 15,000 feet. Looking down a few hundred feet we watch a herder leave his small number of yaks tied together down at the bottom and hike up to visit with us. He shows us how he makes the soles of his shoes with rope. He seems to really enjoy being with new and strange people where we can all use sign language. On the way down the pass to the next plain we are amazed to see telegraph poles made of hardened mud along the road.

In the afternoon we drive through our first Tibetan town, Gyantze. One half is mud-brick Tibetan houses, low ceilinged, flat-roofed, with a group of prayer flags sticking up from the corners of the roofs. The other half of the town is ugly concrete-block Chinese buildings. At the edge of town stands Gyantze Kumbum, a glorious four-story tiered structure, the finest stupa in Tibet. Stupas are usually memorials to people. Sometimes they contain relics of a person.

We drive on to the larger town of Shigatze. Our hotel is actually better than we had ever dreamed. We visit Tashilhunpo Monastery, where Tibetans bring stray dogs and leave them to be cared for. The monks take in any and all dogs because dogs are thought to be reincarnations of monks. "Holy" dogs are everywhere inside the walls. The monastery is one of the great centers of Tibetan Buddhism, and one of the few monasteries that was relatively undamaged by the Cultural Revolution.

The monastic grounds are covered with beautifully decorated buildings, one containing a huge statue of the Maitreya (future Buddha) covered with 280 kilograms of gold leaf. The grounds include numerous impressive chapels and prayer halls. This monastery is the largest functioning monastic institution in present-day Tibet. Again it is so interesting to watch the monks at their duties. While we are here, a large group of them sit in a circle on the floor of the courtyard, chopping up large pieces of meat into bite-size pieces with cleavers. This is quite a project and attracts the dogs who are waiting for tidbits to be thrown to them.

We happen to be here at the moment for afternoon prayers. Monks, including very young boys, arrive at the entrance to the prayer hall where they remove their sandals and don their very large yellow hats, symbol of one of the orders of Buddhism. They enter the room and sit on benches with cushions. We are allowed to stand just inside the doorway at the back of the room.

Monks chopping meat with cleavers. Dogs await their share

All the participants know the chants by heart. The head monk walks up and down the aisles to make sure that all the younger boys are attentive and chanting. He carries a feather to touch the boys whose thoughts may be straying to remind them to participate. We notice that, when he isn't looking, one of the boys blows bubbles with bubble gum! Sacred Buddhist chants and bubbles – what a contrast.

In all the towns we have been driving through we can see that Tibetans are second-class citizens. The Han Chinese that the Chinese government moved into Tibet are definitely better off. They have nicer shops and possessions and a more modern business area.

Along the entire drive across the plateau farmers thresh barley by throwing pitchforks of the grain into the air and letting the breeze carry away the chaff while the grain drops to the ground in a mound. There are no fences anywhere. We see mud-built telegraph poles at one place for a short distance. Crossing two more high passes, we stop at the summits to visit the prayer flags.

Surprisingly we suddenly come upon a few black tents belonging to nomads. Women and children are here, but the men and boys have taken the goats and sheep up higher in the mountains to graze. Inside the tents we see cotton quilts, a stove in the center for cooking, and a few cups and bowls for meals. A large pot simmers on the stove in one tent, probably with stew. There are a couple bags of clothing and possessions. That is all. Each woman wears a silver spoon pinned under her apron. Children have a small spoon pinned inside a jacket. Presumably one will always have this utensil at hand when there is rice or stew to eat.

Three cardboard boxes outside one of the tents attract our interest. They contain the pieces for a new treadle-operated sewing machine, probably the result of a trip to Lhasa or a smaller town.

The nomads' religion is a cross between an ancient shamanic type, Bon, and Buddhism. They put their dead high up on a cliff where birds pick the bones clean. It is called sky burial. Tradition mandates that at least one son from each family must become a monk. Other sons must follow the monastic life for two years. Everyone undertakes yearly pilgrimages. There is a great devotion to natural, sacred places, and all manner of deities.

What a nice opportunity to meet the nomadic women and try to understand some of their culture. Once you get close to people whose lifestyle is so different from your own, you begin to grasp the idea that there are so many, many cultures and religious beliefs; but you feel akin to them all and a spiritual connection with each person. Indeed, Buddha said, "All paths lead to the top of the mountain"!

Down on the flat land once again, we come upon a tribe that is slaughtering sheep, butchering them, and hanging the carcasses on frames. This is my first experience watching the slaughter of an animal. The woman pinches the nose and mouth of the animal shut, cuts through the chest, and pulls out the heart. The animal never flinches. I think it smothers painlessly. This tribe is not Buddhist, so can kill animals. Buddhists, whose religion prohibits harming any living creature, can buy and eat the butchered meat. A good arrangement.

More driving through moonscape-type areas finally leads us to an area of ancient stone forts in disrepair. We climb up in some of them and peer through the slits that archers used against the enemy. Now we sit eating our picnic lunch outside the bus. It is freezing cold and windy. As usual, children arrive from all directions. We share our lunch with them and give them empty water bottles. Most of the children wear heavy jackets, pants, hats and boots. But two boys, seemingly brothers, shiver ceaselessly in flimsy shorts, shirts and sandals. They are so very, very thin and cross their arms as though holding themselves together. It is painful to watch. We ask our guide what we can do for them. She says that any clothes we might give them will be taken by the parents and sold at the market. In effect there is really nothing we can do. I know the sight of them will remain indelibly printed on my mind.

When we reboard the bus, my roommate, Sue, writes the following poem about the older boy.

> Little boy, oh little boy,
> How did you come to be?
> A moment's warmth,
> A quick release,
> A labour in this desert place?
> Yet here you stand
> With hand to mouth
> In silent shivering plea.

103

Little boy, oh little boy,
Who cares that you are cold?
Your tiny feet
And matchstick legs,
Your flimsy shorts
And flapping shirt,
Your hands clasped tight
Across your chest
As biting winds take hold.

Little boy, oh little boy,
This world is never fair.
You stand and watch us eat our fill
In boots and wooly socks and hats
And goose-down jackets, snugly warm.
Our crumbs may fill you for an hour--
But when will tourists come again?
What feelings fill your baby heart?
How may we show we care?

Little boy, oh little boy,
Your hunger sears my soul.
Chance might have been
You were my son --
But, even so, the world is one.
And I have food while you have none.
I feel my shame, my helpless rage --
I cannot make you whole.

Little boy, oh little boy,
Just a few miles from your home
Lies the majesty of Lalung Leh, (a high pass)
Of cloud and frost and sun and snow,
Of dreams and mystery and awe.
But you will never see the sight,
Your heritage, your holy right --

For those few miles might be to you
Another world unknown.

Little boy, oh little boy,
The winter's coming on --
But your small frame
Has no reserves.
The cold will freeze your little limbs,
Your empty stomach bring no warmth.
And when the Spring comes round again,
Dear little boy -- some mother's child --
By then you will be gone.

Used by permission
By Sue Wiggans, Isle of Wight, 12 October 1997

Starving "little boy" and his brother in the poem

Sadly leaving the children behind, we drive to the summit of Lalung
Leh. Down again and up again to Lhakpa La pass at 17,130 feet, the
highest point we will reach on this trip. It is the watershed between

Tibet and the Indian sub-continent. Looking to the north we see the plateau with mountains upon mountains beyond to western China. To the south looms the whole line of Himalayan peaks.

Coming down the south side of the pass, a small village of cement block buildings provides living quarters for a road construction crew. What an utterly desolate place to live.

Suddenly someone calls out, "Mt. Everest"! Sure enough as we stand and peruse the mountains we make out the north col and west ridge of Mt. Everest in the far distance. Both of these are climbing routes to the summit. What a sight! It is so cold that frost lies on the ground, and ice covers the pond next to the road.

Continuing west we pass through a few small, poor, farm villages before climbing to Touo La at 15,100 feet. More prayer flags await us at the top. Dropping down to the junction where the main road from western Tibet comes in, we enter Lhatze, a tiny dusty truck stop town lying at 12,150 feet. After a short petrol stop we head out of town to the west. Now the scenery grows stark, moonscape-like and barren. Very few people live in this area. We climb again, and, as we approach the summit we watch four Japanese bike riders with full bike packs making their slow way up. We pass them, jump out of our vehicle in time to cheer them over the top. They are thrilled with their success of climbing all the passes from Lhasa to here.

After a long descent we reach Shegar at 13,300 feet, our last hotel in Tibet and by far the worst. It lies in the middle of a freezing wind-swept plain. As we walk in the open door to the lobby we notice that all the Chinese staff are wearing down jackets. Why don't they close the door?

Our room is uninviting to say the least, because as we enter, we first walk past the door to our disgusting bathroom. The porcelain (if one can call it that) is peeling and rusty. The tub is so filthy that

106

we know we don't want to touch a toe in it, but it doesn't matter since we discover that the water doesn't work in either the tub or sink. There is a permanent water shortage here. What does work is the toilet. The water in it runs constantly. The beds are covered with pink taffeta bedspreads with a thin blanket underneath. We roll out our sleeping bags on top and know, without being told, that there will be no heat in this frozen place tonight.

Each night in Tibet Sue has requested a pillow full of oxygen for the night. This hotel has no "pillows" but they do have canisters full of oxygen. We both buy one. I am thinking ahead of my trek in Nepal yet to come.

Dinner is unappetizing to say the least. Afterward we retreat to our room and prepare for bed.

A few hours later, I make a trip to the bathroom and find that the toilet has leaked all over the floor. The water is at least two inches deep. If it weren't for the concrete lip between the bathroom and the bedroom, our room would be deep in water.

In the morning our bus climbs to the summit of the last pass, La Lunga at 16,600 feet. To the south we see the road dropping into a gorge between the snow-capped peaks. This is the beginning of the descent to Nepal!

Down, down we bump on very steep, narrow, rocky roads, finally arriving at Milarepa's Cave, the hermit residence of one of Tibetan Buddhism's most famous saints. The story says that he lived here naked for many years. He meditated and composed songs. Many legends abound concerning him, including teaching mountain goddesses with the use of Tantric sexual techniques.

In the late afternoon we arrive at the village of Nyalam. It is bitter cold. Our accommodation is a Tibetan guest house. We must climb up steep steps to the main floor, then again to the second floor, dragging and banging our back packs and day packs behind us.

There are only four rooms. The two married couples each receive one of these. Sue's and my room has a third bed so we get Steve for a roommate, while the other five stay in one room. The single toilet is up on the roof! Megan Hawkins finds a bucket up there, brings it down and "hides it" among the plants in the hall - a fine makeshift chamber pot!

We cross the road to the only cafe in town, bundled in our long underwear, heavy jackets, mittens and hats. Tea is served. The very nicest thing about it is wrapping our cold hands around the hot cups. Soon a simple meal arrives. Then we retire to our freezing rooms.

Thank goodness for our sleeping bags. We put on every stitch of clothing we have with us and wear them all under our jackets, finishing off with hats and mittens. There is a worn duvet on the bed on top of which lies a thin taffeta bedspread. Even these two threadbare layers are welcome!

Next morning, continuing down the narrow road, we arrive at a land slide where the road becomes impossible for vehicle travel. The slide has been here for years. We must leave our bus, driver, and guide behind. Porters wait to carry our large packs. In fact, they and their families live in tents in front of the blocked end of the road for at least the entire "warm season". At the far end of the slide, vehicles wait to load us up to go onward. We "luck into" an ancient truck with a metal bed, no padded floor, and no shocks. The porters attempt to put an entire additional group of people on board with us including all their luggage. But we shout and shout; they finally remove them. A canvas top curves over us from one side of the truck to the other. It is mostly huge holes.

We sit against the sides facing each other. The truck starts off, lurching every few seconds into deep pot holes. This continues kilometer after kilometer. Once we drive under a waterfall, the water pours through a hole in the canvas into the bed of the truck and soaks us. Megan crawls forward to the front, yanks her duffle from under the pile, stands up hanging on to the curved canvas ridge supports and strips down to her birthday suit, replacing everything with dry clothes. The banging and bouncing does evil things to our backs.

We're still on the "Friendship Highway", the road connecting Tibet with Nepal. Slowly the scenery changes from stark grey mountains to a green-forested gorge. It even begins to look sub-tropical with ferns beside the road. Finally we arrive at the Friendship Bridge. A few porters carry our luggage across. The formalities take forever, but at last we are on a modern Nepalese bus headed for Kathmandu.

*   *   *

The visit to Tibet proved to be more than I had ever dreamed. The monasteries and art taught me so much about Buddhism. And the high passes, the scenery, the nomads, the farmers, introduced me to a culture that I had hardly realized even existed. It all exceeded my highest expectations. One more important plus: my friendships with Sue, Roger and Anne, and Megan and John grew to the point that we are still fast friends (I visited them while on my search for stone circles in England at a later time).

*   *   *

Kathmandu Again

The next day is a free day. My tour companions frantically shop while I stay in bed to rest up after the strenuous last few days. Tonight Sue and I have a last meal together and celebrate our friendship.

In the morning the tour group leaves for the airport and I leave for the Kathmandu Guesthouse in the old Thamel area of the city. Although the guesthouse management can't seem to locate my reservation, I happen to appear at the precise moment when some people are checking out. I am in luck, but someone else with a reservation will later be out of luck. This is the way these people do business!

I leave by cab immediately for a small village called Bakhtapur. A young man about twenty-two years old works hard to be my guide, even though I have my guide book with me and feel confident of seeing the sights alone. He finally succeeds, and I am ultimately glad that I have made this choice. He shows me everything. His explanations are complete. Best of all, he takes me down the back streets which are all dirt. The Festival of Durga is still in full sway. Being a holiday no one is working. We watch children swinging, something I have never seen in Asia. And a group plays a game that in a vague sense resembles hopscotch. They slide their "flip flops" along the dirt to a line a few feet away. Those whose slippers don't make it over the line are "out". The line is then moved farther away and the game continues. Several men's groups play cards and bet on the outcome.

We visit all the main temples and stop for chai up on the roof of one temple. A hundred kites fly overhead. On my way back to Kathmandu, I stop at a women's cooperative store of handicrafts filled to the brim with hand-made paper, thin pounded brass animals for Christmas tree ornaments, dolls, and beautifully woven fabrics.

The next day I explore the Thamel section, a tourist mecca, sit and read in the lovely courtyard of the guest house, and find a sort of "chiropractic adjustment" and massage (from the barber in his shop) to put bones and muscles back in place from the horrendous truck ride coming down from Tibet to Nepal.

.

My Solo Trek

At nine the next morning Jangbu Sherpa picks me up in a cab to go to the airport. He is twenty-one years old and will be my guide on my solo trek.

I had written to the local tour operator to request a guide who would show me every monastery, nunnery, and temple on our way. I explained that I was not interested in seeing how high I could climb along the trail. Rather I wanted to be immersed in the Sherpa culture and Buddhist traditions in the mountains.

We fly in a small plane with other trekkers to Lukla, a small village with guest houses and restaurants. It lies halfway up the first group of mountains rising from the Kathmandu valley and is the starting place for treks using the Everest Base Camp trail.

After lunch in Lukla we start out. I have a porter to carry my backpack. He usually follows at his own pace. Jangbu tells me to turn left at the first intersection. I ask why. He tells me we will visit my "first temple". I say, "You read my letter!"

He answers, "Yes. You will see every temple, monastery, and nunnery in these mountains." I know he is the right guide for me!

I brought with me some large Colorado pink quartz stones as gifts for monks. As we enter the temple, I make my ceremonial bow to the keeper of the temple and hand him a stone. He is amazed that I know the correct moves and is most pleased with the stone. Jangbu is also surprised; it cements our relationship. The monk shows us around the small temple; we thank him and are on our way.

The raging river lies deep in a gorge beside the trail. At one point we cross a flimsy bridge from one side to the other. Not for those who suffer from vertigo. The immense boulders and beautiful blue water far below make it all worthwhile.

Mani stone along the trail. Trekkers must circle it three times

About four o'clock we arrive at a small group of guesthouses. When we reach ours we have to climb from the ground to the main floor via an eight-foot high ladder. This is typical Tibetan structure just like the guest house in Nyalam in Tibet. The kitchen and common room are on the main floor. The stove is made of mud and burns wood for fuel. Continuous bench seats line the walls of the room. At night this is where the guides and porters sleep. We climb to the next floor with three guest rooms which are separated by thin plywood walls between the rooms. They all open to one large space above the walls and below the roof.

When Jangbu sets my backpack down in one room, I hear someone with a terrible cough in the next room. With all the open space above the rooms, I can just imagine the microbes from the room next door landing on me, perhaps ruining the rest of my trip. So Jangbu gives me the farther room. It probably won't make a difference, but who knows?

My room has three wooden cots with thin mattresses and a curtain that doesn't reach across the window. But it certainly is adequate.

We climb down the two ladders and check out behind the building where there is a small wooden structure for the cows at night and, beyond it, the latrine. Quite a basic set-up.

We order noodle soup for dinner from the owner of the guesthouse.

In the middle of the night I have to make a trip to the latrine. Even using my flashlight, it is a bit challenging to climb down the ladders, along the path past the cows, who scare me with their rustling about in the dark, to the latrine. Then, of course, with the flashlight in my teeth, I have to re-climb the ladders. One must learn new ways quickly in a new environment.

The trek the next day is all climbing contrasted to the previous day which was just a gentle incline. The narrow path is one huge boulder after another for several miles. We cross the river gorge several times. Hundreds of porters pass us loaded with trekkers' baggage. Some men have high heavy baskets on their backs full of produce, meat, and merchandise of all kinds. They have a tump strap over the forehead to carry the weight evenly. All the men wear flip flops or are barefoot. They have carried loads up from Lukla but, more often, a two-day hike from the flat plain in the Kathmandu valley.

The gorge finally opens up to a large flat area, the village of Namche Bazaar, which appears to be a huge amphitheater, with guest houses rising from one level to another.

Our guest house is a newer building without the usual Tibetan style ladder to the main floor. Instead, a door opens to the street. Inside are rooms for the family and a large common room with huge windows on three sides. Outside the back door are an Asian toilet room and a shower room. Downstairs are the small sleeping cubicles for guests.

Namche Bazaar is a stop for acclimatizing to altitude so we stay here an extra day. It happens to be Saturday which is the day of the market. The porters we saw yesterday were carrying the goods for the market. I think these men spend all their days climbing up with goods for the bazaar, descending the next day, gathering produce from their family gardens or accumulating other goods, for the next several days and then starting all over again. As at all bazaars, almost everything conceivable is available so high up here in the mountains!

The people who live in these mountains belong to the best-known Nepalese ethnic group, the Sherpas. Originally from Tibet, they were nomadic herders when they moved to Nepal 500 years ago. Today most of them are trekking guides or mountaineers, and all known by the same last name, "Sherpa".

After the day of rest, Jangbu and I start once more up the trail. The scenery is incredibly beautiful with many high snowy peaks all around us. After about four hours, we reach the next important point on the trail. Tengpoche, at 12,600 feet, has several guest houses and a famous monastery. I arise at 4:00 a.m. the next morning and take my sleeping bag into the monastery to observe the chanting and sacred instrument playing. Although it is freezing cold, it is definitely an experience not to be missed. A very spiritual event.

During the trek I am reading the book, "The Snow Leopard", by Peter Matthiessen. Since it deals with a very difficult trek in north central Nepal, it seems the perfect book. There are spiritual aspects to it which add much to my experiences during the trek.

The next day we no longer climb higher, but descend a bit and then walk west to the tiny village of Kundjung. Hillary, the famous Everest climber, built a school here. Children are playing in the school yard in spite of heavy snow falling. A short way further we reach a 700 year old monastery. Only one old monk lives here.

Others come from the village for prayers. I ceremonially bow to the monk and hand him another piece of the pink quartz which he obviously prizes. I think this is not an area where quartz is found. He shows us around the small building. There is a glass case with a hairy head of a "yeti" (the traditional "big foot" of Asia).

We walk westward for another mile through the town of Kunde. Fields of harvested barley are everywhere. The people are also raising potatoes successfully. Our guest house is very new, run by a woman in her thirties. She lives there with her two children who attend the school we saw. Her husband built another guest house farther up on the Everest Trail which he manages.

Electricity is available in this tiny village because we are close to a river with a hydroelectric plant. In the common room there is a portable electric heater. I dig some cashews out of my daypack and share them with the porter and Jangbu. We huddle close to the heater trying to keep our hands warm. It is a nice moment for the three of us to be alone together, a moment which brings us close.

A dirty Tibetan mountain man walks in the room wearing a large turquoise stone on a filthy red string which he takes from around his neck. There is a hole drilled through the stone. I certainly am not planning to buy turquoise. But this seems a rather unique situation. How odd to have a man arrive at the building, enter and offer this stone. We bargain for a while. However, I have no idea what such a stone should cost. Finally Jangbu says we have reached the lowest point, and, if I don't buy it, he will because it is such a good price. I'm sure it has been a good luck piece for the man and now it will be for me.

We eat our evening meal by the heater. Noodle soup again. About thirty minutes later, the man returns with another man who has about eight stones on a string necklace! He rolls them off the string so I can examine them. I decide to buy three of these also. Where else would I be visited by a second turquoise seller at my guest house!

115

By this time Jangbu and I have developed a fine friendship. His English is fairly good and we talk about many subjects. He really likes the rock group, The Eagles. We walk along and he sings the first line of an Eagle song and I sing the second. We go on like that throughout the whole song. He tells me about other trekkers he has met and all sorts of adventures. And, of course, he knows that I respect his religion greatly.

So as we walk together the next day, he tells me that he is taking me to his family's village. His family owns the oldest homestead in the village. We stop once on the path as he points out two mountain peaks close by. He says that is where the spirits live that watch over his village. Here I am once again encountering beliefs that are not Buddhist. But this no longer surprises me. One finds this discrepancy everywhere in the world.

We arrive at the family home, climb up the ladder to the main floor which is one big room. There is the kitchen area with a stove plus an oven built of mud. Across the room is a large double bed. In cupboards with glass doors there are many blankets for guests and family members who will sleep on the floor. On one of the poles that support the roof I see all sorts of certificates indicating that Jangbu's brother, who lives here with his wife and two children, has summitted Everest four times with groups he guided. A large chest contains souvenirs from his climbs. In fact, the brother is off guiding at this moment.

The inside walls are painted black and decorated with white dots and lines. I ask Jangbu what they mean. He tells me that people make these "decorations" during religious festivals. I ask him if these are part of the ancient Bon religion and he says,"Yes". This is proof that the Bon religion is still being practiced in the mountains. The book, "The Snow Leopard", devotes much discussion to this practice. I feel so fortunate to see the family home and these designs.

Sacred Bon religious decorations painted on wall
of Jangbu's home

The sister-in-law enters with two small children. At this point I am unloading the "treats" I brought along on the trip for children. I give the children a jar of peanut butter. I also have a couple lollipops left which pleases them immensely.

They go back outside to hang up laundry. Jangbu cooks noodle soup for the two of us. We sit at a tiny table while Jangbu tells me more about his family. The soup is delicious.

We leave the house to climb quite high above the village. He tells his sister-in-law to boil some potatoes for us while we are gone. We reach a nunnery. The nuns have been crushing charcoal to make pigment to paint a black border around the windows of the building, a typical Tibetan decoration. They receive us graciously. We admire their small temple and then start down once more.

117

When we reach Jangbu's house, the boiled potatoes are waiting for us. We dip them in salt and hot sauce and eat them with our hands. Delicious! Jangbu has shared so much of his past, his family, and aspirations with me. And it is so special to have shared the soup and potatoes which are typical foods of the Sherpas. He tells me he would have asked me to spend the night (the first person he had ever invited), but his sister-in-law doesn't keep house like his mother did. He doesn't want me to have to put up with the mess.

Enjoying boiled potatoes dipped in hot sauce and salt

* * *

Namche Bazaar –
and I "Save" a Girl With My Oxygen

That night we return to Namche Bazaar and stay in the same guest house as before. It is snowing heavily and is very cold. Several charcoal braziers are burning in the common room. A British trekking group arrives, and now all the people, including me, are sitting in the room trying to get warm. I notice one girl sitting across from me. She looks as though she has fallen asleep. Suddenly the two people next to her pull open the window above her and hold her outside by her ankles. Obviously the oxygen in the room has been seriously depleted by the burning braziers, something I had worried about the first time I was here. The guest house owner suggests they carry her to his bedroom. Her friends try artificial respiration with no results. I retrieve the canister of oxygen from my pack which is left over from Tibet and blow puffs from it into her mouth. Gradually she begins to recover. It seems strange to me that the owner didn't realize the danger of the braziers. One would think this must have happened many times before.

The snow is falling heavily and is now quite deep. Jangbu goes down into the town to buy some gaitors for me to wear above my hiking boots tomorrow. The owner prepares a delicious dinner. I finish my book and worry unnecessarily about the possibility of avalanche as we go down the next day. The braziers burn all evening and the owner brings in a kerosene heater which people put outside the room now and then because it keeps giving people headaches. It is freezing cold and the owner offers me a kerosene heater to take to my sleeping cubicle for the night, but I refuse for safety concerns. Instead I bundle into every piece of clothing I have.

We start down in the morning and the snow is not as deep as I had feared. We slip and slide through it, but finally arrive in late afternoon at Phakding, the same group of guest houses where we stayed the first night on the trek. There is no room in the house where we stayed before. Jangbu checks out another one -- awful. Finally he finds one with space. It is the usual set-up with the plywood walls between the cubicles ending in a huge open space up high. I think this is going to be a really noisy night. And, of course, everyone in the building is coughing. Our porter doesn't show up for several hours. I think he had trouble figuring out where we finally ended up. Jangbu gives me a big hug when everything finally comes together.

119

We leave for Lukla at 7:30. The trail leads up hill most of the way. But finally we arrive in Lukla. I MADE IT! I think Jangbu is proud of me. I take a hot shower in a hell hole of a hotel and wash my hair! Now I am sitting in a flat dirt area behind the lodge in the sun. People's laundry lies about on the ground drying. Some men are sleeping on camping pads. One plays a drum. Chickens walk around clucking. Mules with bells on walk into the "yard" next door where a string of yaks is being led out. Filthy children with snotty noses play around me. I realize I have slept, showered, pee-ed, even eaten in places I would never have thought possible. I feel almost as though I belong here. It all seems so natural. I guess I have finally" immersed."

We have had to be in Lukla one day before our plane is scheduled to leave. Because of the snowstorm, planes have not been able to fly into Lukla for three days. So in the morning, about one hundred people gather hoping to get on the one DC3. I have no idea how the system works, but miraculously I get on.

* * *

Our cab pulls up to the Kathmandu Guest House. I ask Jangbu not to leave until I know I have a room. I reserved one before I left for the trek, but the men at Reception now say there is no room left for me! I am really furious with them and the way they do business. I angrily let them know what I think. Finally the head man says there is one room in the "annex". "Lonely Planet" warns not to accept a room in the annex. But I check out the room, which is cold and very damp because the sun never reaches it. Mold grows on the stones outside the door. Sewer gas drifts from the bathroom. I feel a sore throat coming on; diarrhea is also threatening. Well, I really have no choice; I accept the room and go to bed immediately in that unhealthy environment. The sheets and blanket are actually wet!

* * *

120

I have one day left in Kathmandu and some important sights left to see. Bengay on my throat all night long and Immodium tablets have done their work. I also started on E-Mycin last night. So I'm off by taxi to Bodnath, the largest stupa in Nepal, and one of the largest in the world. It is huge. People still go here to pray before undertaking a journey in the Himalayas.

On to Pashupatinath, Nepal's most important Hindu temple, and one of the most important Shiva temples on the subcontinent. A man joins me as I start off on a path with my "Lonely Planet" book. It is obvious that he intends to be my guide, but I make no deal with him for remuneration. However, he sticks with me, offering me all the information I could ever want and, even at one moment, picking a handful of marijuana and handing it to me saying, "Smells good." I agree and hand it back to him, hoping no officials saw that little event.

Westerners are not allowed in the temple, but there is much to see along the Bagnati River banks. The Bagnati is a holy river and therefore a very popular place to be cremated. There are four burning ghats and there is almost always a cremation going on. Further along men are ritually bathing in the river. If a person is being cremated, his son has to bathe, have his hair cut off, then don a white cape and live in a mourning building for at least a week.

Further along is a sixth-century temple with erotic Tantric scenes.

We cross the river on a bridge and see eleven stone chaityas, each containing a lingam (a statue of a penis). I stand at the end and look along the entire group. A Shiva lingam stands nearby, a masterpiece dating from the 5th century. Monkeys play around. A snake charmer cajols his pet to rise up out of the basket. There are so many, many temples, images, sculptures all with their own legends.

Back at the main street, my self-appointed guide wants money. We have a bit of a discussion, but I end up giving him something since he was very knowledgeable and spoke good English.

I return to the Guest House, eat dinner in the courtyard, and watch BBC News on the TV in the lobby. The electricity goes off, but there is an emergency generator. I am off to the "wet room" early for bed.

The next morning I fly out of Nepal. Nepal and Tibet have proven to be very amazing places. I know I have truly grown spiritually.

New Zealand and Australia
New Zealand and The Maoris

I n 1998 Jim and I visit New Zealand, camping in the South Island and renting a small car for the North Island. One of my
objectives is to learn more about the Maori people, so we stop on
our way into Christ Church to visit the national Maori "Marae"
(meeting house). When we arrive, the office person seems astonished that we have come. The "leader" of this Marae is not here,
but she calls him and soon he arrives. He is delighted to spend an
hour with us, explaining the intricate traditional wood architecture
of the Marae. The paintings inside the building are very informative. They depict the various migrations from Hawaii and the lead-
ers of the Head Canoes of each migration.

Our guide explains that he himself has the power to look out across
the ocean and "see" the bottom and also to "see" thousands of
miles away. This extra-sensory ability of some Maori must explain
how and why they undertook their extraordinary journeys; some of
them must have actually "known" where they were going as they
set out across the Pacific.

I am thrilled to watch the New Zealand Maori dance traditions and a vibrant drama concerning many of their beliefs and customs. I read several books about their culture before visiting; the story is not new to me. The Maori drama describes disenfranchisement and even enslavement by the powerful colonists who took over the country after the Maori had been here for generations and established their own culture. Happily, the Maori are now gradually retaking control of their lives and living their beliefs. However, their concept regarding right and wrong still brings them into constant conflict with the law of the land. It is frustrating to read about these divergent concepts; just think what it is like for both sides of a legal dispute between the old culture and the white culture.

* * *

Australia
Impulses at Ayers Rock / An Aboriginal Lesson

My spiritual experience in Australia occurs at Ayer's Rock in the Red Center of the country. Jim and I are on an eight-day camping trip with thirteen people exploring the wonderfully beautiful red-rock geological formations in the middle of the desert. Before traveling to Australia, I read four books about the Aborigine culture. Two books were part of a series of anthropological treatises on two different Aborigine cultures, one on Melville Island north of the continent proper and the other the Mardu culture in the Western Desert. Both cultures live today with their own very simple technology and few material goods. Both groups have a complex religious and cosmological system. However, I find that both tribes welcome change as long as it can be worked into their existing social structures and religious beliefs.

A third book, "Aboriginal Australia", discussed family and kinship, environment, health, economics (independence or welfare), and art. A fourth book, "Songlines" by Bruce Chatwin described the uncanny ability Aborigines possess to be aware of their location and how to get to another place simply through Songs passed down through untold generations. They truly seem to have a map in their heads guided by a certain tree, or a certain dry gulch crossing, etc.

Early in the morning our bus arrives at Ayer's Rock. It is huge, smooth, and beautiful with fabulous hues changing as the natural light alters during the morning, noon, and evening. It lives up to its fame. The itinerary says this is our time to climb the rock. I know it is a sacred place for the indigenous people. But I am not aware that these people don't want tourists climbing their Rock. At the foot of the Rock, our bus driver explains that visitors are now discouraged from climbing the Rock, both for safety reasons and also to respect the wishes of the Aborigines.

I am shocked and disappointed; for years I have dreamed of climbing the Rock. Most of the people in our group decide they will climb it, regardless, because they, too, have been planning on this.

So I team up with a woman named Maxine in her eighties from Maine. She is a retired geology professor. We are the only people in the group who are not Australian.

I am a bit nervous about the climb because I know that, if the wind comes up, the excursion can become very dangerous. We start to climb. It doesn't seem as difficult as I had thought it would. As it gets steeper toward the top, there are chains to hold on to. However, when the wind does start to blow, I find myself plastered against the rock, hoping I will not blow off!

The climb takes only about thirty minutes. At the top the surface is surprisingly flat; it is possible to walk around looking out in all directions. We decide to sit down and just enjoy the view and the event. I sit leaning on one arm with my legs curled up under me to the side. As I sit here, I am aware of electrical impulses rising up my arm from the rock! How strange. I have never heard of an experience such as this. I remain sitting here for about ten minutes as the sensation continues to pulse up my arm.

I think this phenomenon is surely something the indigenous people are aware of. And it certainly is a good reason for not wanting visitors to climb the Rock and experience the "sensations". I look over at Maxine and suggest it is time to go down. She agrees. Before we stand up, I ask her, "Do you feel this?" And in her laconic Maine manner, she answers only, "Yes".

We do not discuss it. It is enough that we had the identical sensation. But I feel sure that the spirits associated with the Rock speak to the local people with the electrical impulses. I can't imagine why they "spoke" to us, since we had violated the wishes of the people. On the other hand, the spirits must know we are "travelers", not "tourists", and, therefore, it was alright to allow us into their sacred space. When we return to the bus, no one else mentions feeling the impulses; I feel sure that no one felt them except for Maxine and me.

As I ponder this experience later, I recall the four spiritual vortexes in Sedona, Arizona. At each of these locations on a trip in the past, I found it easy to meditate and always had incredible visions during the episodes. There are dozens of such places on the planet where people from time immemorial have been influenced greatly by such phenomena. I am so thankful that I followed my heart and climbed the Rock.

Another desire I have, as I visit Australia, is to meet Aborigines up close, to hear from them personally about their thoughts on their current life. I enroll in a half day course in Alice Springs during which our Aboriginal teacher discusses and demonstrates "underground cooking techniques", using traditional weapons, and incorporating knowledge gained through thousands of years about edible and medicinal properties of plants. I come away from this "seminar" hoping that this ancient culture will survive for eons to come, enabling visitors to study and appreciate it.

Sai Baba

An Unrewarding Experience in a
Southern India Ashram

In early 1998 it seemed I was often hearing Sai Baba's name mentioned in America. He is a very old, tiny, Hindu saint who lives in Southern India in an ashram. I was very curious about this man who is venerated not only by Hindus but by millions of people all over the world. Devotees make pilgrimages to be in his presence and receive his blessing. Small groups of people in the United States, and other countries, meet in each other's homes and have devotional services which include mostly chanting in the repetitive Hindu fashion. The chants are often traditional Hindu chants, but also some chants authored by Sai Baba himself.

Since I have always been curious about all types of religions and spiritual observances, naturally I wanted to see Sai Baba. I attended a devotional service in Denver and learned about a local woman who would explain everything about visiting Sai Baba in his ashram. I visited her and found her very helpful. All the devotees I met cautioned me about visiting alone – they said I should find a group to go with. I received the distinct impression that it was much easier to have an audience if you were with a group rather than on your own. But I felt that I had no special problems that I needed Sai Baba to help me solve, so it was not important to me to have a private blessing. Also I could not return home with a designated group because I would be traveling onward.

I was planning a trip on the Silk Road that September and would be meeting my British tour group in Rawalpindi, Pakistan. So it would not be difficult to go to India earlier on my own. The woman who had given me information about making a visit to Sai Baba also told me about a Sai Baba bookshop in California. I called them to order a few books. They told me they would keep my name, address and phone number because often people who were going alone would like to know of someone they could join. Half an hour later a woman called me from New York who was going and wanted a companion! Quite amazing.

* * *

We arrive in Mumbai by very different routes, she via Dubai and I via Singapore. I arrive at 8 p.m. and she at 6:00 a.m. the next morning. I have no place to spend the night but sit on a chair in the waiting room trying to stay awake to guard my luggage. It seems almost impossible to do because I began the trip from Denver, Colorado about thirty hours earlier but morning finally comes. The loud speaker calls my name, and I go to meet my roommate for the next week.

Renata turns out to be an extraordinary woman. When the British aide group, Save the Children, was scouting the world over for their very first poster child years ago, they arrived on her poverty-stricken island in the Caribbean. They interviewed several promising children and were most impressed with her, perhaps because her aim in life was to become a doctor. Save the Children provided money for necessities while she grew up and went to school. Eventually, she had an opportunity to be adopted by a family in Wales.

The father in that family was very much into spirituality, so Renata learned about many religions. The family provided funds for higher education and years later she ended up as a physician's assistant in New York City. She was now in the midst of serious marriage problems and was hoping for some help with these through her visit to Sai Baba.

* * *

The plane to Bangalore leaves soon, and an hour later at the end of the flight an English-speaking taxi driver, Suleman, meets us. (I contacted him through the help of the book store in California.) We drive about four hours to Puttaparthi, the village in southern India where the ashram is located. It is our first experience with Indian drivers; they rank up there with the Chinese. Our driver plays tag and races along the narrow road with other drivers he knows. One minute we are the "passing car" watching an oncoming vehicle with trepidation, fearing that Suleman will not be able to pull back in front of the vehicle he has just passed in time to avoid a crash with the oncoming car. Then it is the "passed car's" turn to pass us. All the while both drivers laugh and lay on their horns the entire time. We are exhausted from our plane trips and keep falling asleep regardless of these appalling situations. Everyone I have ever met is sure she has ridden with the worst taxi driver in the world. This thought suggests there are thousands of terrible drivers and ours is just one of them.

It is extremely hot and humid when we arrive at the ashram. Suleman helps us through the red tape to check in, be assigned a room, and pay for it. He finds porters to take our luggage to our room which has a ceiling fan and windows sealed shut with tape so mosquitoes won't come through the screen holes. We have an ensuite room with toilet, sink, and shower. There are two cots and a string clothes line hangs from wall to wall just beyond the foot of the cots. This will be great for hanging up our nuts and trail-mix emergency food with clothes pins to avoid pilfering by the mice we suspect will visit us. The porters help us set up the mosquito netting we brought with us.

Suleman personally takes me to nearby shops where I purchase two inexpensive "ashram-suitable" outfits called shalwar qamiz. They are knee-length tunics with full trousers underneath. I also buy a white nylon shawl. Renata and I purchase two very low camp chairs with supported backrests and cushions sitting inside. The plan is to take the back rest and cushion to darshans at the ashram.

Now it is late afternoon and beastly hot. Back in our room we nibble some nuts, take a cold shower (no alternative available), set our alarms for 4 a.m. the next morning. We fall exhausted and naked, on our cots with the ceiling fan running.

At 4:00 the alarm rings. We dress and find the end of the long, long line of people waiting to get in the mandir. We talk with other people in line and discover today is the beginning of a Hindu festival called Oman and celebrated in some of the southern provinces of India. There are thousands more people here in the ashram than there were yesterday. The Indian women and girls are dressed in gorgeous multi-colored saris. As they come out of their canteen across from where we are standing, they also join the line. Soon it curves around on itself and goes back the way from which we came. After an hour in line we slowly file into a "holding area" where we sit crossed-legged in long lines for an hour. Then each line files into the covered mandir outdoor auditorium where unpleasant women in charge make sure each of us sits down cross-legged, squeezed up as close as possible to the person in front of us, and not saying a word. Mothers with babies are admonished to keep them quiet although I am puzzled how that is supposed to happen.

There is a women's side of the mandir and a men's side. Hundreds, perhaps thousands, of people are sitting crushed together in this area probably intended for less than half that many. We are hot, sweaty, and smelly.

When Sai Baba finally "shows" himself at 7 a.m., he blesses the crowd, then lights two candles in a candelabra without using matches. He waves his hand over them and miraculously the other eight candles light! Baba is a very small, thin man with unkempt bushy hair who is in his nineties. He sits while children sing songs about him (because this is a festival) and perform Indian dances. Then Baba addresses the crowd with his "lesson" in Hindi. After an hour Renata and I get up to leave because we must attend a lecture concerning the rules of the ashram. The women in charge glare at us as we leave. We are glad to be outside since we didn't understand a word of Baba's lecture and it was very hot scrunched up so close to so many people.

We arrive at the lecture venue, but a sign reads that there is no lecture today because of the holiday. We decide to go to the "western" canteen for breakfast. But a sign reads that today the canteen is closed in the morning! Returning to our room, we turn on the fan, strip down, take a cold shower, eat a few nuts, and lie down naked to sleep until lunchtime.

When we awaken we walk out to the stairway where two German women who speak a little English announce we have just missed lunch! So we have not had a real meal since we were on our planes winging their ways to Mumbai. Because I arrived twelve hours before Renata, I realize I have not eaten in 44 hours! Well, nothing to do but go back to our room, eat more nuts and trail mix, drink water, chat, and sleep again. We decide to skip afternoon darshan.

We do make it to dinner, thank heavens. Standing at our places at long tables we chant Hindu prayers written on a large blackboard for fifteen minutes. Then we join the buffet line where we find cooked cauliflower, dahl (beans and lentils), mashed potatoes with tomato and mushroom sauce, and cabbage salad. Delicious.

Conversing at the table with English-speaking women from Europe and South America, we realize they are, without exception, thrilled to be here with Baba. We hear that our spartan room with a private bath and ceiling fan is as good as it gets in the ashram and is available only to western women! Hundreds, perhaps thousands, of people are housed in large sheds with corrugated metal roofs and no fans. They sleep close to each other on the floor and use an outdoor toilet. Just thinking of the heat they endure makes me feel almost ill. Those extremely poor people probably don't have to pay much, but even a little charge would be very difficult for them. Perhaps there are facilities for higher class Hindu women?

We also learn information about having an audience with Sai Baba. We are supposed to write letters to him which we will pass up to the front just before the "showing". If he picks your letter out of the huge pile in the front of the room, he quite likely will choose you to join him in a separate room where he gives private audiences. All the people who arrive in groups will have audiences with many groups at one time. So it is evident now, but too late, that being part of a group is of paramount importance.

Returning to our room we repeat the ritual of turning on the fan, showering, and slipping under the mosquito netting, setting the alarm for 4 a.m. We write our letters to Sai Baba for the next "darshan" (showing).

When the alarm rings, we realize our bottoms and backs hurt so much from sitting cross-legged for such a long period yesterday that we can't bear the thought of repeating that this morning. So we sleep till 8 a.m. We do make it to breakfast, then walk to the site of the compulsory orientation lecture. It is partly over. The lecturer is extremely difficult to understand because of his accent. But at the end we sign our names and get our passports back.

We walk into town to buy some bananas to add to our room food supplies. Suleman arrives when we return to our room. He says he still doesn't have our return airline tickets which he took when we first arrived to have them reconfirmed.

Afternoon darshan arrives. There are still the huge number of festival people here. So the line is as long as yesterday. We are at the head of the line. This time, once we enter the "holding area", we sit in rows. When it is time to go in to the mandir, the first person in each row picks a number out of a bag. The row with the lowest number gets to go in first! The number of our row is the highest, so we go in last, all the way to the back! Our reward for being at the head of the line! Everyone passes her letter up to the front where they are piled in a heap on the floor. Baba arrives, blesses us, chooses a letter, whereupon darshan is finished! All that waiting for a five minute showing.

We have dinner. I sign up to wash dishes tomorrow night. We do our usual routine for bed, write our letters, set our alarm for 4 a.m.

In the morning by 4:30 we are in line with only about 100 people ahead of us -- a good shot at being in front unless they do the "number out of the bag" thing again, which they do. And the person at the head of our line manages to choose the highest number again! As we're waiting the hour before Baba comes out, I notice all the children present. Small Indian children and slightly older foreign children are here. All the children are perfectly behaved. They just sit quietly hour on end. Baba comes out, blesses us, chooses a letter from the pile. At one instant I see energy waves radiating from him in a 360 degree circle around the mandir! I am aware of feeling great peace. So I think there is indeed something mystical about this man.

We go for breakfast, then back to our room. Suleman arrives with a "fax" from Jim saying my British Silk Road trip is really going to "go". Hooray! Because of unrest in Pakistan before I left, the status of the trip has been in question. A change in airline times means we will have to leave the ashram one day earlier, go to Bangalore, and on to Mumbai. It will be another 24-hour ordeal.

We attend afternoon darshan, then go to dinner. I wash all the women's dishes and set them in the drainer. There is no dishwasher. Then its on to the pots and pans. It takes me 45 minutes. Tonight Renata opens up to me about her sad marriage. She is so lonely and frustrated. After listening to her, I counsel her to get a divorce which she has thought of doing but hasn't had the courage to act on it. I feel I have helped her, supported her and given her my love. Finally I think that Baba had it planned. We were to meet, be roommates, and I was supposed to help her.

At darshan the next morning, I pass up a letter I wrote to Baba asking "what is the next step with Renata?" I feel his answer is, "Keep on mentoring and counseling and giving love. That is your path." I suddenly feel very sure and very content and enjoy the beautiful performances: people singing and playing instruments.

Renata and I decide it will make no difference if we stay for the week or, instead, find a way to leave earlier. We decide to enlist Suleman's help. His schedule every day consists in picking people up in Bangalore, bringing them to the ashram, helping them get settled, and then taking people back to Bangalore to meet a plane. For all his excellent English and helpfulness, his compensation does not allow him to even pay for a sleeping cubicle. He sleeps in his car without mosquito netting. I think he must pay for a tiny room where he keeps his fax machine and phone. He has a wife and two teenage boys in Bangalore. Families have to pay school expenses (uniforms, books) for their children. Also they pay more if the school they have chosen is considered high on the list to be accepted into university. The oldest boy is preparing to enter university. I really admire Suleman and all the millions like him who scrimp and save to give their children a better life.

Suleman comes after darshan with another "fax" from Jim saying everything is "go" for the trip. This change in airline departure time means I will have to leave the ashram one day earlier to go to Bangalore and Mumbai. Renata asks Suleman to change her tickets so she can leave earlier with me.

Suleman provided a much-needed connection between, Jim (my husband) the Exodus tour company's head man in London, and myself. The day before I was to fly to LA and India, 31 August, a US missile had fallen on Pakistani territory by mistake. Pakistanis were obsessed with anger by this act. They were rioting in Karachi and burning the American flag. Americans in diplomatic positions were flying out and Americans were advised not to go. The Sunday before I left Denver I phoned Associated Press in Denver and was directed to Associated Press in Cairo. The AP person in Cairo said to go ahead on the trip and just not to draw attention to myself, so I decided to go. Our daughter called from St. Louis to say that her neighbors had relatives in Pakistan. They had spoken to them by phone and the relatives said I must not go. But, by now, you know, I had to go!

I called the man on duty for Exodus in London that Sunday, 31 August.. He seemed rather unaware that this was a big deal for Americans. He said that of course the tour would be leaving Rawalpindi on schedule on 14 September. If we wished we could call Exodus every fourth day in London to check. Well, I certainly would not be in a position to do that. So Jim decided he would call London and then fax Suleman every four days so I would know what was going on. Suleman performed wonderfully in this new responsibility. How lucky that I had made connections with him by fax way back in the States months ago.

*   *   *

Suleman to the "Rescue"

We go to afternoon darshan, then dinner, then pack up for tomorrow morning. Renata now seems to feel determined to get a divorce even though she has a two-year-old girl which her husband will probably insist on keeping. She is a physician's assistant so I am sure she will have no problem finding a job in another community.

It rains extremely hard this evening. This is the first rain we have seen and the quantity is amazing.

We go to darshan in the morning and have breakfast. Suleman picks us up. We are on our way by 8 a.m. with "the taxi driver from Hell" and arrive in Bangalore about noon, delighted that events conspired to make us miss a day at the ashram with no regrets. We've had enough of waiting in lines, sitting and waiting for Baba's showing. I feel at peace.

Suleman gets us a room for the afternoon at the Hotel Roma. No air conditioning, but there is a ceiling fan. It is unbearably hot. Our room faces on the busy street with the honking vehicles. A city street in India is always full of noise, particularly blowing horns. Needless to say we do not sleep.

Renata and I have a farewell dinner in the hotel restaurant. Suleman picks us up and delivers us to the airport in the early evening for our flight to Mumbai where Renata and I will part ways. She will get a plane early in the morning for Dubai and I will be heading to Karachi.

* * *

In the Mumbai airport I discover a small "official looking" group of men at a table who say they can put me in a hotel for the night. The cost is $30, including transport to and from the airport and air conditioning. Sounds wonderful. It is pouring, pouring rain. The hotel is fine, and in the morning, I take a cab back to the airport to get the plane to Karachi, Pakistan.

At the gate passengers wait and wait for the plane to arrive. I luckily am dressed in the "gear" that I purchased in Puttaparti, with my scarf over my head, so am acceptable. After several hours some food arrives in the waiting room at the gate. I wonder what it is like? I pick and choose to find the least spicy, and get enough to keep me going. At last about 1 p.m. the plane arrives and we board soon after. I discover later that Renata's plane never leaves the tarmac that day because a plane slid partially off the runway into the mud blocking that runway. Meanwhile, my plane's late departure is cutting into my connection time in Karachi to catch the plane to Islamabad.

* * *

An interesting sequel to the ashram experience happened about a month and a half later back in the States. While meditating, I asked my two guides with "higher knowledge" for any information they thought I should have. Gradually I saw a picture like you'd see on a greeting card. It was simplistic: two men (pilgrims) walking beside a tall brick wall. They came to a wrought-iron decorative gate. The pilgrims pushed against the gate and found it locked. So they continued on their way. After pondering this "picture" for a while, I figured out the meaning. I was the "pilgrim" on my way to see Sai Baba. But when I got there, the gate was "locked", meaning that I received no benefit from being there because I could not reach the important person (Sai Baba). I left and continued on my way, to discover another of thousands of possibilities that lay ahead that would help me on the "path to the top of the mountain". My spirit lightened. I was "riding my horse in the direction it was going" and ready for the next spiritual adventure.

Pakistan and the Silk Road

Karachi Airport "Scam" and a Day in Islamabad

After the Sai Baba episode, I am flying to Mumbai, to Karachi, and on to Islamabad. Arriving in Karachi, I hand my passport to the official at the arrival gate, and receive my stamp. Then all hell breaks loose. Two young men in uniform have been standing behind the official. Now they intercept me saying that I am not on the passenger list for the plane going to Islamabad! I tell them it is impossible since my ticket was reconfirmed in the US, again in Bangalore and also Mumbai. They say, "Look at the computer. Your name is not listed"!

I read the passenger list on the computer; unfortunately my name is missing. I believe one of these men deleted my name. One says he will "work" on getting my name back on the list! The other man "helps" me find my backpack on the carousel. Of course, I need no help but he "assists" me anyway. He says we must now go to the top floor and talk with the airport manager. I ask him how much baksheesh (or bribe) I will have to pay to get my name back on the passenger list, but he doesn't answer. I ask if $100 is enough and he indicates it probably will be.

139

The airport manager is out to lunch. Of course! The minutes tick relentlessly away until the plane for Islamabad will leave. We sit outside the manager's office, waiting.

Finally the manager arrives and talks to my "guide", and then to me. Things begin to happen. My guide steps up to the "Caisse" (bank). The person inside claims I need to pay $100, no explanation offered. I give him $100 American. I ask my guide how one minute there is no seat on the plane, but the next minute it appears there is. He claims there are always three seats unsold, so government officials can get on at the last minute. The lady in the "bank" suddenly needs $100 more cash which I provide. By this time the plane is definitely ready to depart. A loud speaker calls out, "This is the last announcement". It is imperative that I get on that plane because I arranged, via Jim and Exodus (my tour company) to have a person in Islamabad meet me. The last news I have had about the situation in Pakistan was very bad; people were demonstrating in the streets and burning the American flag.

At the last moment, the announcement calls for "Joyce Rasbach" to pick up her ticket at the Caisse and go on to "boarding". I grab the ticket, race through security, and can see the plane ahead of me beginning to pull up the steps. I run as fast as I can, and get there in the nick of time.

Well, one can say this was all staged so a group of people could get their share of the baksheesh, and I am certain this is true. What a scam! To watch for American women traveling alone and put them through what I have just been through! The two young men, the woman in the "bank" and the "manager" will all receive a nice cut from the $200 I forked over.

I have to put this episode behind me so I can contemplate now on what it might be like when I disembark the plane in Islamabad. Will there be bedlam, chaos? Actually, everything is calm. I pick up some Pakistani money at a "change" place between the plane and a sign that reads "Rasbach" and also "Karakorum Explorers". A vehicle is picking up other people also. The local tour company is attending to the needs of people in various groups. But eventually I am delivered to the hotel where I will meet the Exodus tour group in two days. Quite an adventure!

I wonder if Sai Baba made everything turn out alright in Karachi in addition to bringing Renata and I together at the ashram so I could mentor her. Perhaps he put a charm on this whole trip. After all, seven flights in seven days could have produced mayhem for me. But it all worked, including the tour company's vehicle in Islamabad to meet me!

I sleep late in the morning. The tension from the prior day has exhausted me. I spend an hour or so writing post cards. Then I ask the doorman if he can find someone to take me on a sightseeing tour. One signal from him and a taxi pulls up. He tells the man what I want to do and Shahid and I are off.

Our first stop is the Folk Art Museum. We see magnificent costumes, musical instruments, ceramics made of a combination of wood and metal, and weaving equipment. Excellent reproductions of a tea room, a kitchen in a house, the interior of a nomad tent, and a desert adobe house. A fantastic museum.

We drive up in the Margulla Hills for a panorama of the city, and then through the government diplomatic area with impressive buildings.

Islamabad, "the new city", is next to the old city of Rawalpindi. It is beautiful with wide streets and lovely buildings which house most consulates from various countries. We visit the incredible modern mosque, built of blue and white tiles. It is the largest mosque in the world and can accommodate 100,000 people at one time. Very impressive.

We drive a few miles outside of the city to the ancient town of

Taxila. Excavation shows three eras, the oldest before 4000 B.C. In the museum we see marble sculptures and relics of the three periods. About 300 B.C. Alexander The Great came through Taxila, so there is a synthesis of Greek and local art. Sculptured figures from that period are shown with clothes such as the Greeks would have worn. Some present-day people in the area of Taxila have blue eyes and claim heredity from Alexander and his troops.

The Buddhist teacher and missionary, Ashoka, lived here in the third century B.C. Buddhism began in Pakistan and was exported to the east along the Silk Road. At Taxila, there is a village excavated from the second era, which reminds me of Pompeii in ancient Italy.

Part of the excavation includes a Buddhist monastery from 200 A.D. in excellent condition. One can distinguish the individual cells, the dining room, and the kitchen.

I enjoy Taxila immensely because there is the evidence of Alexander the Great and Ashoka. I love historical and ancient religous places and get my fill of it at this site.

On the way back to the hotel Shahid tells me about his family. He has seven children, aged five to twenty-two. Two are girls. He himself has only a primary school education. He taught himself English. He is putting all the boys through public school, a very expensive endeavor. His wife observed purdah until she was 50; now she goes out with her head uncovered. They live in a mixed neighborhood of Muslims and Hindus. Everyone gets along together – nice to hear a positive fact in this era of Muslims and Hindus clashing so often.

Next morning Shahid picks me up at 10 a.m. to go to the open air market in Rawalpindi. He buys a white, sleeveless shirt with many pockets. I think it is an undershirt. We watch a man pressing sugarcane to make a sweet drink.

Back at the hotel, the owner of Karakorum Explorers joins me for high tea. Apparently Britain is now in disarray because of the Pakistani political unrest. The British tour company, Exodus, discovered that their insurance won't cover the terrorist problem. So Exodus requested of Karakorum Explorers that when the tour arrives by plane in the morning, we will all fly north to Hunza instead of driving the road from Rawalpindi to Hunza to avoid possible political trouble along the way. The tour operator/owner says he purchased tickets for the flights. However, there are frequently problems with bad weather along this flight route. So he feels it is doubtful that we will fly. Apparently, if the weather were bad for several days in a row, the prospective air passengers would back up waiting for a flight, and ironically, the passengers booked for the day the airline company resumes operations would be served first!

* * *

The Silk Road
Karakourm Highway, Khunjerab Pass, into China to Kashgar

My host goes on to say that, because of the unrest, the two Exodus Silk Road trips scheduled for later in September have been canceled. The British passengers are now nervous because their government has told British citizens to leave Pakistan. Two members of our tour from England have canceled. Well, I have been through all this commotion earlier in the month, and am not in the least bit worried.

The tour group arrives at 7:30 a.m. from London. They transfer to the hotel for breakfast. We learn that the first daily flight to Hunza has been cancelled due to inclement weather. So the decision is made to use the bus. There are nine tour members plus Jenny, our twenty-five year old Exodus tour leader. We will pick up two more people in Gilgit who flew there earlier in the week in order to spend more time in the northern area.

We embark on the two-lane, 1200 km Karakorum Highway which will eventually go over the Khunjerab Pass into China to Kashgar. The road is also called the Friendship Highway; it was begun in the 1960's as a joint project between Pakistan and China and is one of history's biggest engineering projects. The Chinese engineered and built the many bridges. Many workers were killed during construction, and there are memorials in their honor along the way.

It is quite a thrilling trip because previous landslides, rockfalls, and mud conspire to narrow the road to a path right at the edge of the Indus River gorge! It is also a beautiful trip. I calculate that I may be among the first 5000 travelers to see this road from start to finish.

The path has a huge drop-off on the river side. It follows the Indus River. We see terraced fields and rice growing. Large trucks drive straight through the night from Rawalpindi to the Chinese border. Apparently they can make it in sixteen to eighteen hours, stopping only for fuel. How can they see to drive this curvy dangerous road at night?

The scenery changes from rice cultivation to no cultivation at all in many places. The river gorge is very far below us. We stop for the night in the town of Beshem.

Our Pakistani guide, Cesar, understands English very well, but speaks it poorly. He is very friendly, as are the driver and back-up driver.

The next day is a twelve-hour ride. We have an opportunity to walk through a very poor village. It is like traveling far back in time. Ladders outside the houses lead to the second floor. Fifty percent of the population is conspicuously missing -- the women. The men wear an infinite variety of hats and various colors of punjabis, the long shirt

144

and loose trousers that are common in India, Pakistan, and Afghanistan. Each school has a unique uniform its students must wear. The girls do not attend school, but remain home with their mother. Many small shops open onto the street. Two men are grinding tobacco into a paste which will become snuff.

Gradually the road climbs ever higher following the river. Soon we are above the lush valleys and now drive through stark brown mountains. The road runs right on the very edge of the drop-off. The Indus River below us is now very brown because of glacier melt and runoff.

We drive through an extremely narrow chasm with spectacular high walls, stopping two times to see rock art from the first through the fourth century A.D. There has been a rough path along here for at least 1500 years. Pictures of Buddhas, stupas, all kinds of information and mantras for the traveler, plus animals seen frequently in that bygone time are abundant as we drive along. Really marvelous. Bridges crossing the river are very few and far between. People living on the far side have to walk miles carrying their produce to get across.

Along the way we begin to glimpse Nanga Parbat, 24,000 feet high and rising by seven millimeters every year. It lies at the extreme western end of the Himalayas. The name means "naked mountain" in Kashmiri, because the southeast face is a sheer wall 13,500 feet high.

We stop at a site where three major mountain ranges come together: the Himalaya to the east, the beginning of the Karakorum to the north and the Hindu Kush to the north west. Tectonic plates are always shifting. One part rises, another falls a bit. It is an awesome place.

We stay tonight at a lovely, clean hotel in Gilgit. The evening meal is delicious. Here we pick up the two men for the tour who flew to Gilgit earlier. They are Ishmaili Muslims. This is a sect of Islam that recognizes the Aga Khan as their leader. The Khan is a very rich man who helps the poor people by building hospitals and schools. The world headquarters of Ishmaili Muslims is in the area of Gilgit. This Muslim sect has no mosques and is not required to pray daily.

In the morning we drive out of town to see a huge Buddha carving on a rock from 400 A.D. Walking back though the residential part of the town, we meet a woman with her three children standing at the gate to their house. How nice to at last see a woman instead of just men and boys. And what a different culture this is, when the mere existence of a woman makes one take notice.

We drive ever upward and stop for lunch at an astonishingly beautiful spot at the foot of huge Rakaposi Mountain, and the glacier below the summit. In fact, it seems as though the glacier is just a couple hundred feet above us. Very tall pink cosmos flowers grow in a garden beside our outdoor tables. Across the road six children, four boys and two girls, stand watching us. I ask the children if I can photograph them -- I really want the girls because I have plenty of photos of boys. The boys push the girls out of the way, but the older girl, maybe about seven, pushes the boys away and the two sisters pose for me. I wonder if the girls will receive a beating from their father after the brothers "tell" on them. I hope not, because they are such sweet, smiling girls.

We arrive at Karimabad two hours later in the very middle of the Lower, Middle and Upper Hunza Valleys. We have a pleasant hotel with beautiful flowers in the garden. The weather here is perfect for growing all kinds of fruit and other crops. I take a jeep trip with two people from the tour up to the "Eagle's Nest". We drive up a dirt path past houses and walled yards. Men have been digging potatoes all day and putting them in bags beside the path, waiting for a tractor to take them down. A very sweet, young girl stands guard next to her family's bags. Girls have become a special thing with me, and I quickly snap her picture. Women and children bring down loads of greens on their backs to store in small stone barns so the goats and sheep will have food in the morning before they are driven up to the high pasture in the afternoon. Many activities occur on the flat roofs, including drying vegetables and fruits. There are also small storage tanks for water on the roofs.

Little girls who pushed brothers out of the way

At the end of the road we walk to the Eagles Nest, a point where we can look down on the Karakorum Highway, the river, and the town. It is sunset. There are snowy, sharp peaks in all directions of the compass and all are shining gold. How stunning!

On the way back down we stop at Altit Fort, built about 1000 years ago as a dowry for a princess. Inside the one big room there is a fireplace in the center of the floor with a hole in the ceiling for smoke to escape. A niche in the corner was used to store kitchen utensils, food and candles. Nasar, our guide, says it is a typical Tibetan house, and that his is like this, but it certainly doesn't look like houses I saw in Tibet or the Sherpa houses on the south side of the Himalayas.

We are up early in the morning to take a jeep to Rakaposi where we hike two kilometers each way to the glacier, which is nothing but black, dirty ice. The next morning we visit Baltit Fort, a newer building than Altit Fort. There is a roofless room facing south where people would sit outside to be warmed by the sun, even if the temperature might go down to minus ten degrees Fahrenheit. Those were the people of James Hilton's "Lost Horizons" (Shangri La). Some of the local people today live to be 100 years old and many to more than 100!

Starting out at 5 p.m. to drive an hour to our new hotel in Gilgit. We stop to admire amazing animal petroglyphs made by pilgrims on the road at least 1000 years ago. We stay in another beautiful small guest house with a lovely garden. All the hotels in Pakistan have clean carpet. Jenny says this will change tomorrow once we enter China because the Chinese are fond of spitting, due no doubt to all the respiratory diseases they endure. So they just hawk and spit wherever they are, even if it's the carpet of their hotel room.

In the morning we start up the last five hour segment of the road before we reach the Kunjarab Pass. We are engulfed by outstanding scenery above tree line. It's snowing on top, and at the border we transfer to a bus that simply plies the road between the two national borders. A five-hour trip one way! The driver must drive ten hours round trip to get back in time to get through Pakistani customs so he can do it all over again the next day, and, in fact, seven days a week!

148

He drives like a banshee, and refuses to stop for photos, although there are glorious possibilities. Such a pity.

Going through customs into China is excruciatingly slow. Now we have a Chinese bus, and a beautiful young Chinese guide named Hue. She is tall, willowy, and so graceful. To me she seems like a princess.

In the late afternoon we reach Tashkurgan, the Chinese border town, and a hotel that is one of the very worst places I have ever stayed. It is seemingly the only hotel in town. Apparently "high ranking Chinese officials" arrived today unexpectedly in this god-forsaken place and confiscated the best building in our complex. So everyone else staying here has had to drop down a "notch" in quality of accommodation. There are enough rooms in the second-quality building for all but four of our group. Jenny and I plus Karim and Amin are "quartered" on the second floor of a third building. The man in charge of keys on the main floor of this building helps me find my room because there is no hall lighting. One has to feel along the walls and doorways trying to identify the raised numerals on the doors. The first few rooms on this second floor are large dormitories with open doors where men sit around on their double-decker beds smoking and trying to watch the one television in the room. The key-keeper man opens the door to our room; it is dark inside even when he turns on the one lamp. There are three beds; the pillows are filled with dried beans! The pillows and sheets are filthy, but Jenny and I have the answer to that. We will crawl inside our sleeping bag liners. The bathroom is the dirtiest I have ever seen. The tub is unusable because pieces of the tile above it and in the tub are missing, leaving gaping views of the inner walls. A teakettle, of all things, sits on top of the radiator. There is water in the spigot, but only cold, naturally. The whole room is disgusting. The only time we enter the bathroom is to use the toilet.

Jenny and I were to have been housed in the "first" building with our entire group, not the third. Jenny asks me if we can invite our lovely guide, Hue, to sleep in our room because the quality of the fourth-class rooms is such that the mattresses are straw filled and adjacent to the stable. These rooms are for bus drivers. I am delighted to ask her to join us.

Amin and Karim are in the room next to ours. In the morning Amin says he didn't touch anything in the bathroom. He used his bottled water to wash his face and hands and placed his soap on the top of the bottle! He never used the dirty towel filled with holes but, then, neither did we.

The next day we drive mostly through fog and never see the jagged-peaked mountains of the Pamir Range, which form the border between China and Tagikistan. Now and then, as we descend from the summit, we catch glimpses of stone and mud houses and herds of yak, sheep and goats. The herders ride donkeys and wear clothing very different from the Pakistani men, actually western style. Late in the afternoon, Hue explains that we have some time to explore a small village beside the road. The people living here are Tajiks. Tajikistan is just a few miles away over the mountains. The women and children adore the color red, so their clothes are bright, cheerful, and mostly red-patterned. This is a marvelous opportunity to observe the people up close. As we board our bus again, children cluster around the door to sell bread containing omeletta and sweet pastries.

Late in the day we reach Kashgar, a fabled stop on the Silk Road, and a place I have always dreamed of visiting.

We do better with our rooms tonight, but Jenny falls apart before dinner. Too much stuff is going on in her life right now. A year ago she was hiking in the mountains of South Island, New Zealand, and fell in love with a New Zealand dairy farmer. They will be married next summer in England, but she has three more Exodus trips to do this fall, and no time to prepare for the wedding. I am able to calm her down somewhat.

150

The Kashgar Market

The next day is Sunday. The great event of the day in Kashgar is the exotic Sunday market, known as the greatest market in the world. We go as a group and then are turned loose on our own after about an hour. I wander off and see everything under the sun which could ever be for sale. Rows and rows of donkeys, horses, goats, sheep, camels, and cows all tied together. Pony carts (the mode of travel in western China), colorful cradles for babies and beds for children, and painted chests and wardrobes which look just like those in Mongolia. There is hardware for every use imaginable laid out on the ground, and men making horse tack and farm utensils. There are felt hats and orange velour fabrics for draperies. On and on the market stretches.

Kashgar Sunday Market - goats tied together at the neck

After several hours, I decide it is time to return to the hotel. I tried to keep my bearings all day, but, in the end, I cannot find the main street which runs in front of the market and eventually about a mile later reaches the hotel. I have a card with a picture and name of the hotel. Since I'm not on the main street, no taxis are available. I ask a young man if he will take me. He is riding a bicycle and towing a very small wagon which he uses to carry produce. He indicates I can get in the wagon. We agree on a price and off we go; I sit cross-legged on the metal floor of the wagon covered with green stains from lettuce and cabbage.

Gradually, I realize that we are not heading in the direction of the hotel at all, and I know the boy can not read the name of the hotel on my card. I tell him to stop at a corner where there is a traffic policeman. I jump out and show the policeman the picture of the hotel. He has no idea where the hotel is located. But, at this moment, a taxi driver next to our bicycle and wagon, jumps out. He looks at the picture and says he knows where the hotel is! And he does! He takes me there. What a relief!

Later in the day five of us are on a pony cart sitting along the sides with footrests. Our Uighur driver is taking us to the outskirts of the city. Uighurs form the majority of the people in Western China; they are all Muslim. Our guide, Hue, told him to return us in two hours. Our pony plods along on dirt roads lined with poplar trees grown for fuel. Ditches on each side of the road irrigate the maize and cotton growing in the fields. We stop to visit a tiny adobe mosque next to a cemetery, and climb a ladder to the roof to get a better view of the surroundings. All houses are hidden behind mud walls and made of adobe and brick.

Hue had told the driver to arrange for us to visit a family in their home. After what seems an eternity, I touch the man on the shoulder, point to the houses behind walls and open my hands wide in a questioning manner. He jumps out and knocks on the gate of the house beside us. A woman answers and invites us into the courtyard where two small children are playing. A second woman, who I think is the grandmother, arrives with a huge bun-

152

dle of cotton on her back that she has apparently picked today. Perhaps the pickers were given some amount of the cotton for their family?

The women offer tea and grapes picked from the vines on the lattice roof of the patio. Then lead us into the house. There are two rooms, one with Persian rugs on the floor, and the other with a sofa in addition to the rugs. The people sleep on the rugs on the floor. Cooking is done outside using a mud oven and a couple of gas burners. Our hostesses are so very gracious.

Already we have been gone two hours. We say "Kashgar" to the driver and he nods. But first he stops to buy a watermelon from a vendor. Our driver has a long dirty curved knife in his belt. He cuts wedges of melon and, of course, we eat them; they are delicious. We arrive back at the hotel after about three hours. It has been a great afternoon.

Tonight our group goes to "John's Cafe" near the old Russian embassy. It is one of a series of John's Cafes along the Silk Road. Travelers can post messages on a bulletin board concerning selling their shalwar qamiz, or trying to find partners to do this or that side trip.

I watch a man painting tee shirts picturing the Silk Road. I choose the scene I want and what it will say. On the back he paints a proverb in Uighur script: "You are fortunate to be born into this world. You should show your gratitude by doing good deeds"!

I try sending a fax to Jim from the cafe, but it comes back indicating, "poor quality". Four of us go to a folk dance and singing show performed by Uighurs. Fantastic. Great costumes and dances. Very different from anything I have ever seen, but with a tinge of Russia in it all. The men are extremely graceful in their movements and very handsome.

Back at the hotel I try to send a fax again, but the machine is broken.

The next morning we visit a Uighur primary school which proves very interesting. The children, six or seven years old, are learning to read Uighur script from back to front of the book, and from right to left on the page. They appear to be very industrious.

Kashgar school

Then we visit a Uighur home. The people always have a china cabinet with their cups, saucers, and rice dishes displayed on the open shelves. Again there are Persian carpets on the floors for sitting and sleeping. The women are gracious and offer us tea.

Walking through the old narrow streets of the city we watch men crafting and repairing shoes, making metal pots, and fixing watches. Among all these activities dentists are pulling teeth. Interesting signs on walls of buildings depict, by simple pictures, what the merchant's craft is.

Back to John's Cafe tonight for another great meal al fresco. Some of our guys play pool. This place is a real haven for Englishmen.

Off we go the next morning leaving Kashgar on a paved road along the north side of the Taklamaken Desert which is all gravel with no sand. The name means "If you go in, you will never come out". The desert is so different than I had imagined, and there is lots of white salt on the ground everywhere.

In the oases they actually grow crops using water from the streams coming down from the mountains. Farmers get one crop before the stream dries up for the summer.

At lunch time we stop in a nondescript hamlet. There are several tire and truck repair shops and a tiny cafe. We watch as the two cooks choose from among the most beautiful, brightly-colored vegetables I have ever seen. They chop them and cook them in the wok which no kitchen in Eastern or Central Asia would ever be without. In fifteen minutes from start to finish a most delicious soup is ready, prepared just for our group!

There is mammoth road construction going on. The road is being dug up and rebuilt. Also a railroad is being installed beside the road which will finally reach Kashgar, and people will be able to ride from the extreme western end of China to the central and eastern parts of the country! Construction means blowing sand and dust. In some areas there is no longer a road, so vehicles are forced over into the fields until the road reappears. However, there is a complication: Vehicles going in both directions are driving in the path in the field. How we avoid head-on collisions hour after hour in the blinding, blowing sand, I will never understand.

Because this road is the only link between eastern and western China, there are literally thousands of trucks on this highway. This means that besides the dust from construction, diesel smoke also permeates the air. The air is so polluted that you can't see the brown Tien Shan mountains a short distance north. These mountains form the north boundary of western China.

Double-tiered busses also ply this road. People riding in both levels are confined to a small "bed" so they ride propped up by their belongings all day and all night. These busses are definitely long-haul vehicles. I think it is rather a new phenomenon because the busses look quite modern.

After ten hours of driving, we arrive at our first oasis -- Aksu. I am surprised to discover that these oases are not tiny villages, but large towns with shops, schools, day care centers, and hotels.

As Jenny and I walk down the hall of our hotel looking for our room, we notice a door with many windows at the end of the corridor. We see strange shapes through the windows. Walking closer we realize that these are children's faces pressed against the glass. As we stare through the glass, we slowly begin to understand that what we are looking at is a playground and day care center. We are excited to think that we might have interaction with these children. So we quickly walk out the front of the hotel and around the school to the playground. We enter the gate and say "Hello" and they amazingly call "Hello" back to us. We share some cookies with them. Quickly we figure out some action songs we can do with them. First we sing "Head, Shoulders, Knees and Toes." They know this song in Uighur!

Hue arrives on the scene and the three of us sing "I'm a Little Teapot" with actions. They sing it back to us in Uighur! We sing "Happy Birthday" and they repeat it. How can these children in the middle of the desert in western China know these songs? And how does Hue know them? She says she learned them in daycare when she was a little girl.

What fun we have with these children -- precious moments I will never forget.

The daycare teachers are so kind, easy-going and happy. How nice for the children who come at 8:30 in the morning and perhaps are not picked up until 9 p.m. One child calls me Granny and another Auntie which I believe they also call their teachers. The teachers do not teach them to paint or dance or to know their alphabet or numbers. They simply babysit them. The children in the group range from two (still in diapers) to four and a half. There is no limit to the number in the class.

When we finally enter our hotel room, we find it disgusting, along with the bathroom, which has only a toilet and sink. Obviously the sheets have not been changed for months. Again our sleeping bag liners will stand us in good stead. How fortunate I never threw away the foam rubber from the cushion I bought at Sai Baba's. Here on this trip I use it repeatedly for a pillow, covered with my towel.

However, one takes the good with the bad. Jenny and I buy dry, red wine (impossible in Western China?) in the hotel shop before dinner! We finish it off in record time, and no longer care about the filth.

The next day is another long ride in the desert. Now there is no longer construction, but instead hundreds of barricades which lie across half the road because of washouts. We have to drive out around them on the desert gravel.

We stop in a tiny hamlet, another truck stop. Again we watch the cooks in the only cafe in town make a vegetable stir fry and home made noodles in record time. Delicious.

Late in the day we leave the main road to reach ancient Buddhist monasteries, the Kizil Grottoes, dating from the first to the fourth centuries. A king had had caves dug in the cliff and frescoes painted on the walls inside. There are over one hundred caves. Years later monks arrived to care for them and build monasteries. Early last century archeologists came, peeled the frescoes off the walls and carried them off to Europe! Members of the Cultural Revolution committed the final destruction leaving little to see today.

After driving through gorgeous red rock scenery, we arrive at Kucha for the night. Our hotel is quite new, but in remarkably bad condition. The Chinese seem to know nothing about maintenance. You would think an army went through here and destroyed everything.

I shower with some dribbles from the shower head. Our hotel is "on the highway". How can there be so many loud vehicles at 10:30 in the evening? I realize most of them drive all night long.

Today is another long day beside the desert. But, because there is no construction, we can see the brown mountains clearly. Sometimes we can even see snow on the peaks.

When we stop for lunch, we see hundreds of vehicles lined up in town, with loads of cotton. The farmers owe a percentage of their crop as tax to the government. Quite an extraordinary sight.

By now three people in our group have bad colds. It is probably just a matter of time till we are all sick!

Tonight in Korala our hotel looks beautiful from the outside. And even the lobby is nice. But I know the score by now! Jenny gets an electric shock while in the shower. It burns her finger and almost scares her to death. Needless to say, we change rooms. The sheets are clean in this hotel. The "top sheet" is simply a towel.

Before dinner several of us walk with Jenny to an underground mall! Once we walk down the steps, the mall seems to go on forever. We take special care to remember the landmarks near the set of steps we used so we can find our way back again.

Our entire group sits at a round table for dinner. The people at the round table next to us are Inner Mongolians, having a celebration and singing. Three people received khatas (the white silk scarves I received in Tibet and Mongolia) from the rest at the table, and now all are doing the Mongolian toast. I walk over to their table and tell

158

them I spent time in Mongolia. They are thrilled. They put a khata around my neck and take my photo with the group. Then we all toast with a "small brandy". How special. It is obvious that the more one travels, one finds interconnectedness.

Farmers lined up to pay their taxes with cotton

Turfan lies at the bottom of a large depression. We arrive in the afternoon and walk through an ancient deserted city, more like a military citadel -- dating from 100 B.C. and not well preserved. Chinese walk all over the part that is left!

Here in Turfan we find our second John's Cafe. On the blackboard is a message written by someone advertising shalwar qamiz for those travelers going east to west who will need them in Pakistan! This is also a backpacker restaurant, because Turfan is within two hours by bus from the railroad terminus, the same railroad we saw under construction farther west.

The next day in Turfan we visit another deserted city, then an ancient underground water system called a kerez. A long, long tunnel is constructed to divert water from a river in the mountains and bring it to an inhabited area needing water. Vertical shafts (wells) are dug down to intersect with the long horizontal tunnel. I have seen this system used in several places with desert climates. What a clever idea.

Turfan is a very important raisin-producing area. There are drying barns with holes in the walls where bunches of grapes are hung to dry. The grapes are then removed from the stems and shoveled into piles. Men turn the piles several times during the day to ensure adequate drying.

We have a long siesta in the afternoon. Women in the group have one hotel room and the men another; this will prepare us for the late boarding of the train tonight.

Dinner at John's Cafe one last time. I notice that a celebration is taking place in the restaurant next door. I walk inside and find it is a wedding. The bridal couple welcomes me to their table where I snap a picture of them and their attendants! To me it is such an adventure to walk in and be welcomed by whomever is there, just like when I walked over to the table with the Mongolians last night. Why not use an opportunity when it comes your way? The British are loath to interrupt a group like that. It's part of their national character and I am fine with that. I love to travel with them because they are so easy to be with. So there are plusses and minuses and it's not a big thing one way or the other. I'm just glad I have found a nationality of people that I feel easy with. And with a little extra effort on my part, I can usually form lasting friendships with very special people.

It takes two hours to reach the train station by bus. After an interminable time in the crowded station, we board a special foreigners' tourist train. Some of us are such good friends by this time that we have a fantastic party in the guys' compartment next to ours.

A bus picks us up in the morning and drives us two hours to Dunhuang. It certainly doesn't make much sense to build the railroad two hours from important Silk Road towns! Now we are driving in the Gobi Desert and it is all sand, the same Gobi that is in the southern part of Mongolia which is just over the mountains to the north. The town is surrounded by beautiful sand dunes where we take a camel ride after siesta. My camel is tied to the camel ahead of me, but there is nothing behind me, so the camel's rear end is "loose" without a line. He derives great pleasure from running up next to Karim just ahead of me and agitating his camel. After a succession of these antics I am sure I will fall off. Thankfully, I manage to stay in the "saddle".

When we reach the dunes, we climb wooden steps that have been fastened into the sand. At the top we pay ten yuan for a wooden sled to slide back down.

Our newly carpeted hotel is gorgeous and the plumbing actually works! I guess we are finally far enough east that modernity has reached this point.

The Mogao Grottoes are on the schedule in the morning. Our guide speaks German to Hue who translates into English for us! Not the best way to learn about these magnificent caves which were dug out of a cliff wall. Rich "sponsors" paid to have the frescoes painted and Buddhist statues carved. The first cave was built in 366 A.D. One thousand more were dug over the next thousand years. We brought our flashlights to see this gorgeous artwork. The caves provide one of the largest art museums in the world. Four of us return in the afternoon. This time we have a Chinese guide who tries very hard and speaks passable English. She lovingly explains all the incredibly beautiful paintings to us.

In our hotel room in the late afternoon, Jenny and I drink a whole bottle of dry, red wine. Very nice. As we leave the hotel for dinner, we chat with two British cameramen who are filming a documentary of the last 1000 years in China. It will be shown at the millenium in England.

Next morning we fly to Xian, the eastern terminus of the Silk Road and the following day on to Beijing. I am laid up by the stomach flu, but two days later I feel much better and join our group on the bus to the Great Wall. We begin at a spot less visited and touristy than the usual location. I have great fun climbing with Jenny and Bill Johnson all the way up till the reconstruction suddenly ends with piles of stones ahead of us.

Back in our room just in time for wine with Jenny and Hue. Hue gives me a little canvas purse she had purchased in Turfan. It has four different scenes stenciled on it. How lovely. What a special woman! I give her a poem I wrote about her:

> I have found a real-life Princess.
> She is a Chinese princess but not from
> a far-off time of this dynasty or that;
> she's a princess of "today."
>
> She is as beautiful as any princess you
> could imagine anywhere.
>
> But more important than her beauty is
> her kindness and grace, her ready smile,
> her genuine desire to help.
>
> She stops whatever she is doing to discover
> what she can do for you at this very moment.
> This princess is the true kind that makes
> your heart fill to overflowing when you think of her.
>
> How fortunate to have met her in this lifetime.
> Now I can carry the image of the perfect
> princess with me forever.

Jenny (Exodus guide) and Hue (Chinese guide) - my princess

The three of us go our own way, Hue to return to her home in Urumchi by bus, Jenny to move to a different hotel where her parents are staying while her mother delivers technical papers, and I to my plane.

The Quest For Arthur and
The Stone Circles

O n 13 May l999 my British Airlines flight lands at Heathrow Airport and I pick up my rental car, a Fiat Punto. I don't leave the parking lot immediately as I want to make certain that I know where all the controls are. I call the man back out of the office several times to ask him this and that about the controls. I know he thinks I have never driven a car before. I am chagrined to find I can't figure out how to put the car in reverse. I decide not to ask him for yet more help. I am simply driving north of London to the home of Anne and Roger, a couple I met on the Tibet trip, and I can't imagine that I will need to get into reverse in that short time.

* * *

Now I need to step back in time briefly. I have always been enthralled with King Arthur since I was a small girl, and I always knew that sometime I would have to seek out all the locations in Britain that had anything to do with Arthur. In preparation for the trip, I had read :"The Historic King Arthur" by Frank D. Reno. I also read "The Druid Tradition" by Philip Carr-Gomm, "The Celtic Tradition" by Caitlin Matthews, "Pagan Celtic Britain" by Anne Ross and "West Country Wicca - A Journal of the Old Religion" by Rhiannon Ryall. I subscribed to a one-year course from England to become a Bard, the first of three levels on the way to becoming a Druid. Lastly, of course, I read "The Mists of Avalon" by Marion Zimmer Bradley.

My other great fascination has always been the ancient stone circles found all over the British Isles and even in northern France. I found a book, "A Guide to the Stone Circles of Britain, Ireland, and Brittany" by Aubrey Burl. In this book are descriptions of each circle, detailed directions of how to find it, dates of construction (which prehistoric period), and the number of people who would have used a circle at one time (determined by equations). The book also gives the astronomy of each circle, which depends on its latitude, and the physical condition of the circle today. There are also admonitions: always carry a compass, always have a water proof and heavy jacket, always carry extra food and water because it is so easy to get lost up on the moors, especially in heavy fog which is a common occurrence.

So on this trip in 1999 I had many places and circles to look for. I was aided by the long days close to summer solstice and my Ordnance Survey maps of Bodmin Moor, Dartmoor and Southwest England. I planned to start in May hoping to avoid the out-of-sight prices of high season. I found extremely high prices anyway, which made me wonder how outrageous they really got in high season.

* * *

Visiting Anne and Roger -
"I Can't Get Into Reverse"

With directions in right hand, map on the seat, left hand on the steering wheel and gear shift, I arrive at Anne and Roger's home about an hour after I leave the airport. Anne stayed home from work to show me around the house. Then she leaves as I settle into a nice nap following a hot shower. After a couple hours I hear Roger walking around downstairs and get up to greet him. I mention that I can't get my car into reverse. He walks outside and is back in a moment. The simple solution: push down on the gear shift while pulling it into reverse! Why didn't I think of that? After all I owned a foreign car in the past. But I am a totally non-technological person and this is just another example of my limitations.

Roger and I walk the two West Highland terriers. Then he offers to take me up in his WWII Piper Cub plane. We go "for a spin" and it is delightful. All three of us, Anne, Roger and I, visit a pub for a drink and then head home for dinner.

The next day we drive to Oxford to pick up their daughter, Katherine, who has finished her last exam. We visit a beautiful old town for a drink at a pub, and then go on to a huge supermarket the likes of which I have never seen before. Then home to prepare dinner for Andrew and Celia, a fascinating young couple who were on the Tibet tour with us. Great fun to see them again.

Early the next morning I am on my way on the M4 going west. I have a good map of England but I must say it is a bit difficult to hold the map in front of me and watch the road and the road signs at the same time. The hardest situation is when I come to roundabouts and have to drive left, watch for the correct road number on which to exit and operate the manual shift.

I am compelled to stop in Bath where the cult of the local nymph goddess, Sulis, was observed by pre-Romans and Romans alike.

She was the goddess of the healing hot springs, Aquae Sulis. Before the present resort buildings were built, one might now and then have found a votive statue in the stream leading up to the sacred pool. Naturally I have to visit Sulis's site and pay tribute to her .

On to Bristol, where I get lost repeatedly because of construction. But finally I am on the M5 driving northeast through Gloucester, Worchester, then Birmingham where I exit and follow a small country road west. I find a trail leading up a steep hill and deduce that it goes to the Celtic Bronze Age hill fort known as The Wrexin which the Saxons occupied at the time of Arthur. From that vantage point at the top they could watch, as I now do in my imagination, when Arthur and his men rode toward them on the south bank of the Severn River, coming either from Cornwall or Wales. I am sure the hearts of both armies were pounding as Arthur's group crossed the river. The great battle of Badon ensued on the plain below the fort-- Arthur was victorious!

Then a short drive to meet Meg and John Hawkings, another couple from the Tibet trip. I follow them south to the fairy tale, half-timbered, medieval town of Ludlow, then west a few miles until we arrive at their beautiful home right at the base of another Bronze-age hill fort. They take me to dinner at a local pub and then I need to get to bed because I am still recovering from jet lag. In the morning we climb up the sheep path to the summit of the fort. I think we can see the other fort I stood on the day before. I hate to leave them because they have traveled to so many places and it's fun to hear their stories. John helps me find my way out of town to the south after we explore the streets with half-timbered houses.

* * *

Glastonbury - Poems and Musings

I reach Glastonbury by 3:00 p.m. The tourist bureau finds a room for me in a B & B.

It's rainy and misty this morning, perfect weather for visiting the holy Tor, an ancient tower atop a high craggy hill. I walk up the back side and, at the top, I can hardly discern the outline of the Tor. A young man from Buenos Aires is standing and meditating. I decide to do the same. Suddenly the sun shines through the mist. It is spectacular and we are both transfixed.

> Heavy mist encircles me
> As I reach the top.
> The sun struggles
> To pierce the haze.
> Suddenly appear dark outlines
> Of the ancient monument.
>
> Standing before the tower,
> Facing the slowly gaining sun,
> I feel the power, the energy
> Of the holy Tor rising within me.

Driving north through a market town, then a deep gorge with big-horn sheep, I finally arrive at the stone circles of Stanton Drew. There are three rings, a gigantic central one and two smaller ones. My book explains that there are several alignments between the circles, one of them looking through the centers of two circles and two pillars a short distance away. The southern moon sets between the pillars. There are many other intriguing possibilities.

I continue on a very narrow, straight, ancient Roman road to Cadbury Castle, another Bronze Age hill fort which many people believe is Camelot. I walk the ramparts and imagine life in Camelot. There is very little left, but the romance is still there for I am sure in my heart

169

this was the home of Arthur, Guinevere and the Round Table.

Glastonbury Tor emerging from heavy morning fog

Back in Glastonbury I visit the Abbey, the oldest in Britain. I'm very moved by the tomb of Arthur and Guinevere, the Lady Chapel and the thorn bush which is the descendent of the branch that Joseph of Aramithea planted at the site of the Abbey when he founded it very early in the Christian era. The Crown of Thorns on Jesus' head is said to have been part of that same thorn bush.

> Fragmented walls beautifully crafted,
> Lady's chapel, remnants of a nave.
> The Abbey towers over the ancient grave
> Of England's hero and his queen.

170

I just have time to visit the Chalice Well (a holy Celtic spring) to collect some water to take with me tomorrow on my drive to Cornwall and Lands End.

The following afternoon I am enchanted by St Michael's Mount, a sister castle to the famous fortress of Mount St. Michel on the coast of Normandy, just across the channel from Cornwall.

Madron Wishing Well is one of my special destinations. It is located inside a tiny ancient Celtic temple open to the sky. A Wishing Tree stands just outside the door where visitors from time immemorial have tied bits of cloth on branches and said prayers of supplication. I enter the small temple which is probably six by four feet. Two stone benches line the walls and a low stone alter stands at one end with visitors' messages written on small pieces of shale. There is a small spring of water in one corner -- the sacred well of the Great Goddess. Gorgeous wild flowers grow out of the top of the walls.

> I follow the path
> Birds singing,
> Foxglove blooming everywhere.
>
> There it is
> The ancient Celtic temple.
> Walls of stone, open to the sky.
> The doorway beckons me.
>
> Inside in the corner
> The holy spring of The Goddess,
> The Wishing Well.
>
> Such a tiny place;
> yet a stone altar
> At the far end
> Holding prayers of love
> Etched on bits of shale.

Two stone benches
Line the other walls.
I sit, meditating.
Bird voices, glorious flowers
Flow among my prayers.

Black firmament, silver stars.
A wooden bucket, tips.
A shower of beauty, love, integrity, peace
Pours down on me.

I lay a yellow daisy
In the Well.
Slowly I leave
The most mystical, holy place
I've ever known.

I drive on to Lanyon's Quoit where King Arthur is said to have celebrated his last feast with his soldiers before they fought the final desperate battle.

Three legged it stands;
The table balanced above;
A huge monument
Built eons ago.
Some say the hero and his men
Feasted here
The night preceding
The last dismal battle.
Silently the stones stand
Still mourning the fabled King.

My last stop for the day is close to Land's End. It is the Boscowen-Un stone circle. I walk through many fields and am sure I will not find it. But finally here it is.

Nineteen stones stand mysteriously;
Silent tribute to the druid priests.
One of quartz tells when
The May Day sun rises.
Another in the center
Guards the sacred site.

What long-forgotten rituals
Were chanted here?
What haunting rites performed?

Mystical energy envelops and heals:
The ancient power of BOSCOWEN-UN

The next morning I drive to famous Tintagel Castle, the site of Arthur's birth, a place that I have always known I must visit.

Crossing the isthmus
To the enchanted place,
I stop to watch the waves
Break and crash far below
Against the headlands.
The fog envelops
The ruins and me

But for one brief moment
I can see the cave
At the water's edge below
Where once the magician
Slipped through
With the precious babe.

A magical birthplace
For a legendary king.

* * *

Bodmin Moor – Many, many Stone Circles
"My Hero is Indeed Dead"

If I had the time, I could spend days on the moor admiring the many archeological sites. Looking down on the first one, I see moor ponies and sheep everywhere. I lay the "Circle" book and the compass down on the grass to take some photos. About fifteen minutes later I realize I never picked up the compass. I return to the area where I had put it down, but everything looks the same: rocks, clumps of grass. There is no chance of finding the compass.

I spend several hours the next day driving south to Liskeard, a market town, trying to buy a compass. I determine that compasses are not found in market towns. Finally a nice lady clerk sells me her own.

A few miles north in the tiny town of Duloe I discover a circle in a farmyard, split in half by a row of poplar trees. Certainly the location is not as picturesque or thought provoking as if it were up on the moor. But I sit in the circle and meditate, then leave a tiny strip of green ribbon tucked in the grass beside a stone.

> A small comfortable circle:
> Eight quartz stones shining white.
> A Bronze Age urn found
> Buried near one stone.
> Visions of people arriving
> At this holy place
> To honor their Goddess,
> To request "good happenings"
> In the year ahead.
> What rites did they follow?
> What ritual did they chant?
> We can only imagine.
> But we can sense their hopes
> Their joys, their sadness.

174

Filled to the brim with rewarding, interesting speculations, I continue north and approach Bodmin Moor once again. Soon I arrive at a group of three circles named The Hurlers. Because of their accessibility, these circles are perhaps the most renown of all the monuments in the area. Two other women are sitting here, enjoying the tranquility of the place. As one leaves, she places a bouquet in the center circle.

> Three stone circles side by side,
> Silent sentinels of another age;
> The middle circle, the largest,
> With a stone in the center.
> Visitors who came before
> Left flowers, bouquets
> In honor of The Goddess
> And of those who built the circles.
>
> Two ley lines cross here.
> As I meditate,
> The energy envelops me.
> I lay my green ribbon
> Amidst the flowers
> And reluctantly step
> Out of this magical place.

My next destination is Dozmary Pool where the Lady of the Lake reached up her hand from the water to retrieve the sword of the fallen king. As I sit to meditate I suddenly burst into tears. All my life Arthur has been my hero. Now, however, the certainty strikes me that he was a mortal king, that he died and here is the resting place of his sword Excaliber. It is a devastating realization.

> Here it is at last
> Where the Lady reached
> Up her hand to receive
> The hero's sword.
> My quest is ended:

My hero indeed died.
He did not live forever.
A part of me dies this moment.
And I cry silently.

*　*　*

The News Agent and the Green Grocer

When I finally compose myself, I continue on to a tiny town with an imposing Roman name, Altarnun, where my directions indicate I will find the next circle, "Nine Stones". Unable to figure out how to proceed, I walk into a News Agent's shop and ask him, "Where is the circle?" He answers, "There is no circle"! I am astonished because my book has specific information about this circle. As I am about to leave a sweet lady customer suggests that I visit the Green Grocer, Richard, for information because "He knows the location of everything in this area."

Richard's shop is two doors away. I walk in with my map unfolded, lay it on his counter, and ask Richard if there is a circle. He says, "Of course there is" and proceeds to give me complicated directions.

This is a very rural area of the moor. I follow his directions: under an underpass, to a rustic roundabout, to a dirt road (really a dirt path) and eventually run out of landmarks. Returning to the roundabout I take another dirt road which attempt also proves futile. Back to the roundabout and another path. This time I stop at a farm a couple miles along to inquire where another certain farm is located. This farmer feigns ignorance of his neighbor.

But I continue on this path to the last farm where I park the car and walk around to the back of the farmhouse. Peering through the backdoor windows into the anteroom, I see high boots and yellow

176

rain pants and coat, excellent gear for a sheep farmer in this cold and rainy region. When I knock, a man answers the door and looks at me suspiciously. "I'm looking for a stone circle called Nine Stones", I say. His response: "It's up there on the moor. You walk around the end of the wall, go left, cross a creek, and it will be right there". I tell him I don't want to block his driveway. He answers gruffly, "No, I don't want to be blocked". He can see I am confused about where to leave the car. He takes pity on me and tells me I can park in his field which proves to be nothing but rough, muddy ruts. As we walk out to the road he tells me that his name is Ian and I say, "Oh, I have always wanted to meet an Ian!" The ice is broken. Ian says he knows that British people are always treated nicely in the States, so he thinks he should do his part by me.

As he returns to his house and probably to his supper, I start along the wall which separates his farm from the common land of the moor. The wall makes a left turn and I continue along it for probably one mile. Soon I see the creek which is rather swollen by recent rains. I can't see a bridge or logical place to cross. There is nothing for it but to risk soaking my hiking boots as I perch precariously on small stones in the creek. Reaching the other side without an accident, I expect to see a stone circle just ahead but there is nothing except gorse bushes. The hill rises to the right away from the wall. I wander up amid the scrubby plants for a way, then down again and farther along the wall, up again, down again and back to my starting point at the creek. I am beginning to think I might have to return to Ian for help. I feel so helplessly stupid. I know the circle has to be here, but have no idea where to look next.

Deciding to try one more time I walk determinedly up the hill for an eighth of a mile. I cross over a tiny ridge and there it is! A small flat area. A perfect location for the ancients to build their sacred monument.

The perfect circle is fifty feet in diameter, built of eight granite stones with a ninth in the center on a very evocative, isolated site.

It is the smallest, most perfect ring on Bodmin Moor. One of the eight stones has fallen; a gap exists at one point and is probably the location of a missing stone. A row of small stones runs from the ring toward a nearby ridge where there are cairns. Hut circles are obvious to the north and east of the circle where people lived either during construction of the circle or when they would gather to have ceremonies.

This description sounds so unimaginative, but the real scene is quite lovely. Moor ponies and sheep graze around and in the circle. The sun is getting low and there is a faint tinge of pink in the west. I sit down in the circle with my back to a stone, contemplating the people and events that might have led to the construction in such a beautiful spot. I meditate on their sacred philosophy.

> The News Agent said,
> "There isn't a circle"
> Richard the Green Grocer, said
> "Of course there is.
> Ian, the Farmer, in whose field I parked,
> Said "One mile along the edge of the moor,
> Ford the stream, and up on the flat,
> There it will be."
> It is indeed.
> Eight stones in a circle,
> A ninth in the center,
> Silent, lonely, remote.
> But the moor ponies and sheep
> Gather and join me silently.
> In my meditation
> I feel the same peace, solitude,
> The mysticism, the builders knew
> Thousands of years before.

Nine stones –
eight in a circle and one in the middle – plus moor pony

It is difficult to tear myself away from such a peaceful place. But as the sunset continues to brighten, I realize I must descend before nightfall catches me in such a bewildering place.

I spend the night on the other side of the highway in an old inn where I enjoy a five-course meal before retiring to mull over all the day's events. I am very fortunate to be able to feel the amazing energy in special places like stone circles. While everyone admires the physical accomplishments of moving and placing these large stones, few imagine ancient uses and celebrations with them, few say they can actually feel the energy like a palpable substance. It is a joy, an honor perhaps, to sense these wondrous feelings. When I am enveloped by the energy of a place of power, I feel a sense of completeness, as I am filled with its light and beauty.

I wish I could spend more time exploring Bodmin Moor, but my schedule says I must go east to Dartmoor, to seek out circles there.

Next morning as I drive to the new moor, a thick fog descends. I know I will encounter a difficult search just as the "Circle" book mentions. I find a parking area along the road right where I think the Merryvale Circle might be. Merryvale means "Pleasant Valley". Today it's not living up to its lovely name because of the heavy, dense fog. A sign warns not to leave valuables in the car and, moreover, not to leave the car here. I drive a short distance farther and come upon a farm with a wall outlining its boundaries between the buildings and the moor. I find a woman inside the house and ask her where to park. She kindly says to park right in front of her house. I inquire about where I should start looking for the circle. She suggests I simply walk up along the wall on the moor side till the wall turns left. The circle will be in the area of the corner.

Well, I nearly wear out the pages of the "Circle" book, reading and rereading the instructions many, many times. The book says that Merryvale is a complex of two stone circles, a stone avenue, a double row of stones, a single row, standing stones and hut circles. It calls it a splendid complex and deserves a lengthy visit. The settlement of these huts of the Bronze Age is known locally as the Plague Market. In 1625 the farmers left food here in exchange for money from inhabitants from a nearby larger town where 575 deaths had been recorded.

After crisscrossing the entire area over and over for more than half an hour, I finally stumble upon one of the stone avenues. Following along it, I come at last upon a minute circle eleven feet in diameter. Also, peering through the dense fog while feeling increasingly chilled, I begin to discover many standing stones, another avenue. Eventually 100 yards to the south of this entire area, I come upon a second circle, a flattened ring (67 feet in diameter by 58 feet). At this point I decide that I have been successful to some degree and call off the search. The fog has truly been too much for me. The magical energy of these circles will have to await the appreciation of another visitor.

As if this lack-luster search hasn't sufficed, I embark a half hour later on a second one, this time with no fog but pouring rain. The book named the circle Drizzlecombe and said it was very easy to find! Again I tramp here and there in tall wet grass, over stiles into new fields, with no luck. Finally, two drenched people approach me. I ask them if they have seen the circle. They have and tell me it is in an entirely different place than I have been searching. Finally I find it, but it is quite a disappointment. A stone wall cuts it in half! There is a wagon track through part of it. I don't stay. I am soaked through even though I have good rain gear on. Unfortunately the rain has dripped down from the lower edge of the rain pants into my hiking boots.

It is a long walk back to the car in the deluge. Finally I reach it and drive immediately to the town of Yelverton on the edge of the moor to a B & B. It has not been a rewarding day in any respect.

The morning dawns with blue sky and sunshine. Undaunted, I start driving again, this time to the north area of the moor and Fernworthy Forest. There are many tiny dirt lanes to negotiate, but finally I arrive at a lake and parking area for the forest. I walk through the trees toward the moor and come upon Fernworthy Circle with twenty-seven granite blocks of varying heights. I do not feel attracted to it at all and continue to the edge of the moor where a dirt path strikes out up the hill to the top of a small pass where there is a stone wall and gate. Once through the gate, I see two glorious identical circles below the crest of the hill. Named Grey Wethers, they are 107 feet in diameter and 15 feet apart. They lie in magnificent isolation where people from the valleys on both sides could have come for ceremonies. I meditate at length on my back in the tall grasses and wildflowers.

.

> I leave the forest behind
> And walk out on the moor.
> The narrow path winds
> Upwards towards the pass.
> A gate in a stone wall

Opens to the holy place.
Two elegantly perfect circles
Stand side by side,
Magnificently hand-crafted stones.

I lie in the deep grass
Imaging tribes climbing
From two valleys.
Old friends reuniting,
Bringing gifts to the Goddess.
The priest chanting the rituals.
Smoke stealing upwards.
Fulfillment for these people;
Fulfillment for me.

It is a glorious end to a holy search which has led me to innumerable spiritual places in wild and isolated southwest England.

I still have plenty of hours of daylight in this season of longest days. So I head toward the east. I purchase raspberries in the market square of a tiny village and eat them by hand out of the box while I drive toward Exeter. I get slightly lost during the rush hour traffic in the city. Once out the other side I head for Badbury Rings. It is a triple-ringed reinforced grass battlement where Arthur is said to have surveyed the Salisbury Plain before his final battle was fought and lost. I wander upward through the three rings and gaze out over the plain. Looking northward I realize sorrowfully this is where Arthur's life ended.

The next day I visit Avesbury Circle close to Stonehenge. I soon decide that there are too many people; there is no way to feel the vibes of tribal people from eons ago.

So I proceed to Waterlooville near Portsmouth to visit with Jenny and Bill Johnson, a very dear couple I met on my Silk Road trip. And then across to the Isle of Wight for a visit with Sue Wiggans, my roommate from the trip to Tibet. How wonderful to see all these intelligent well-read travelers again.

I couldn't have had a more rewarding trip than this has proven to be. It is one that had to be undertaken alone in order to afford me time for meditating at the archeological sites. I leave England fulfilled beyond belief.

Iran

The Western Mountains /
Fighting with Sara / "Arrested"

This chapter is an example of how a trip can go disastrously wrong. After all, not every traveling experience turns out to be "the best trip one has have ever taken".

*   *   *

In January 2000 Marilyn, my fellow traveler whom I had met five years ago in Mongolia, and I were trying to put together a trip to Iran. We considered joining a British "Explore" trip. We proceeded with our applications and were ready to send a payment. But then we began to worry about the visas. We had no idea how hard it might be for us, as Americans, to obtain a visa. Explore said that first we would have to pay the total cost of the trip. Then Explore would collect everyone's passports and send them with visa applications to Tehran. However, if our visas were refused, we would lose our entire payment! It hardly seemed fair; but those were the rules of the company.

So we decided to search for a local Iranian tour company to work with. The Internet provided a name: Caravan Sahra. We decided that this would be better than joining a tour group because we could visit any sites we wished and not be confined to a standard tour itinerary. The usual itineraries visited the five most prominent sites in the country, but we also wanted to go to historic sites in the western Zagros Mountains. Caravan Sahra complied with all our wishes and soon we had tied up all the loose ends. Unbelievably we didn't have to pay any money up front. We ordered our visas from the Washington, D. C. Iran embassy, received them quickly and were almost ready to travel.

We had to get proper clothes together. Marilyn's mother and my seamstress made us black polyester long sleeved cover-ups which started at the neck and ended below the knee. Trousers were imperative. It was alright to wear other clothes under the cloak which is called a mantle. We needed a scarf for our heads.

We left from Miami in April, stayed overnight in Istanbul, and had the next day to visit the city. In Asia, not all flights operate every day. Those that are operating usually fly around the skies from midnight to five in the morning.

* * *

Our plane arrives in Tehran at 2:00 a.m. from Istanbul. It's sinks down, down through the thick dense yellow-green layer of smog. We check to see that our new costumes look proper and that only a small amount of hair peeps out from under our scarves. A very nicely dressed young woman with white gloves named Sara meets us with a car and our driver, Mashid. They take us to our hotel to catch up on our sleep. They are very late picking us up the next morning because they, too, had to get some sleep.

186

All day we visit the main sights in the city, stop at an Internet café to send messages home, and then stop at Sara's house to pick up money. We push her to let us go in. We know that she doesn't want to or have to let us in. We are aware it is inappropriate on our part. But we have items on our agenda that we know we are not supposed to ask for. The tour company had written us that Americans are not allowed in an Iranian house no matter what. Sara's parents are not home, but her two sisters are; one of them makes us some tea. We enjoy their pet cat and look around. The furniture in the living room is all lined up along the walls. Brightly colored Persian carpets cover the floors. The bedrooms are on another floor of the apartment building! We are happy because we have gotten inside an Iranian house and also won the first of many unpleasant battles with Sara. I cross this item off the list of things I want to accomplish in Iran.

The next morning Sara, the driver and the two of us are driving on a divided highway west toward the mountains. Sara tells us that none of the regular guides in her company had wanted to do our tour because we are going to the western mountains. The standard tour of the country includes about six cities and none of the guides want to vary from that, particularly because they have never been to the west! Sara is still in travel school but finally the tour company asked her if she would like to do it. That is how we happened to get the tour guide from hell!

Our first stop is the Ali Sadr Caves. It is not a simple endeavor to find them. We drive miles out into the country. No signs at corners. Mashid constantly asks peasants for directions. We drive a while on one road, then turn around and head off in another direction. Finally we arrive.

The arrangement is that Marilyn and I will sit in an ancient rowboat pulled by a still older motor boat until we arrive deep into the cave. Then we'll walk around the lake in the cave and view the rock formations for one kilometer at which point we'll be back where we started. At some point the boats are to come back for us.

Once we reach the cavern and disembark, we notice a tremendous amount of construction, or perhaps deconstruction with workers using jack hammers. The smell of gasoline and exhaust and the noise are nearly unbearable.

At the end of our walk among the unremarkable stalagmites, we can't help but think that at some point the exhaust and gasoline fumes could be dangerous to those inside the cave. I also notice that there is no phone or other emergency method of reaching people outside the cave. As we continue to wait, we're feeling more and more concerned about when or if we might be "rescued". After about forty-five minutes I can hear the little "put-put" sound. This was our first visit to an "important" site in rural Iran!

Early in the afternoon Sara and Mashid spend about forty-five minutes trying to find our hotel in the town of Hamadan. They ask many people, each of whom gives us a new direction to try. Back and forth, up and down the main street we drive before we locate it. We arrive at the beginning of siesta hour which means that all stores and restaurants are closed. We realize that Sara brought lunch for Mashid and herself but not for us. She cautions us not to speak to anyone on the street as we search for food. Then she goes in for her nap.

We're on our own now. We're disgusted with Sara and hungry because no shops are open. We walk across the street to a park. Many children run up to us, some greeting us with "Hello." They all know we are foreigners after one look at our outfits, which make us look like refugees. College students are walking home through the park and they want to talk to us. We spend at least an hour getting acquainted with the very friendly people of Iran who say over and over that they love Americans. We are having our first forbidden conversations with Iranians! They give us their addresses so we can send them copies of the photos we have taken in the park.

Sara and Mashid are ready to proceed around three in the afternoon. We visit a twelfth century mausoleum of the Alavi family. Avicenna, the most famous member of the family, was a doctor but was very curious about plants that might prove to have medicinal qualities. His search lasted the rest of his life. He wrote a medicinal encyclopedia which was published in Europe and is still read by medical students the world over. It's hard to imagine the importance this individual had in history. In many town squares in other cities we later see statues of him.

In the center of a round-about we see ruins of the very first city built in this place, Ecbatana. There is a hole-riddled stone lion guarding what must have been a gate. The lion may have been carved at the behest of Alexander the Great!

It's evening now and cooler breezes are coming up. We drive into the mountains surrounding Hamadan and stop to admire a pair of Achaemenian rock carvings (bas- reliefs) commissioned by Darius I and his son, Xerxes I. They are inscribed in Old Persian, Elamite and neo-Babylonian (cuneiform) and have to do with the fact that each one is king and the just ruler of all the great lands listed. I am thrilled to see these carvings ordered by these great men -- up until now they were just names in a history book.

We drive further to an outdoor "restaurant". It's our first experience with small platforms on which the patrons sit with rugs and pillows and a low table. Kabobs seem to be the only thing on offer so we order them. As we are finishing our meal, I ask where the "toilet" is. Mashid accompanies me down a steep hill in practically pitch blackness. Finally we reach a tiny stone hut. He leaves and, since I can't see inside where the hole in the floor is, I "go" by the open door then slowly scramble up to the restaurant in the dark. We are getting our Iranian "legs" in a hurry.

Arriving back in Hamadan, Sara and Mashid are lost again trying to find the hotel. In our room we don our long underwear. The information in our guidebook said it could get very cold during the night because of the mountains surrounding the city. We had been

189

assured in our emails back and forth to the tour company that all the hotels have central heating. Well, they may have it, but they're not using it!

The hotel provides continental breakfast and now we're off on the day's excursion. Our destination is the area of Kermanshah about 300 kilometers south on slow bumpy roads at approximately thirty-five miles per hour.

Overlooking the road as we near a town called Bisotun is a bas-relief from Parthian times showing King Mithradites standing before four supplicants. I can't believe that such a marvelous sculpture would exist just anywhere unannounced by a sign. A little farther along, and 150 feet up the cliff is a tablet commissioned by Darius I representing one of his hard-won victories. The symbol of Ahura Mazda is at the top of the panel. This is the Supreme Being in Zoroastrianism, the first monotheistic religion of the world. Next we drive through a small town, Tagh-e-Bostan, and stop to admire the bas-reliefs and carved alcoves from the fourth century A.D. which are among the highlights of western Iran.

During all this sightseeing we stopped once for a cup of tea. But now it is 5:00 p.m. and there has been no lunch stop. Fortunately Marilyn and I have plenty of snacks with us, so we've been alright. But now it's getting dark quickly. Sara says we must drive back to Hamadan for the night, and we're trying to figure out why the people in the office of Caravan Sahra didn't arrange for lodging at a hotel in this area per our itinerary. We say we need to have dinner and Sara says there's no time; we can eat when we get back to our hotel! We say it will be midnight by then and the hotel restaurant won't be open. Sara says we can order room service. We say room service probably will be closed. Sara doesn't like this logic, but finally she tells Mashid to find kabobs (again) for us. He brings them to the car with a huge container of yogurt which sounds wonderful until we discover it is heavily flavored with garlic! Nevertheless, we share it using one plastic spoon.

We start back on the road to Hamadan. After four hours we arrive at the outskirts of the city. But now at midnight neither Sara nor Mashid can remember how to get to the hotel once again. Back and forth, up and down and around we drive. It is so late no one is to be seen. Now, half an hour later we find the hotel. How, I don't know, since no outside lights are on anywhere.

The next morning Marilyn and I are doing some long-term planning. We know we have at least 400 kilometers to drive today and we're not going to be caught short of food this time. We fill our day packs with hard-boiled eggs, rolls and cheese from the breakfast table. Off we go to the south, turn off at Bisotun and now head southwest to Khoramabad. We eat our lunch about noon in the car and at two o'clock Sara says we're stopping for lunch! We tell her we have just eaten! But she says the driver needs some food (she needs none because she is dieting all the time). The lunch stop takes at least an hour. We wait while Mashid eats his kabobs.

Three o'clock and we're off once more on the bumpy, potholed road. We finally reach Khoramabad but the usual scene evolves. Where is the hotel? We drive around for half an hour and finally, here it is. However, there is no one to answer our loud poundings on the doors and windows and our shouts. Finally we see what appears to be a gardener and he says the hotel is closed! Not temporarily, but permanently! What were the people in the Caravan Sahra office thinking? The gardener suggests another hotel not far away. We find it and register quickly. Because rain and thunderstorms are threatening, we race to the museum which is supposed to be excellent. It is 4:30 and the museum closes at 5:00. We rush through it at top speed and rue the fact that Sara spent so long at the "lunch" stop. Once the museum guards close the doors we visit the bazaar which is a superb idea, since the downpour has finally unleashed itself on the town.

By this point in the trip, we are exasperated with Sara. We tell her we will eat alone in the dining room and she tells us it is not safe because men with black beards (secret service / religious police) are spying on us everywhere! We think that she fears repercussions for herself and her family if she allows us to be on our own. We insist and she goes off to her room in a huff. Every twenty four hours she must report to the travel office that our behavior is not unseemly.

The torrential rain drips through the dining room ceiling into strategically-placed buckets while we happily enjoy our dinner alone.

At breakfast the next morning we again fill our day packs from the table with food for lunch. We head south for about 300 kilometers to Chogha Zambil, a beautifully preserved ziggurat from the 13th century B.C. It is the best surviving example of Elamite architecture anywhere. King Untash Gal built it and dedicated it to the chief god of the Elamites. It was covered by wind-swept sand for 2500 years and is now registered as an UNESCO World Heritage site. Originally the building had five levels, but only three remain. This area was fertile and lush when the ziggerat was built; but now it is in the middle of a desolate, dry, nothingness. I think it is fascinating, nevertheless, because of the reading I have done about early religions in this area of the world. I'm very happy to have seen it.

We're about ready to drive back up the road 40 kilometers to the next location on our itinerary. I tell Sara that I want to use the restroom located in a brand new building next to the ziggerat area. She says I can't go alone, presumably because she thinks someone will kidnap me even though there is a French tour bus parked next to us and some of the French women are using the restroom. I go alone anyway and now the level of our disgust, and Sara's unhappiness, has risen to a new high.

We head up the main road to where the next ruins appear on the map. But Sara and Mashid can't find them. We drive back and forth, down a side road a few kilometers. We find a man to ask, but he has never heard of the ruins of the ancient palace of Shush.

Back we go to the intersection and find another person who does know and soon we arrive.

We know there will not be much to see because of destruction by Alexander the Great in 331 B.C. Despite this, it is magical to stand in the ruins of the winter capital built by Darius I in 521 B.C. and, at one time, similar in grandeur to Persepolis.

We meet a twelve-year-old boy who speaks English. He tells us his family is living temporarily in this area for his father's business, but they really live in Esfahan. We take his picture with the idea of sending it to him once we are home.

Now we begin the tortuous trip to our hotel for tonight. Sara and Mashid cannot find the name of the community on the map. We leave it to them and enjoy our packed lunch. However, about an hour later, Sara is searching for a place that makes kabobs. Mashid orders his lunch; we while away an hour during this stop.

Mashid begins driving northeasterly down a number of secondary roads for an hour. Finally the search switches to a hunt for a tele-phone. Alas, this takes a long time, but we are successful and Sara calls her office for directions. The location of the hotel seems to be rather in doubt by the company staff that happens to be in her Te-hran office at that moment.They have a few suggestions which we try out one by one. By six o'clock we accidentally come upon a very small town where we find the hotel at last! But it is not a fin-ished hotel! People working here right now are doing cement work in the lobby area. No tile has been put on the floors inside or out-side on the steps. A collection of about 100 chairs has been piled in one section of the lobby, presumably for a dining room which doesn't yet exist.

A worker calls some women from the town who arrive to say that we can stay here in uncompleted rooms without functioning air conditioning and they will arrange for a local restaurant to send in a meal to our rooms. This sounds do-able, especially in light of there being no alternative.

Thankfully the plumbing works; we have cold showers. There is a balcony off our room, but the air inside and out is like a furnace. We work on our journals until the meal arrives. Happily it is not kabobs but rather a meat and rice dish that tastes delicious.

When we go to bed, we do so in the nude. We don't dare leave the balcony door open because we are only one flight up from the ground. It is breathless but at least we have comfortable beds.

Next morning the hotel provides breakfast for us, some of which we pack in our daypacks. We're off by 9 a.m. and soon driving on a superb two lane road (not yet on the map, which could create a problem). But Sara says, "No matter, we are going east regardless". The scenery is incredibly beautiful. We go up and down over hills, then down to cross a stream bed. Soon we are going up and down over passes. This takes a long time because up and down means little movement to the east. It is a very isolated area. We pass a large string of nomads along the side of the road. Women and girls are riding in the bed of a pickup, while the boys and men come along slowly behind herding the sheep and goats.

Suddenly there is a gas station and the nomad truck stops there to wait for the rest of their group. Mashid stops for fuel. Marilyn and I open the car doors and start to get out to visit with the women. Sara yells that we are not allowed to talk with nomads. We ignore her totally, and walk toward the women and girls all dressed in peasant blouses and many-layered flouncy skirts such as gypsies would wear in Spain. It seems that the government doesn't try to control their dress. They are delighted to see us and form a circle with us holding hands. They indicate we should all sit down on the grass. One women asks with hand signals where we are coming from, saying "Teheran"? We say, " Khoramabad". The women smile and nod their heads. Then we point east and say, "Esfahan" and then "Yadz" and "Shiraz". Every time we mention a place, they smile and nod their heads. We suggest taking photos. We all stand up for a number of shots. Then, the women notice that the men are catching up. It seems they are forbidden to talk with us; quickly they jump back in the truck and we get in the car. Sara is furious, but we pretend not to notice. We have completed another of our plans for this trip, meeting and talking with nomads. Sue, my roommate from my Tibet trip, who went to Iran a few weeks earlier with Explore, wrote me and said her group twice had spent the night tenting with the nomads!! Once again we wonder what is wrong with Sara, or is it the entire travel company?

We continue eastward. Gorgeous wild flowers of all hues bloom beside the road because we are at such high altitude above the desert. A magnificent experience. Never mind that we don't know where the road goes or how far it is to Esfahan which is our destination for the evening. We begin to laugh and Mashid laughs with us because we don't know where we are. Down we go again and up again, over and over. Suddenly Sara spies a narrow road that turns off to the right going south. She tells Mashid to go that way. We eat our lunch from the hotel breakfast selection. About two hours later we reach the main road, the one we were supposed to have been on. Sara, however, in her "infinite" wisdom, thought that the shortest distance on the map between two points must be the fastest way to go. She had no idea how slow a road can be when you're going up and down over passes and down to stream beds.

We turn east toward Esfahan and very soon see a restaurant beside the road. It looks quite classy, certainly not the kind of place we have been frequenting. We order a lamb stew which is delicious with all the added spices. There are dried red barberries in the rice which add interesting color. This is absolutely the best food we have had in Iran. That wouldn't be hard, since all we have eaten are kabobs and the one nice meal in our room last night.

About two hours later we enter the outskirts of Esfahan. Mashid is happy because he knows his way around now. He takes us to our hotel and then Sara says she wants to take us to the nicest hotel in the city for tea. But we saw a guest house on the street when we were approaching our hotel with "Internet Cafe" written below the sign. We tell Sara that first we have to visit the guest house.

Each day Sara dresses impeccably in the most expensive clothes she can buy, and always wears white gloves! At the top of the stairs leading up to the guest house, the manager meets us and looks with disbelief at Sara and her gloves. It is embarrassing for us to even be with her. The manager says to come back later because someone just got on the computer. On the way down the stairs Sara asks us why anyone would want to stay in a place like this. The fact of the matter is that this is exactly where we wish we were staying. We will return when the guests are back and we can talk to them in the courtyard.

Mashid whisks us away to the expensive hotel where we have a cup of tea in the courtyard and watch the wealthy tourists. This is where Sara wants to be, and we do not.

Now on to a pizza restaurant. The pizza is good. While Sara is paying we quickly leave the restaurant. She calls after us that we can't walk back to the hotel by ourselves, but we call back and say we are going alone. We stop in a shop to watch two men making gorgeous wooden furniture with carved details. Sara would have been furious had she known, afraid of possible kidnapping.

In the morning we go to the main square which is very beautiful. Our local guide is an hour late meeting us; this is aggravating because we are itching to visit the shops after the tour. But he knows what he is doing. At the time we finish, he takes us to a marvelous restaurant where I am sure he gets a kick-back from the owner. Then we tell Sara we plan to shop. She says she must go with us to negotiate the best prices for us! We tell her we want to do our own bargaining because it is fun. She reluctantly leaves us.

In the first shop we ask the man what happens when a guide accompanies the customers. He says it is terrible; he cannot discount by way of bargaining and the guide gets thirty percent of the paid price! We had figured that was the case! But we have outsmarted Sara once again!

Marilyn now starts on an interminable search for a carpet to buy. I stick with her the rest of the day, but vow to myself that I will be on my own tomorrow. We return to the pizza restaurant for a late meal because every other restaurant is closed!

We join the local guide once more this morning and have another interesting tour which ends just at the lunch hour. But this is fine because he takes us to another superb restaurant. In the afternoon Sara and Mashid drive us out of town to visit the ruins of a Zoroastrian fire temple. These truly are just ruins, not much to see. Then we're back in town, and Marilyn continues her indecision about the carpets.

Sara has asked us if we'd like to ride horses while we are in Esfahan. She will have to make an appointment. We say to make it for early the next day. At breakfast we ask about the horses and she says that this day is for men to ride; tomorrow is for women! So she will try again. She is catching a terrible cold. We can tell that she certainly doesn't want to be out and about. We tell her we will go shopping alone. She says it isn't possible. We tell her that we're going whether she likes it or not. Our relationship continues to disintegrate. However, she scores a point by making us promise that we will never, ever go to the bridges over the river - under where the tea houses are located--it is very, very "dangerous"!

We go to the square and visit a tea shop where we are alone until three local college-age men come in and sit down two tables away. We start to chat back and forth and learn that they are studying film-making at the university. I am enthusiastic and mention an Iranian film I have seen lately. But they say that is not the kind of film they want to make. They want it to be like American films with some sex. We figure out that their plan is to make a film and smuggle it out of the country so that the bootleg businesses can re-import it. Customers will call on the phone to order the film which is delivered to them in the dark of night because Iranians are not allowed to see films with sex scenes. We wish the young men success in their endeavors. We're extremely pleased because, once again, we have talked to ordinary Iranians. We agree that Iranians are very pleasant, and much like Americans.

Marilyn and I go different ways to shop. Down an alley I discover a tiny shop. It requires climbing an extremely high step to enter. Through the window I watch the craftsman painting "miniatures". He invites me up to the shop to observe more closely. He explains in Persian about his technique and the many different brush tips he uses. He shows me one made from the whisker of a cat. As usual I can make myself understood with my hands and using English words slowly. And I can similarly understand him. I choose some miniature paintings and he makes frames for them. It is gratifying to know that he makes each one expressly for me.

Later I sit down on one of many grass terraces above the square proper. Leaning my head on my arms folded on my knees, I close my eyes. I am really tired. Our schedule has been exhausting, especially with all the driving we did in the mountains. I hear someone approaching, look up, and see two young Iranian women. I think they think I must be very hungry as they point to food they have left over from their picnic on the grass. I shake my head "no". Nevertheless, they spread their table cloth next to me. We all take off our shoes and kneel on the edge of the cloth. They produce some pistachios and I find cashews in my pack to add to the "repast". One of them speaks somewhat passable English. I discover she is married and the other girl is her sister. Both go to the university and this is siesta hour so they usually have a picnic here each day. I tell them about myself. They rummage through their packs to try to come up with some article they can give me as a memento of our meeting. They give me an old coin; I give them a pen. The girls initiate the old hand-stacking game normally played by children the world over. When we have all the hands stacked in a "tower", we swear we will always be friends and write to each other forever. We exchange addresses. I always put addresses of people I meet on trips in my journal so I can send them copies of photos of us together. We ask passers-by to take pictures for us. Then it is time for them to return to school. We hug each other and sadly say "Goodbye". I am so thrilled to have gotten to know two young Iranian women so intimately!

I meet Marilyn. We decide to return to the hotel by taxi for a rest. While riding we pass a large group of religious men marching along, chanting loudly, and shaking their fists in the air. Now we are seeing the other kind of Iranians. It is quite disturbing. We stop at the guest house to check on e-mails and sit in the courtyard where several guests are having tea. They are British and American. They tell us that they have been traveling independently, hitching rides and staying anywhere they please. We are shocked and tell them of our "incarceration" by Sara. They can't believe us. They tell us to grab our luggage and catch a bus to anywhere! We would truly like to do that very thing, but we don't know what the consequences might be. One French couple comes in and tells us that this is their third trip to Iran. They come each year for six weeks and travel a different part of the country. Inevitably they meet Iranians who invite them to stay at their home overnight. Once a week they stay in a guest house to have a bath. This is indeed what Marilyn and I would like to have done, but we are completely ensnared in this tour operated by Caravan Sahra.

Another taxi takes us to the river after a rest. We find a "forbidden" tea shop-restaurant under one of the bridges and have something to eat. Then we order a hookah with peach peelings. When it arrives at the table I see it has tobacco in the bottom of a pipe with the peach peels on top. When you draw on the pipe, the tobacco and peach tastes go through under the water and arrive in one's mouth as a very mild sensation. This is where the locals go. There are families at other tables with young children. This is the "devil's pit" that Sara had warned us about!

Stopping by Sara's room in the hotel, we tell her we'll meet her by 9:30 the next morning in front of the hotel and that we hope the arrangements will have been made to ride horses by 10:00 at the latest. Next morning we get in the car and ask her about the horses; but she has been unable to arrange anything! She says she'll call now. We are disgusted and tell her not to bother. Instead we opt to visit a huge aviary in the city, and then are on our way to our next destination, Yadz.

Yadz is three hours across the desert which is mostly gravel with some desert bushes growing here and there. Once in a while we can see tiny red poppies blooming, even a miniature rose bush. As we approach the city we stop at an ancient Zoroastrian site. This was the main religion in Iran and other parts of the Middle East until it was pushed out by Islam. The leader, Zoroaster, preached about an omnipotent, invisible god called Ahora Mazda. Fire is the symbol of god and is worshipped at an eternal flame in the temples. Zoroastrians placed the dead at the top of a high hill with a wall around it. These are called Temples of Silence. It was felt that burial contaminated the earth and cremation the air. So the bodies were left to the work of vultures. Mongolians and Tibetans also use this "Sky Burial" idea. Marilyn and I climb to the top of the hill and, with great difficulty, we crawl through a tiny hole in a wall and then over the precariously higher wall itself. Not a single bone remains. However, we can look over the city to see many windtowers on roof tops designed to catch the breeze and direct it to rooms in the houses -- ancient air conditioning!

Before entering Yadz proper we stop at a modern Zoroastrian temple. An eternal flame burns here. There is a painting of Zoroaster. Large pockets of Zoroastrians exist today in the Mumbai area of India and Singapore. We meet some pilgrims from Singapore who had arranged for a guide to take them to every Zoroastrian temple in Iran. Sara confesses that she is Zoroastrian.

There is a very ancient city within Yadz proper. UNESCO says it is one of the oldest towns in the world. It is made of adobe and has many twisted, narrow alleys. We want to explore at length, but, of course Sara says it is dangerous; we might get lost! Or someone might kidnap us! We want to walk up to the roof of a large mosque, but the iman says he is busy digging a grave in the floor of the mosque for a follower who must be buried yet this day; so he can't take the time to unlock the door to the roof! We walk through the market where the women are wearing mantles and scarves of thin fabrics with light, colorful designs. The government allows Zoroastrian women to wear them in deference to their religion.

In the morning we drive on to Kerman over another long, hot, dusty, desert road. We stop for lunch at a very nice restaurant in the middle of nowhere! Long ago Kerman was an important city on the Silk Road; now it is known for its carpet making.

Once we reach the city we find that most hotels, including ours, are filled to the brim. Sara fortunately finds a room for us at the hotel across the street. There's no room for Mashid and Sara. That suits Marilyn and I just fine. We eat alone in the dining room of the hotel we were supposed to be staying in, because ours has none at all.

In the morning a short drive takes us to the town of Mahan, where there is a beautiful palace with lovely gardens tucked into a series of pools. Lunch is very pleasant, sitting in the gardens. We have been harassing Sara endlessly because we want to stay for sunset at our next destination, the ancient city of Bam. Sara says it's not possible. We insist she call her office so we can talk to the director. She calls; I am sure she calls him every day and tells him how very unruly we are. Now I get on the phone and tell him that our guide book says we must stay for sunset, and my friend on a recent Explore trip wrote me that their tour stayed for sunset. I can't persuade him. He says it is dangerous to drive the desolate road back to Kerman at night. We might be stopped by military police or kidnappers!

As we approach the red clay desert city of Kerman, the sun makes it resemble a fiery red fairy-tale fortress. It is magnificent. Sara tells us we have 45 minutes to look around before we must start back! We are furious with her. Why didn't we get there earlier to have more time? We cover as much as we can of this incredible place. We find stables and rooms of the guards that were billeted there once. We walk up and down and around. Suddenly on the highest level we find a delightful room, a tiny cafe with a glorious view over the ruins. This would have been a perfect place to have lunch. We are thinking maybe we can squeeze in a beer, but Sara finds us and coerces us into moving down to the parking lot. In spite of all the hassle, this has been one of our favorite places in Iran.

We have driven only a short distance when the sun sets. Realistically we are only half an hour away from enjoying the sunset at Bam. What insane rules! At a mandatory check point on the way back, the official wants to know why we are so late returning on the road. It seems like everyone is crazy.

Preparing for an early morning departure the next day our memory jars us into taking bread and cheese from the breakfast table. The plan is to drive about 350 miles to Shiraz over a boring desert road in terrible heat. We had read that there is a huge, salty lake on the way but well off the beaten track. It is on the path of migratory birds and the home of 50,000 flamingos. So naturally we want to drive over to the lake, but Sara is not in favor. We argue at ever higher decibels; finally she gives in. She and Mashid drop us off on a forlorn dirt path not too far from the lake, saying they will be back in half an hour. We walk a bit along the shore. There are no flamingos. We are nevertheless amazed at the caked salt along the edges of the lake and a distant island. It is unbearably hot; there is no shade. About an hour later we see the car parked half a mile away. They didn't even bother to pick us up! They have had lunch somewhere in this barren wasteland, but brought nothing for us.

Sara finds a phone to call her office. While she's gone Mashid looks back at us, "Sara bad, Mashid good? We agree heartily and all laugh.

Now it's only a short distance to Shiraz. Our local tour guide is waiting for us at the hotel. She is an old friend of Sara's, but she is so sweet we love her right away.

Shiraz has been a center of learning since medieval times. The two most famous Iranian poets, Hafez and Sa'di, were born here. The next day we visit their mausoleums with Sara and our local guide. The gardens surrounding the small, beautiful buildings are superb. The rest of the city is lovely as well, with gardens and flowering trees everywhere. We visit many buildings; the most impressive is the Bogh-e-ye Shah-e Cheragh, the famous tomb of the King of the Lamp. Today is some sort of holiday so the crowds are unbeliev-able. Attendants hand us special mantles and chadors. At the women's entrance we are checked to make sure we are properly at-tired. The thousands of shoes outside are an unbelievable sight. The walls inside are covered with minute mirror tiles. Ceiling lamps create myriad dazzling reflections. Innumerable women and girls sit jammed together on the floor. There are many babies-in-arms but also crawling toddlers. It is like a furnace inside the shrine. After a short stay we gratefully leave the building.

It has been a perfect day which we enjoyed tremendously with our local guide.

Next day is our long-awaited trip to Persepolis. Trouble erupts as we all try to fit inside the taxi. It is really a narrow car and we tell Sara she can't sit in the back with us because it is so hot and there really is no room. She goes up to her room and comes down with a thin pillow from a chair which she places on the console housing the gear shift!. We tell her we can't see past her and also it is not safe. It should not be a big deal; after all Sara must have seen Per-sepolis many times. Finally she leaves the car; we start out on the rather long trip to the ruins.

As we arrive at the site, Sara descends from a private, hired taxi!

We can't believe it.

In 512 B.C. Darius I began constructing this massive palace which was to serve as his summer residence. It took 150 years to build with Xerxes I and II and Artaxerxes I, II, and III all contributing to the finished product. Alexander the Great is thought to have burned it to the ground in 331 B.C. Walking with map in hand, it is not hard to figure out where the various rooms were. A magnificent stairway flanked by columns still stands. There is a bas-relief on each column, and sufficient reliefs for the viewer to understand the story of subjects from all over the empire bringing gifts to Darius. What a glorious place this must have been!

Like so many sites in Iran, the land was at one time much more fertile and therefore more welcoming than now. Deep sand eventually covered the site until it was rediscovered in the 1930's.

As we leave the area (Sara in her cab and we in our car) we stop to gaze up at a cliff where high alcoves show us the tombs of Darius I, Artaxerxes , Darius II and Xerxes I! They are called the tombs of Naghsh-e Rostam. Eight reliefs cut into the stone below the tombs depict scenes of conquests and investitures. All in all it is quite an amazing sight.

We drive a few miles north to the ruins at Pasargardae, site of the earlier capital of the Achaemenian empire, and used from 559-330 B.C. This was Cyrus' palace. All these famous men seem to me to be right here with us all during the day. They have come alive for me. What an experience!

The next morning as we board our plane for Tehran, Sara unbelievably tells us to buckle our seat belts! Where does she think we've come from and how many planes we've ridden?

Mashid is there to welcome us in Tehran, having driven there while we visited Shiraz. We do a little more sightseeing. There are paintings on the walls of buildings showing Iran dropping bombs on the USA during the war the US fought with Iran. We even jump out and take pictures of the paintings. But a policeman angrily stops and says, "no photos". A motorcycle policeman again stops us when we try to photograph the old US Embassy.

In the afternoon we arrive at our hotel. We have a couple hours to repack our suitcases before it is time for dinner in the dining room downstairs. At one moment the nice manager calls us on the phone to tell us he needs our passports. He hadn't taken them earlier because we aren't spending the entire night there. I tell him we are almost finished with our packing and will be coming downstairs, but he says he will come and get them immediately. We sense a note of urgency in his voice.

As we walk downstairs a while later, the manager comes up to us and suggests that we go to a table in the parlor and join three men that are sitting there! We look at him in disbelief. Why would two women want to join three men? We tell him we'll just sit at another table and write in our journals. We are writing industriously when suddenly we are aware that the three men are standing behind our chairs. They are very large and burly and speak almost no English. They grab our journals and motion that we must go to our room! My mind is racing. What is going on? We walk to the elevator and somehow five people squeeze into a space meant for two. We lead them to our room and unlock it. The men motion to us to sit on our beds.

Our suitcases are lying open on the floor. The men start to rummage through our belongings, disrupting everything we had so carefully packed. We have no idea what they are looking for. I suspect they think we have drugs. But Marilyn hears one say, "Computer?" and she shakes her head, "No". They continue to tear through everything, but they don't find what they want.

Our daypacks are on the foot of the beds, neatly packed with the tops open. Our film, used and unused, and our cameras are right on top to remove at the airport to avoid the X-ray machine. The men produce a large garbage bag throwing in all the film and one of Marilyn's cameras plus our journals. After an interminable scary period they leave!

Marilyn and I look at each other, shaking with fear. It takes us quite a while to settle down, hash it all over, and try to make sense of it all. Finally we figure out that our "good" friend Sara must have called the police to tell them we are photo-journalists! She finally got back at us for all the discord we had had during the trip!

Finally we compose ourselves and go down to dinner. The manager comes over, apologizing profusely. He says every now and then police raid the guests. He never has any idea what they want.

After our meal we go to our room to rest until midnight when Sara and Mashid will pick us up to go to the airport. We are still upset from the shock, and really can't fall asleep. When our ride arrives we don't give Sara the satisfaction of knowing she turned us in. We give Mashid a large tip, and of course nothing to Sara. But we do give her the money we owe for the trip (we had paid nothing to date).

Surely this must be the end of the adventure. But as we work our way toward the gate with other passengers in the airport, a burly man pulls us out of line. Each of us must go separately into a small room to have all ten fingers fingerprinted! I do believe this is our final message: you are personae non gratis. Never mind, we are not planning to return!

Once the plane takes off, we immediately remove the mantle and scarf, our uniform for two weeks. And we have a glass of wine to celebrate our freedom. Our sad thought, however, is that we no longer have the journals with the addresses of the special people we met. They will forever regard us as crass Americans who don't keep their promises to send photos and letters. And we have no pictures of our trip in Iran. But we have indelible memories of the worst tour guide ever.

Khumbh Mela and Rajasthan

I had been hearing about a huge Hindu festival in India that would take place in the middle of January 2001. There would be more people there at one time than had ever been together before on the face of the earth, and would not be repeated for forty years. Marilyn's friend, Carol, had written her that she was thinking of going. I emailed her and told her I wanted to go. She decided she would not go. But I was "hooked" by then and decided to work out my own plans to attend. I also had to think of another place to travel once it was over to get my money's worth from the huge flight expenses. It would be Rajasthan.

Some friends had traveled in the area and gave me the name of a travel company in Delhi. So I began to plan. First of all I had to find a person who could act as my guide at the festival. I found Suez on the Internet. He wrote me that he would meet me at the Allahabad train station and take me to my hotel. The following day he would take me along the Ganges River to show me the festival happenings and explain everything to me. It sounded perfect. I could tell by his name that he was Muslim and not Hindu; however

I figured that people of both religions know a lot about each of them. I decided he would be just fine for me.

*   *   *

The Khumbh Mela Festival - India

On January 21 in the evening I arrive in Delhi and meet a driver from the Hotel Regent. I change some money and he drives me to the hotel. My room is appalling. Sheets are grey, walls are dirty, light switches filthy, bathroom fixtures leaky, corridors noisy, loud commotion outside the building. But I'm so tired by this time that I simply pull out my sleeping bag liner and fall into bed about 11 p.m.

In the morning I drag myself out of bed to have some breakfast in the dining room and return to bed, after complaining to the tour company on the phone about the condition of the hotel room.

At one o'clock a guide arrives for sightseeing in Delhi. His name is Mukesh. He is 28 and extremely intelligent. I learn a great deal of his personal philosophy and about Hinduism. We drive around the city of New Delhi which is all parks and trees and beautiful old monuments, mostly Muslim. One was built by Akbar, the same architect who designed the Taj Mahal. We see Nehru's memorial and the eternal flame that burns there in his memory. Bunches of bright orange marigolds lie everywhere, left by Hindus at the site. We visit a huge new Hindu temple which is very beautiful, and pay homage to the Hindu gods. Outside I suggest that we sit down and meditate together. He is pleased to do so. A very nice experience.

We don't finish our tour until 6:30 p.m. Two managers of my tour company are waiting at the hotel. The hotel management switches me to a different room-- best one in the hotel! What a difference. This is the bridal suite! The sheets are clean, the bathroom OK.

However, the room is cold and noisy and there is the smell of sewer gas. In India one cannot expect perfection.

One of the two managers of the tour company, Plukesh, stays to help me order dinner: dahl, yogurt, and curd in gravy which is delicious. We talk about his family while I eat. He has a twelve-year-old boy and seven-year-old girl. Plukesh explains that the reason the hotel is so noisy is that it is filled with a large group of Pakistanis who are drinking alcohol and carousing because they're outside of Pakistan and no one at home will know.

Plukesh leaves and I have a bath and go to bed. Several times during the night I jump up and open the door, hoping to find the noisy culprits in the hallway but to no avail. I think they are partying in the rooms with the doors open. The dogs that were sleeping outside the building during the day are now busy with` barking, yelping, fighting, and scrounging for food in the garbage piles in the street.

I'm up at 5:15 a.m. and leave for the train to Allahabad by six. The hotel staff hands me a box breakfast and lunch to eat on the train. I share a compartment with two middle-aged Indian couples also going to the festival. I sleep the entire train ride from 6:45 a.m. to 3:45 p.m. in part because I took a sleeping pill! My daypack provides an adequate pillow. There are no real compartments in this car, just bench seats and another bench up above. There are various floppy cloth barriers here and there. We arrive at Allahabad about 4:00 p.m. My ride is waiting to take me to the Hotel Sarap. This hotel is also filthy; I guess third-class hotels in India are always pretty bad. The shower drips loudly and constantly. In one corner of the room there is a shelf where someone tore out the television, all the wires, and ripped up some of the red shag carpet.

I try to reach Suez. The deal we had made was that he would be ready when I got to the hotel, but he is in Varanesi picking up clients for his tent camp at the airport. I eat in the "hotel dining room". There are two tables. I order dahl and raita. Back in my room I keep calling Suez as I prepare for bed. I find my sleeping

209

bag liner and then two extra blankets in a cupboard. As I slip into my liner, the phone rings. Finally it is Suez. He has the details for tomorrow. We can't take the private boat he had described on the Internet because new restrictions say we can't drive close enough to get to the boat. We'll have to walk to the festival from where the rickshaws must stop and the path becomes a pedestrian area. Now that I know the plans, I can go to sleep. The shower runs and drips all night long.

Suez picks me up at 8:00 a.m. and is carrying lunch. We take a rickshaw for about three miles; then we walk three miles to the edge of the Ganges. The crowds are immense. The sight that we see as we approach the water is spectacular. People mill around everywhere. Some are bathing in the river to erase their sins. Some are cooking lunch. Clothes lines hang here and there. Women have washed out their brightly-colored saris and hung them out to dry after bathing in the river. Magnificent bright colors are every-where. Millions of people are walking in our direction with bags of clothes, cooking pots and food to stay overnight or at least eat lunch on the wide sandy shore. Other millions have already bathed and are walking in the opposite direction. Such bright colors, myr-iad men's outfits, unusual hats. Extraordinary! We are more or less locked into our area since we can't get near a bridge to cross to the other side of the river.

Contrary to what Suez had told me, there are now restrictions on photographing close to the water where people are bathing. Appar-ently the media had photographed a naked man and printed it in the newspaper! There is so much to see: parents cutting their chil-dren's hair to donate to the Ganges, even some adults cutting their own hair. Marigolds wrapped in leaves are being presented to the Mother Ganga. As we walk along, we see women cooking for their families. When they made the trip they packed one cooking pot and a flat plate to knead chapati dough which they fry in oil. Or once here make soup with rice and vegetables. One young woman insists she'll make a chapati for each of us. She puts some brown

210

sugar on top. How delicious! Suez and I sit on a plastic emergency blanket I carry with me and eat potato chapatis and bananas which he has brought for lunch.

I wish I could participate in the bathing ritual. I dip my right foot in the water. It looks much cleaner than most of our rivers at home! I think I could perhaps wade in the water up to my knees; but after all the things I have read about the organisms that live in lakes and rivers in the Third World (or even perhaps in our own world these days), I decide not to take the chance.

Hundreds of stalls line the shore. People are selling all manner of things. One man has a myriad of necklaces. I decide that I need one made of orange beads and a couple of snake eyes to commemorate this fabulous celebration.

Many Hindu home decorations are for sale. One man puts a holy mark with ashes on my forehead. I purchase marigolds to toss reverently into the river as I offer prayers to all the deities in the world.

We gaze at the bridge that we had planned to cross and see hundreds of people walking back and forth across it. But we cannot get there because the police have seemingly divided this huge area into parcels and we must stay in the one we entered.

Along the river there is a fort built in 1583 by Akbar. We climb up to the ramparts to look down at the teeming masses of people engaged in all manner of interesting activities.

Several hours and several miles after we arrive we start back to the rickshaw area. I figure that I have walked possibly 10 miles today. Every single one was worth it. Never have I seen so many people in one place in my life. A great festival!

People bathing at Binares

All the time that we have been walking today, Suez has been constantly answering his cell phone or is making calls on it. He is truly a wheeler-dealer. On his phone he has found a car for a client to rent; so we have to wait about an hour for the client to arrive at the rickshaw station. All four of us drive to Suez' tented camp which he owns. It is very upscale: gorgeous large tents with living space plus bedrooms inside and a little porch outside. Suez had asked me in an e-mail before I arrived if I wanted to stay in his tent camp; but when I inquired about the price, I decided I would do better price-wise in a cheap hotel.

Suez's parents are delightful people. His mother gives me a dish of rice pilaf which is delicious. Some Japanese clients who are staying at the camp are going via the camp's van to the river for a boat ride. Then it seems the van will return and pick up some other people and myself and take us to another boat. It is getting later and later and I'm wondering if I should even go on the river because I don't have a jacket or sweater with me, and I think it's going to get cold. Finally the van arrives. The other people and I get in. Traffic is unbelievable. I can see it's going to take a long time to get to the river.

There are two couples and myself. One couple is a young Mexican woman who just graduated from the University of Mexico and her father who has quit his job. They will travel around India until July visiting ashrams. Both couples have been at the mela for several days. Yesterday they crossed the river on a bridge and visited the sadhus' camp (Sadus are itinerant holy men). The girl and her father stayed overnight there. Why didn't they freeze? All night there was chanting. Then at 4 a.m. the nagas, who are naked men covered with ashes formed into a huge line hanging on to a long rope and carrying pitchforks. The couples were also put in the procession. Nagas have the right to be first in the water. They all ran here and there in a long line hanging on the rope, shrieking, and finally dashed into the Ganges! Both couples bathed today and other Westerners were bathing also. So I'd missed the "spot" where the action was! But how could I have known and, being alone, I would never have dared to stay the night. Also Suez had never dreamed we wouldn't be able to get across the river to see the sadhus and nagas this morning. The rules seem to have changed by the hour.

I get out of the van about 45 minutes later to take a rickshaw to the hotel, foregoing the boat trip because it is now much cooler. The crowds make it impossible for cars to progress. My smaller rickshaw has a better chance to move ahead, and I arrive about 15 minutes later.

This has been a stupendous once-in-a-lifetime privilege for me. I have developed such a respect for the Hindus -- always quiet and peaceful, no shoving. Lovely, lovely people, acting out an amazing sacred ritual. A very spiritual happening! I have certainly felt the energy the whole time I have been here. Incredible!

Every western nation except the United States has media at the festival with coverage sent to its country. One does wonder, doesn't one?

I am in bed at last in my filthy room. But -- I am warm.

The next morning is Republic Day. I am wondering if this could possibly be a holiday? Two young men from the hotel take me to the train station. What a sight! Millions of people everywhere. We climb many steps to the correct platform for the train to Benares (Varanesi). They leave me there with my backpack and day pack. I find an empty cart and sit on the edge.

As I look about I see many sadhus in their saffron clothes, with wild unkempt hair, and a tin cup for donations. They are waiting for trains that perhaps will never come; but, never mind, they will camp on the platforms along with millions of other pilgrims. Some people are reading the newspaper and I can see there are many photos of the mela. I ask one couple if I can look at the paper when they are finished and they generously hand it over. I really want to have the photos and finally I dare to ask them and they just give me the paper! How nice.

As I wait and wait, I realize that not one train has arrived at the station. And here are all these people waiting in vain as I am. Some people are saying the train is five to six hours late; if ever, I am thinking.

About 1:30 in the afternoon the two young men return and take me to the hotel manager's house. The front room has inexpensive posters on the walls depicting various Hindu gods and goddesses. There are people standing around in the next room. I think they must be family members who have gathered together perhaps for the festival and also National Day. Two children talk a little with me. Finally, the hotel manager comes and asks how he can help me. I tell him that because the trains are not running, I need a taxi to Benares where my guide is already waiting for me to go sight-seeing. The manager tells me there are no taxis; they've all been reserved. But he starts to make phone calls and eventually, amazingly, is able to get a taxi. I agree to pay both ways for the driver so he can get back to Allahabad.

The taxi comes soon. I immediately feel ill in the back seat and although I lie down, I know I am going to vomit. At first I use the newspaper with the photos from the mela. Then I pull out my windbreaker, lay it on the floor of the car and start having dry heaves. At one point when I raise my head slightly, I see a huge camel caravan moving along beside the road in the direction of Allahabad. All the camels are heavily loaded as though they have come a long way. I try to sleep. At first the traffic is really thick and slow, but as we move farther south, it thins out. However, when we enter Varanasi, after four hours, we find ourselves in a traffic tie up. The driver does not know where the Hotel Praqdeep is located. He asks several people, and finally finds it at six p.m.

The manager of the hotel says he will call my guide to let him know I have arrived. I receive a beautiful room and go down to the restaurant; amazingly I am over my digestive problems. The guide arrives to eat with me which I think is very nice of him. He says he has been waiting for me since noon! We plan a very early departure for the morning so I can recoup at least a small part of what I missed today. My room is incredibly clean and lovely. I enjoy a fabulous shower with hot water. The water pours down from the shower head in the middle of the bathroom ceiling which, of course, soaks the entire bathroom, an extremely common arrangement in Asia. As I crawl into bed, I realize that no dogs are barking, another great plus!

In the morning I feel a bit nausous and take a compezine pill just before meeting my guide at 6 a.m. First we walk down to the ghats, where they cremate bodies right next to the water. We take a boat, resembling a gondola, and watch the people bathing in the Ganges. I even see a naked man bathing. The sunrise light is so beautiful, great for photos. The people here are still celebrating the mela.

We walk back to the hotel, quickly eat breakfast, put the luggage in the car, and drive off to Sarnath outside the city. This is where Buddha gave his first sermon in the shade of the bodnath tree where he was enlightened. Here at last is the Deer Park (of the Buddhist symbols)! We take a look at the stupa there in honor of Buddha and rush off to the airport.

Security here like I can't believe just to go to Khajuraho, a thirty minute flight! My new guide meets me and takes me to the beautiful new Hotel Clark, then to the one and only Internet cafe. The young owner has only had the computer a week and is not familiar with the workings. I finally get on line and write to Jim for an hour telling him all that has happened since I arrived in India, but as I try to send it, I am disconnected! This is par for the course for me at foreign Internet cafes. Quickly I write a short email and send it. Back at the hotel, I do some laundry and rest a bit. Then I'm off to a great folklore show. The costumes are just glorious. Dinner at the hotel: deep-fried potato and corn pancakes and yogurt with marinara sauce. Delicious. To bed at 9 p.m. Everything works in the bathroom including the hot water. The shower head in the proper place. Perfect!

A very nice man, Sarvesh Shukla, picks me up at 8:30 in the morning. We walk to the ancient Hindu temples which are part of this UNESCO World Heritage site. The temples were built around 1100 A.D., similar in time to Angkor Wat, but have no similarity to the Cambodian temples. There are no bas-reliefs, just thousands and thousands of carved human figures, many of them tantric. Sarvesh and I discuss Hindu principles including non-violence, Muslims, Kashmir, and our feelings of God within us. We sit on the ground and meditate, talk of our personal philosophies, of sending unconditional love to people everywhere, and of sending light to other galaxies (he had never considered that). We discuss feeling the spiritual energy at holy sites, no matter what the relig-

216

ion practiced there. Here at last is my spiritual connection on this trip!!! Truly a meeting of souls. He says he felt my energy during our encounter; and, as we talk, I feel his.

The second area of the heritage sites contains Jain temples. The temples were constructed between 950 to 1050 A.D. They are of monumental size, built of white marble. The decorations are fantastic delicate carvings which show many aspects of Indian life 1000 years ago. Stone figures of apsaras (celestial maidens resembling angels) and erotic figures in all types of sexual positions and possibilities appear on every temple. What a marvelous assortment of buildings and sculpture.

The Jain priests are celibate. When alone they are always in meditation and always naked. Two robed priests outside the temple meditate in Buddha position, sitting on the platform of their temple. Their beautiful skin is rich and dark.

The most wonderful part of this day has been my SOUL CONNECTION! Just unbelievable.

Sarvesh takes me back to the hotel where I realize I forgot to eat breakfast. So I order scrambled eggs and toast for dinner.

I am up early the next day, and my laundry is dry! I have packed up and returned to the infamous Internet cafe whose owner has learned a lot in these two days. I discover there was a big earthquake in Ahmenabad, in the western province of Gujarat. Jim had sent an e-mail inquiring about the quake to Intrepid, the Australian tour company I intend to join when I get back to Delhi. As it turns out, the quake was farther west and south than Rajasthan where we intend to travel. I ride back to the hotel on the back of a tandem moped, owned by one of the cafe owners.

At the airport we must surrender all batteries in our possession for security reasons! This includes all camera batteries in the cameras or not yet removed from their cardboard containers! Another inane

217

idea. We are told we can pick them up in Delhi when we land. Naturally I forget to pick up my batteries when I arrive at 4:00 p.m.

The Hotel Regent driver is here to pick me up at the airport. I am given the same bridal suite I had before I left for the mela. I check out the window to see what progress has been made by a demolition crew which is tearing down the building next door, with the use of only sledgehammers and pick axes. I am not particularly surprised to find that only one floor level has come down. I see that the dogs are all sprawled out in the yard next door, sleeping so they can begin at nightfall to bark and fight for food in the nearby garbage piles. I will always remember the barking dogs of India.

I am exhausted but pleased to have accomplished the first part of the trip successfully. And I have found the Indian people to be friendly and helpful.

* * *

Rajasthan
Western India, Including the Holy Rat Temple

In the morning I move to the Arpit Palace Hotel where I meet the members of my Intrepid tour of Rajasthan. Our group visits the Friday Mosque, climbs the minaret, and walks through the market, including the wholesale spice area. The chilis make everyone sneeze and cough constantly, including the workers who are unloading them from trucks.

Some of us visit Indira Gandhi's house which brings India's history close. I find an Internet cafe, and decide not to join the group for dinner because I know it will end up being late. I order room service: porridge and yogurt.

The next morning we are up at 4:15 a.m. to get transport to the train station and a train to Agra. The train ride takes only about an hour, but the rickshaw trip to our hotel at the other end is interminable. Once we get our assigned rooms, we are off again in rickshaws to the Red Fort. Akbar began the construction in 1565. His grandson, Shah Jahan, finished it as a palace. After years as the ruler, he was dethroned by his son and imprisoned in an octagonal palace tower for seven years before his death. As consolation, he could look through a window far down the river and see the Taj Mahal, which he constructed as a mausoleum for his second wife. A sad story.

The next day we visit the Kealadeo Bird Sanctuary. The bus is so late leaving that we have an opportunity to observe a number of Indian people at the bus terminal. It seems that all Indian men wear a scarf around their neck or their head to keep warm. At the sanctuary we ride in rickshaws with driver-guides and see many beautiful huge winter birds. However, the water level has been dropping drastically over the past three years, so not as many migrating birds stop over here as in the past.

The people on my tour are amazing travelers. Robyn (American), my roommate, is expecting to travel at least one year. Joe and Rita (American) have already been traveling a long time as has Tom (American). Julie (American) has traveled for at least six months and more to come. Ginelle (Australian) is here with an old schoolfriend, Jackie, who traveled with her husband a great deal before he died. Nadyne (Australian) has been on the road for months. Ross (Australian) left home three years ago, saw all of Europe, worked in Scotland and London for two years to sock away money for this trip and the rest of India, southeast Asia, Nepal, and Tibet. Rachel (British) has been working in Australia and is going home after this trip. Sue (Canadian) has a year off from her teaching job, and has been traveling in Australia and now in India. Only one married couple among them. Everyone uses a backpack like me. These are "real" travelers.

We stayed last night in a small hotel near the sanctuary. There was a mosque close by where a loud continuous recording played religious music all night long. Accompanied of course by barking dogs, fighting as they rummaged for food. Terrible.

Today we are on the local bus to Jaipur. Totally crammed full; three people in a seat for two and many people standing. I am in the middle seat, and one of my seat partners keeps wiping his runny nose on his hand and rubbing his hand on the fabric back of the seat in front of him! We stop briefly in a busy market town to pick up and let off passengers. I see Ginelle and Jackie get out and head somewhere for a bathroom stop. By the time I climb over the snotty-nosed man in my row (he seems determined not to move an inch to facilitate this), the other two are out of sight. I ask a man outside and he directs me to go to a place behind some buildings in the other direction. I expect a toilet, but this is a field with high walls and no doors except for the one I just came in. Men are peeing all over, mostly against the walls. I keep indicating to the man who directed me in here that I can't find the toilet, but he keeps making signs that I should go back in the field. I believe he's saying, "Just go anywhere", with all those Indian men. I wonder if it is taboo, and if I will be apprehended. So I don't go. I finally run back to the bus which is pulling away. Members of our group are calling to the driver to stop since I hadn't returned. The driver slows slightly as I run alongside the bus and finally jump and climb up to the bus floor with great effort and no help from men near the door.

We reach Jaipur and are staying in a nice haveli. Rajput rulers and other rich men owned gorgeous houses and furnishings. When they realized they would lose them all to new rulers if they stayed, they moved out. Years later they returned when the political situation was safe and converted them to hotels (havelis). The inside walls are painted with interesting views of everyday peasant life. Really supurb. Outside at the end of the drive is a huge pile of garbage. Dogs and even a holy cow are rummaging through it.

After a trip in rickshaws into the old part of the pink city (Jaipur), filled with myriad bazaars, Ross and I decide to visit the astron-omy-astrology observatory built about 1728 by Maharaja Jai Singh, who also laid out the city. Each gigantic construction in this outdoor museum has a special purpose. There are all manner of ways to figure out the time of day, hour, solstices, and equinoxes. It is essential that each Hindu know the very hour of his birth. Very complicated. The gigantic sundial is simply incredible. The sun moves along it in incremental distances, four yards in one hour. What an interesting place.

We still have time to visit the City Palace, which is really the Ma-haraja's Palace. He and his family inhabit only one wing. This is a fabulous museum. Our guide has been guiding for twenty-five years and his English is perfect. What a tour: art gallery, arms col-lection, and clothes collection. The school of arts and crafts here is sponsored by the Maharaja. We meet the man who won the na-tional prize for art and see his paintings. He demonstrates his miniature painting techniques with a brush having only one hair. A woman sells boxes containing a tiny grain of rice on which she has written a proverb; she sold one once to President Clinton.

The next morning we take an elephant ride up to Amber Fort, a gorgeous palace in perfect condition constructed in 1592. After-wards we have lunch at a small restaurant not far away.

Suddenly I hear drums, cymbals, and horns and run outside to see a wedding procession! The groom is on a horse with a small boy rid-ing on the saddle in front of him. They are on their way to "kidnap the bride." The child has some symbolic reason for being there. All the people in the loud band are dressed in colorful Rajput costumes along with the groom. The horse has majestic trappings. Old women dance and follow along behind the band "trying to prevent the kidnapping". The rest of our group does not come outside. I never fail to take advantage of a situation, but most other people are reluctant.

After dinner our group attends a movie at the largest and most sumptuous movie theater in the country. It holds thousands of people. Tickets must be purchased in advance. Our guide says, "Viewing an Indian movie is just something one must do in India". This one is a rather stupid boy-meets-girl story. The songs and dancing are western style. Guys wear western clothes and the girls wear a new outfit every other minute that is pretty and a cross between western and Indian. The movie lasts from 9:30 pm till 1:30 am. Some of us leave after one hour -- long enough!

Back at the haveli, I am just climbing into bed when I see a rat running all around in the room. Visions of his running over my face while I am sleeping and rummaging through my food supplies prod me to take action. I get dressed (no phone in the room), walk past some other buildings to the main one with the reception desk. A man walks back with me. Of course, we can't find the rat. A large bathroom floor drain would be the perfect passageway for him to explore each room in turn -- unless someone happens to be taking a shower at that particular moment. The man says my roommate Robyn and I can move to another building with a different drain system. So he and I gather up all my things and Robyn's and carry them several buildings away to another room.

Today is Sunday and all the shops are closed, whereas in Delhi they were closed on Monday. I am at an Internet cafe and have just about finished a long letter to Jim when the electricity goes off! Guess that's common on holidays and Sundays. It usually stays off two hours. Well, there goes my letter. Seems this happens wherever I travel in the world.

Ross and I take a three-wheeled vehicle (called an auto rickshaw) to visit the "milk market". All types of trucks and vehicles arrive with large un-refrigerated milk cans. The milk might be from buffalo, cow or goat. It seems the holy cows are allowed to perform this task. People buy the milk and boil it before using it. The driver says the pasteurized milk at the store isn't good because the cream has been poured off.

In the morning, Tom, one of our group, is in an auto rickshaw ahead of us in the front seat with the driver. Tourist police stop them, pull Tom out and "pat him down". This procedure holds up our entire group waiting for him. When he finally joins us, we arrive at the train station too late to get "soft seats". Instead we settle for third class wooden seats for the six hours it will take to get to Junjunu. It is a nice opportunity to visit with the Indians in our compartment. We have an "elder" and his wife, grown daughter, her baby and three other men. Very crowded train!

We have another gorgeous haveli in Junjunu. Two jeeps drive us the next morning to the town of Mandawa which is only about 15 kilometers away, but the road is unbelievable -- bumpy, narrow, and pot-holed. The ride takes an hour. The town is tiny and very remote, full of havelis with exquisite paintings on the exterior walls. Some of the paintings are comical. We lunch in a lovely haveli followed by a tour of it's many huge sumptuous rooms and bathrooms.

We visit a school for children who supposedly come from mon-eyed business classes? There are 75 children to each teacher! The children are excited and I have a wonderful time putting my "happy face" stickers on their hands.

The next day we arrive by bus at the town of Bikaner. We have lunch on the roof of our hotel. A guided walking tour of the old city reveals beautiful havelis. No one lives in them except the caretakers, because the owners live in the big cities. A goldsmith working in his house makes very expensive jewelry. He has to sleep on his roof with his jewelry to prevent thievery. We see women who do henna designs on hands. And we are surrounded by lots of filth and animals, animals, animals everywhere and smelly trash in every gutter.

In the early evening we leave for a farm and a camel wagon ride. There is a large bonfire and gypsy dancers. Many, many children show up from the surrounding countryside and sit near where the musicians play. We sit in uncomfortable chairs and drink beer followed by a delicious buffet. More gypsy dancing follows. Each of us has to follow the movements of a dancer. It truly is gypsy music and dancing like you'd see in Spain. The music goes on and on, a fun evening.

In the morning we visit the "holy rat temple", a highlight of the trip. We are allowed to keep our socks on and wander around on the carpet of the building. Hundreds of rats are scurrying everywhere. Holes in the walls have been provided for them to run in and out. Rat devotees bring food offerings to the rats. Huge pottery saucers of milk sit all over the floor with rats drinking from them. The rats perch all around the edges of the saucers, looking like birds at a bird bath. These rats are considered to be reincarnated musicians. There is one white rat. If you can manage to see it, it is very auspicious. A young boy offers to help me see the white rat. It peers out from under a door sill and the boy makes sure I see it. I make the compulsory wish -- mine is to visit India again. I give the boy a tip.

Visiting the "Holy Rat Temple"

A wedding is occurring in another of the temples. Very interesting to watch. Priests offer us special wedding candy and one puts a tika on my forehead. The guests are very friendly.

We left Rachel (27 years old) at the hotel for the day. She has been deathly ill -- vomiting and diarrhea -- for two days. Yesterday morning before we got on the bus I gave her cimatide to stop the nausea and cipro for the diarrhea. She improved, but then refused to take any more medicine, not even rehydration salts. She hasn't eaten or drunk fluid in all this time. Big mistake!

I've been trying to figure out why I am the only person without bronchitis and cough. I took cipro for a cough before I left home. Maybe it is having residual effects?

We catch an express bus at 5 a.m. which isn't even jam-packed. It is really rolling along. At a rest stop I make a trip through the dining room of a restaurant, on through the kitchen to a back room with a hole in the ground and no door. Young men are filling basins with water at a sink. There is nothing to do but squat.

Off we go again but are almost immediately apprehended by the police! Our driver apparently forgot to drop some passengers off a few miles back in the desert. They complained to the authorities at the rest stop. Now the driver's crimes grow more serious. The policeman discovers he has no permit to transport passengers and is 18,000 rupees in arrears in his taxes. So we have to return to the village. Miraculously the next bus is here already. The first driver runs away with the keys to the bus, so it is determined that our load will squeeze onto the other bus. Brian has to smash the lock on the back of our first bus so we can get our luggage out and shove it in the new bus. Two busloads in one is not much fun. Brian and Tom sit on top of the bus; Ross is in front with the driver and locals. I have a seat with a broken back at the very rear. It smashes back against the metal box of the vehicle at the slightest bump. There are thousands of huge potholes. I believe the springs are broken; everyone and everything inside bounces up two feet and then, of course, has to come down again every time we hit a bump. We are only going about twenty to thirty miles per hour. A slow, painful trip.

Rachel hasn't been with us today. Brian arranged a taxi to take her to our next overnight stop to see a doctor.

We arrive at Jaisalmer-- a fairy-tale stone fortress on a high hill. We stay inside the walls of this tiny walled city. Our rooms actually have been dug out of the wall proper! Fabulous! The rooms are spartan but everything works! I wash out some clothes and hang them on the balcony. Ross, next door, is working on his laundry but is perplexed how to deal with a wool hand-made sweater. I tell him to just keep wearing it.

The next morning is free. Genelle and I investigate the old alleys. We go to a German bakery for lunch -- two big pastries and a banana lassi (bananas beaten with yogurt). Delightful. This is a good day to relax and regroup. Genelle, Jackie, Robyn and I take a jeep ride out into the desert about thirty-eight kilometers from our town. We want to find the houses that are painted with designs on the outside.

The first one belongs to a Hindu family. It looks to be adobe, but is actually built of cow dung. The people add a new clean floor and inside walls every few days. There are some dung shelves built into the walls on the inside. Blankets are piled in a corner. There are two rooms for ten people. A woman is spinning thread with a spinning wheel. There is a grinding stone for the wheat which is stored in huge dung containers with tight covers to keep out insects and mice. We take photos of the house inside and out and of the people who keep asking for "rupee, rupee, rupee". Once we're out of 10 rupee notes, our guide-driver produces a bag of wrapped chocolate candies for us to use instead of money.

The outside of the house is painted in geometrical shapes and even some village scenes with bright colors.

The second house is in a tiny Muslim village close by. These people are wearing darker clothes. The women are wearing shalwar kamiz, and the men wear long white shirts over their trousers. These people are not as friendly as at the Hindu house, and the designs painted on the house are nondescript. These houses are not of dung and not nearly as nice looking. There is a small oasis nearby with a few goats around it. No greenery at all.

The next morning we drive out into the desert about forty-five minutes to meet our camels and guides for our camel safari. One minute we see no one and the next minute all the handlers and camels appear seemingly "out of the sand"! All the camels are males. I have a very nice one named LaLu. I brought a thick piece of foam to sit on. It certainly helps. But I also think that single-humped camels are more comfortable than two-humped animals.

On the camel safari

We ride for about one and a half hours, stop for a rest, and then ride another one and a half hours. The guides make lunch under an acacia tree: fried hors d'oeuvres, cooked vegetables, and rice pudding.

On our way again. The afternoon sun is scorching: even with all the sunscreen I have on, I expect a bad burn. We women create make-shift veils out of our jackets.

When we arrive at the dunes, our guides set up camp: blankets laid side by side on the sand with another blanket for a cover. We play on the dunes until we are called to eat. More fried appetizers, dahl, veggies, a fried sweet. Some of the food is quite spicy, but I am finding that I can handle it. There are unusual long shadows on the dunes; it's hard to choose which ones will make the best photos.

As we sit around the campfire after dinner, the guides sing many Hindu songs. We try to contribute some songs although we don't know any special ones. It is full moon and stars are everywhere. Unbelievably beautiful! This could not be better.

Up at 7 a.m. I heard camel bells tinkling all night long. Breakfast is porridge with bananas.

The handlers saddle up the camels. I love LaLu, I ask to not have a man lead me so I can really truly ride him by myself. The safari is a brilliant success.

We go to dinner outside the walls of the city. Brian sets such a late starting time. Then it takes forever to order drinks, then the food, then to get the food. The worst is trying to get the bill and pay it. To deal with the bill usually takes one half to three quarters of an hour. And always there is one person who gets his meal when everyone else is finished. We get home about eleven. Then half the group have a room party afterward, but not in our room!

Everyone now has been sick at least once on the trip. Some are on their second ailment. I believe Nadyne has pneumonia. But Rachel is finally better.

We leave Jaisalmer by 8:30 the next morning on the best bus yet. Attractive new seat upholstery and clean windows which work. The locals get on, get off, more get on. The bus is always crowded. A woman with a small, perhaps three-year-old boy and holding a baby is standing. I offer to hold the baby. Rachel and I "ooh" and "aah" over it. Finally the baby starts to cry and I hand her back to the mother. I just can't believe that no Indian man gets up to give her his seat!

We arrive in Jodphur, where our hotel is very nice and clean. The shower floor has a lip and a shower curtain and, best of all, hot water!

In the morning we have a lovely breakfast on the veranda of a beautiful palace. Soon we leave in jeeps for Mt. Abu, a six-hour ride.

There are many, many goods carriers and no busses on this twisty road. We wonder if the lorries are delivering emergency supplies south to Ahmenabad where the earthquake occurred about two weeks ago. The last part of our drive is so curvy that Ross is violently carsick. It seems as though the drive will never end. Our driver is good, but there is the usual horn tooting, passing on curves, and driving too fast. I guess the other jeep driver is worse, so Brian makes him drive behind us.

Finally we arrive at the town of Mt. Abu, which looks rather shabby. We are here to see the most beautiful Jain temples in India. They are gorgeous, covered with white delicate marble carvings.

After seeing the temples, I take a taxi to a dirt path off the main road and climb up and up hundreds of small steps to a tiny temple honoring Devi, Shiva's wife. It is quiet and peaceful. I stand and meditate.

229

Back at the hotel, the group walks out to Sunset Point. This is a honeymooners' spot. They arrive on horseback with women sitting in front of the men; or the women sit in little carts pushed by the men. There is quite a bit of activity. We chat with one couple who was married in Ahmenabad three days after the quake with all their relatives there. So I assume there are some parts of the area that are not totally damaged. It's hard to imagine this couple, having just met each other in an arranged marriage, trying to have a nice time here on their honeymoon. The woman's hands are beautifully henna-ed; both the woman and her husband are quite proud of them.

On the way back to the hotel I stop at a little stand. I ask the man what he is making. It is a "bang lassi", a lassi with a lump of marijuana mixed in it. I try it; I have a choice of one or two lumps and settle for one. I feel nothing strange for the next two hours, and then perhaps a tiny bit as our group eats at a fabulous restaurant called Bikaner House. Jackie also partook of a bang lassi, and can't keep her wits about her!

The "Bang Lassi" stand

The next day is Valentine's Day. There are protesters demonstrating in various cites in the country against this occasion, of all things.

We have a nice drive to Udaipur on narrow, country roads. Many, many more goods carriers. One has a sign on the back, "Supplies for Gujerat" (the earthquake province).

We are staying at the Ratan Palace Hotel. I go alone to a cultural show -- dancing, musical instruments, and acrobats. A flavor of Central Asia. One man balances all sizes of pots and pans on his head, then walks bare foot across broken glass and daggers. However, walking on hot coals is prohibited tonight as a memorial to Gujerat.

The next day I visit the large Hindu temple in the town and meditate briefly. A sadhu puts a tika on my forehead. I decide to stop at the tiny "Internet cafe" next to the temple. Actually the "cafe" turns out to be a single computer in a miniscule boiling-hot cubicle with the door open to the outside. As I compose my e-mail to Jim, I am suddenly aware of something large directly ahead of me and am quite startled to see it is a cow's head, more or less lying on the computer keys. The cow has pushed in the room as far as it can. This is indeed an up-close and personal encounter with a holy cow.

In the afternoon I visit the puppet museum which is quite fascinating. The puppet show is fun. We have our farewell dinner tonight because, once we reach Delhi, some of the group will be leaving immediately.

In the morning we board the train for an overnight nineteen-hour trip to Delhi. The train is extremely crowded. Our area is a facing three-tiered set of bunks. I have mandarins, bananas and hard-boiled eggs for the trip. We play cards including "Presidents and Idiots" which Brian taught us on the camel safari. Gin rummy continues long into the night. I climb into the top bunk and eventually fall asleep. Robyn sleeps on the bunk below me. She reports in the morning that a man climbed up to her bunk and lay down cross-wise on her legs where he spent the rest of the night!

We arrive at the Arpit Hotel about 1 p.m. A shower with hot water! In the morning we have breakfast on the roof and say our good-byes.

Uzbekistan and Turkmenistan

Two Weeks After 9/11 – Should We Go?

I n the spring and summer of 2001 Marilyn (my frequent traveler partner whom I met in Mongolia in 1995) and I planned a trip to the Central Asian countries of Uzbekistan and Turkmenistan. Both countries border Afghanistan. One might think that because we had not experienced the best trip ever in Iran the year earlier that we would be happy to leave Central Asia alone. However, there was so much more to explore that we decided to put Iran behind us. We planned this trip via Internet with Salom Travel, based in the Uzbek city of Bukhara.

We were due to leave September 27 for Tashkent, the capital of Uzbekistan, for a three week trip through these two countries. Then came the tragedy of "9/11" just sixteen days prior to our departure date. Of course, everyone assumed that we would cancel. However, I called Associated Press in Moscow. A business-like reporter answered; I told him our plans. He said, "Fine, go ahead. Just don't wave the American flag"! He even gave me his cell phone number. Our decision was to do the trip. So off we went from Miami, twelve hours to Istanbul and another eight to Tashkent.

* * *

Uzbekistan

We are met in Tashkent by our first guide, Romil, who takes us to our guesthouse for a short rest and then gives us a tour of the city. Romil is full of stories of his ancestors. Listening to him is so fascinating; I vow that I will have him document part of his family tree. I include it here to show an interesting family history, dotted with many political conflicts, and destructive elements which caused his family to move here and there in Central Asia.

Here is Romil's family's story on his father's side:

My father Ismail died in 1988 at the age of 76. I knew three of his uncles. His Uncle Mirsoly was the source of most of my information. He died at 90 in 1965. For the last 40-45 years of his life, Mirsoly lived in Jambul which was part of Kazakstan. He had a business in the local bazaar, selling handicrafts and spices. He would come to Tashkent to buy goods to take back to his market stall. In the evenings when I was a boy, Mirsoly, Mirazam and Mirsultan, the three brothers, would tell tales of the ancestors who lived so long ago. And I listened very attentively.

The name of the father of my great-grandfather was Sultan-Murad bek. Bek means ruler of the city, Talas, in what is now Kyrgyzstan. Sultan-Murad was the brother of Kokand Khan Hudoyar, an important man. Sultan-Murad bek was concerned about education of the people. He constructed a big school for boys in Kokand which was destroyed in the 1930's. During the last period of his life until the Russian invasion he was the bek of Margilan. When the revolt started in 1882, he joined it, but he understood the senselessness of the resistance and abandoned the revolt. However, the leader of the revolt, Mulia Iskhak, executed Sultan-Murad with three of his sons.

234

One of his sons, (Tokhta bek) , escaped to Kashgar where he married a young Uighur girl, Ayam-bibi. They had a child, my grandfather Ibragim.

Soon the Chinese came to Kashgar. My grandfather, Tokhta bek, was executed because he didn't want to change his religion. But the main reason was his wealth and that he was part of the royal family.

His wife, Ayam-bibi, ran away with her child to the territory taken by Russians, the land of Kyrgystan near Lake Issyk-Kul. She married one of the richest men of the city, Mirazimbay. The word "Mir" at that time was added to the name of people who had some connection with the royal family. This word means Mirza - the title of a local feudal lord.

So Mirazimbay became step-father to Ibragim, gave him a good education, and married him to one of his daughters whose mother had Tajik origin. The number of wives in that time depended on the richness of the person, so Mirazimbay had seven wives. Ibragim worked in one of his private offices.

But then came the 1916 Revolution. Mirazimbay was shot, his wealth was nationalized, and his family crushed. Four years later when Lenin's decree about a new economic policy was announced, my grandfather Ibragim's family situation improved. Ibragim opened his own shop and had his own business.

It didn't continue for long. When Ibragim's son (my father Ismail) was ten years old, he witnessed a terrible scene. Drunk Kyrgyz militiamen severely beat and kicked his father. Ibragim survived and took his eldest son Mohamed away. They have never been heard of since.

Later Ibragim's wife (my grandmother) married a Tajik man and went to live in Ura-Tepa (a city in Tajikistan). She left her young son Ismail with old Ayam-bibi for upbringing. Due to Ayam-bibi's gold and silver jewelry, they didn't die of hunger. In 1928 Ayam-

235

bibi died and Ismail was left alone and began to work in a canteen as a cook's helper.

Due to Ismail's job, he did not die of starvation in spite of the great famine in the European part of the USSR during which millions of people perished. His life looked like the lives of millions of Soviet people. He was a soldier from August 1941 until September 1945. After the war he returned to Uzbekistan and met a young Tatar woman who became my mother. So now you can see my blood consists of Uzbek, Uighur, Tajik, Tatar and Russian.

* * *

Romil puts us on the plane the next morning for Khiva, in the western part of Uzbekistan. Khiva's historic heart is entirely preserved. A Soviet conservation program in the 70's and 80's converted it to an official "city museum". We meet our next guide, John, who takes us to our guesthouse which is owned and operated by an Uzbek family. An eighteen-year-old daughter caters to all our whims, trying very hard to speak English. We grow very attached to her. This is only the third time in all my travels that the thought comes over me about women always being so considerate to me no matter where in the world I happen to be.

Most everyone who had been planning trips to Central Asia have cancelled them because of the 9/11 terrorist attacks. As a result there are virtually no customers for the vendors and crafts people. While we were here in Tashkent, the huge market there was not suffering because it was a market for the city inhabitants and did not depend on tourism. But in Khiva, merchants put out their wares but there is no one to admire them. It is a very pitiful situation. How will these people get through the winter with no money coming in during the fall from their handiwork?

There is even an acrobatic act on a tight wire -- two men and a twelve year old boy-- but no one in town to pay to watch it. So we decide we should watch. It is presented in one of the large squares and is excellent.

Marilyn and I walk through the city. It reminds me of Disney World because the complete reconstruction of the city makes it appear new, clean, and beautiful. It is an excellent example of how an ancient Central Asian city really looked.

John spends two days with us showing us the city and driving to ruins of old forts and castles far north of the city. Very early the morning of the third day he drives us to the Uzbekistan - Turkmenistan border where he helps us switch between one country and the other. We simply walk across, pushing our luggage along on a conveyor belt.

* * *

Turkmenistan

On the other side of the border, Kemal, our new Turkman guide, awaits us. He proves to be one of the nicest people I have ever met. His travel company, Ayan Travel, was very cooperative with Salom Travel. Between the two of them they put together this extraordinary trip for us.

Our first stop is lunch in a guesthouse run by a Korean woman. The Russian government in the past moved large ethnic groups of people so there would never be a huge number in one place to rise up and revolt. Consequently, there are many Koreans in Uzbekistan and Turkmenistan; Korean food is available in many restaurants and markets.

After lunch we visit incredible ruins dating back to the 12th and 13th century in Konye Urgench. The Torebeg Khanym mausoleum is the family tomb of the Sufi dynasty. Torebeg Khanym was the daughter of Khan Uzbek, the leader of the Golden Horde who converted the people to Islam (and from whom the modern Uzbeks trace their origins). The mausoleum is one of Central Asia's most perfect buildings. Its geometric patterns are a giant calendar: 365 sections for the days of the year, 24 arches for hours of the day, 12 arches for the months of the year, and four big windows for weeks of the month.

The Kutlug Temir minaret across the road is all that is left of the main mosque. It is decorated with bands of brick and turquoise tiles and is 220 feet tall, the highest minaret in Central Asia. Further along we see Konye Urgench's oldest standing monument, the Il-Arslan mausoleum. Its twelve-faced conical dome is unique, and the floral terra-cotta molding on the facade is spectacular.

Kemal takes us to a holy spring. A "wishing tree" stands beside it with probably a hundred tiny fabric cradles tied on it. Women who fail to conceive place them here with wishes and prayers for a baby. A cup upon a stone in the spring allows supplicants to drink the holy water. The Goddess tradition is here and very much alive! I am truly amazed and try to figure out how what I have thought of as a Celtic tradition appears here in this place. Finally, I remember that the Celts came from Africa and took one of two paths northward. One went through Central Asia and the Middle East, ending in Austria; the other went up through France to Normandy. Some of the Celts crossed the Channel to England and their religion became the prominent one of the British Isles!

Once again I have experienced a mixture of religions in one place. Spirit worship and shamanic healing is prevalent in South East Asia, South America, Africa and other places. Even though people in these places may say they are Christians, Buddhists, Muslims, Hindus, etc., they also often reserve a place for goddess and spirit worship. The Great Goddess is not far away in these peoples' spiritual lives.

Round and Round -- Again and Again
(Thoughts about religions)

What goes around truly comes around in countries the world over. Spiritual traditions resurface in other places and other times which show us that no religion is pure, all are interconnected and come to us from a dim mysterious past.

Perhaps Tibet is a Buddhist country -- But what about the black dot patterns painted on walls by worshippers today -- a heritage from the ancient Bon religion?

The British Isles were peopled by Celts who worshipped the Great Goddess and found Her in holy springs beside which were "wishing trees" with knotted fabric strips tied prayerfully by pilgrims -- But what about the holy wells and springs and wishing trees found all over Central Asia? And what about the holy water of Lourdes? And what about the Virgin Mary? -- simply another name for the Great Goddess, shocking though it may seem!

Mongolia is a Buddhist country -- but what about the ovoos (piles of stones placed one by one by travelers as prayers for safe journeys)? A hold-over from animistic traditions.

Southeast Asia is Buddhist, but everywhere there people have a small "spirit house" on a pole where they bring offerings daily to Quan Am -- the goddess of love and fertility. The Great Goddess again!

Peru and Ecuador are said to be Christian countries -- But what about the shamans there who use spiritual powers passed down to them through past generations?

Indigenous people in Guatamala revere the corn god and elevate him to a higher level in their churches than Jesus.

Uzbekis consider themselves Muslims. But what about the tradition of the bridal couple jumping across the fire? A heritage from the ancient Zoroastrian fire worshippers.

People call themselves Muslims, Buddhists, Hindus, Christians. In reality these religions are mixed with age-old rituals from past spiritual traditions.

Perhaps if we meditate on these thoughts, we'll gradually see that people everywhere are connected in their deepest souls.

*   *   *

We reach Darvaza - but where is it?

Already I have a soft spot in my heart for Kemal for showing us this tree. Most men, I am sure, would not have considered it important.

Now we start to drive south across the Karakorum desert to the extreme southern part of the country. The road is a mass of potholes. Having been paved by the Russians at one time, it has received no attention in ten years although it is the only road south from Uzbekistan to the capital of Turkmenistan. When the Central Asian countries broke away from Russia in 1991, they found themselves in desperate economic straits. Suddenly no one was paying for education, health care, or infrastructure repair. The Middle Asian countries are crumbling in many ways.

Beside the extremely rustic road, there is nothing but sand, sand, and sand as far as the eye can see. However, many trucks and a few busses ply this 700-mile road because it is the only way from the northern border with Uzbekistan to Ashgabat in the south.

About six in the evening just before dark we have a flat tire. Tuya, our driver, has all the necessary tools and the spare tire to make the switch. However, darkness drops like a curtain. The one thing the driver does not have is a flashlight. Marilyn and I have small ones which help. The vehicle is Russian, resembling an SUV today. The driver has a difficult time with this repair. As we are stuck here at the side of the road for an hour, it is amazing to see so many vehicles on this desolate, desert road.

Finally we are under way once again. Our communication with Kemal is not a "complete" thing. We misunderstand each other many times. As far as we know and according to our map and our itinerary, the first community to the south is Darvaza. That's where we are to spend the night; it is about 300 miles from where we crossed the border. As the hours drag on, we are understandably eager to reach Darvaza. Tuya pulls up beside a lonely isolated building about eleven p.m. Kemal announces that this guest house-cum-restaurant offers a very nice meal. We are not interested because we think we will eat when we arrive in Darvaza. So we tell Kemal to keep going. The men must be rather dismayed that we turn this place down, because they know what Darvaza is really like -- and we don't! Communication doesn't seem to exist. We envision a small town where we will walk along in the morning and visit shops.

About midnight Kemal announces that we have arrived at Darvaza. But where is it? We see a lonely yurt here and there, certainly not in a neighborly group. No shops. Nothing.

So Kemal begins knocking on doors of yurts as we drive slowly along the path. No one answers his knocks, but we hear plenty of snoring at each yurt! Now the truth dawns on Marilyn and me. There is no town, no guest house. Kemal says we can drive back to the guest house we rejected about an hour ago. We are emphatic but stupid; we want to be in Darvaza! We creep along the road, Kemal knocking on doors. Finally we see a young teenage boy walking beside the road. Kemal asks him if he knows any family that might take us in. The boy says his family will. He jumps in the front seat and guides us to his family's yurt and small group of out-buildings. He calls to his parents inside. They jump up and welcome us. Immediately the family begins clearing out of their yurt.

In Central Asia, in isolated areas, people inevitably welcome strangers and share all they have. Marilyn and I notice that two of the out-buildings have separate rooms with broken windows. The family explains that they use them when distant members of the clan visit. We say we will just use one of the rooms. We certainly don't want the family to turn itself up-side-down for us at one-thirty in the morning. We choose a room and lay our sleeping bags on the linoleum floor. The host builds a fire in the stove. There is so much heat and smoke in five minutes that we ask him to put it out! The family does provide a thermos of boiling water. We pull out our emergency packets of dry oatmeal, add water, and eat our "dinner" by flashlight!

Because Kemal is our guide, it is his duty to provide some sort of breakfast for us. He requests eggs; the family has none. But a family member is happy to ride off on his horse to "some" place and come back about an hour later with eggs, which must have been very expensive, because in this environment we have seen no chickens. Kemal pays them well for their inconvenience and food.

The woman of the family takes us on a stroll up a sand dune to look around. How kind everyone is. As time goes on, we know that someone will always take us in, even though we are strange Americans.

We are unaware that the plan for the day is to leave the "road" and enter the sand track using four-wheel drive. We drive bouncing along, all the while leaving the "security" of the "road" farther and farther behind. Eventually we actually come to a cluster of buildings, a village so to speak. A village without shops, only yurts. Women and children come out to see us. They are very friendly and polite. The children lead the way to a SCHOOL of all things.

It is quite a large school with perhaps at least fifty children. The head master comes out and politely offers a tour of the classrooms. The children are all outside in the "playground". The rooms seem well enough equipped with double desks and seats and a desk for the teacher. There is even a map on the wall. After our tour we go outside to photograph the children. At this point the headmaster goes berserk; it is not permitted! He shouts to the children to head home. What can the problem be? Kemal finally discovers it. This school is so poor and the children so destitute that they do not have uniforms or shoes. Unpardonable. The headmaster is afraid that our photos might appear somewhere public, perhaps a newspaper, and the government would see that these children are not attired according to the national laws, and that he will probably lose his job and perhaps even something worse.

It certainly makes sense. It's just that we have a language problem!

Kemal tells us that the desert people have to drive out to the main road frequently to obtain potable water stored in a large tank truck which is parked out there.

We drive onward in the sand and eventually come to a larger group of dwellings, Erbent. The children from this village have to walk or get a ride to the school we have just visited.

Here the women and girls are very busy making felt. They place wet pieces of sheep's wool on a large, flat, concrete "table". They roll the wool over and over with a finished roll of felt until the pieces begin to join each other in one piece. The rolling continues on and on. Finally the piece of felt is deemed satisfactory. They then put wet salt on the fabric followed by natural colors for designs. More rolling is necessary until the product is finished. It will not be used by these people who make it. It will go by truck out to the main road and south to the capital, Ashgabat, to the huge Sunday market. This is their paying industry, along with raising sheep and goats.

Girls of desert family "felting"

The children of all ages are so happy to see us. I always carry pages of stickers with me on trips. The children are invariably excited when I put a sticker on the top of their hand.

The stickers prove an easy gift for them and are a great way to break the ice anywhere. But here we do not need to break any ice. The children want to lead us up a high sand dune where we can see the whole surrounding area. Up, up we walk with the dirty urchins in tattered clothes and no shoes. We must resemble the Pied Piper.

The children love us unconditionally and we fall in love with them. There is much photo taking and laughter and, as we descend, a song. A very warm experience.

One of the village women and her sister volunteer to make lunch for us. They busy themselves in their yurt for about half an hour and then they invite us inside. We sit on the floor beside the piece of oil cloth serving as a table cloth and enjoy soup and bread. Looking around we see a western stove with oven underneath! The stove saves squatting and cooking over a gas burner. The oven is used for storage because people in this part of the world and, indeed, in most parts of the world, have no oven and prepare their meals in a wok. Two long braided pieces of colored wool reach from the floor to the center of the ceiling to keep the "evil eye" away from the house. Also, the children all wear a talisman to deter the evil eye, be it a braided bracelet or necklace. This is common in many countries.

A produce truck is parked here in the village. The driver came from the main road and is selling tomatoes and melons out of the back of it.

On our way again, this time following the truck, we come to a huge, gaping hole in the earth which extends about 50 feet by 100 feet. Natural gas is escaping and burning. There is no way to extinguish it!

We push on to Bekuria, another small village, again without shops, made up entirely of camel breeders. Kemal knows the school headmaster and so arranges for us to stay in one of the family's yurts. He is excited to finally have a chance to drink camel milk which he dearly loves. I try it, but find it very salty and sour.

Marilyn and I sit outside the yurt writing in our journals. A number of young teenage boys fool around, but really stare at us. They start a fire and squat and hang around interminably. It begins to get dark so Marilyn and I retreat inside but soon notice that every crack in the yurt has eyes peering through. At some point we open the door and the boys immediately scramble inside and start picking through our gear. I yell at them and go over to them, threatening them if they don't get out. It is like trying to move molasses. But as I travel more, I realize that all objects in a house are common property and subject to "search" by curious children.

The woman of the family is not feeling well. She just had a baby. After a couple hours it is evident that no food will be forthcoming from that yurt. Kemal comes to apologize to us. We tell him we have more emergency food supplies, and we cook up reconstituted dry soup. Kemal and the driver also have emergency food in the car which is good in case we get lost or have car problems. So they are fine with that.

Very early in the morning the camel owners take the camels out to pasture. "What pasture?" we wonder. The camels subsist on bits of dried bushes here and there. The owners milk the females first, then separate the babies from the mothers and take them to different areas for the day because they don't want the babies to drink the mothers' milk all day long.

After breakfasting on reconstituted oatmeal, we follow the produce truck out to the main road by a different sand path. As we approach the road, a huge black cloud covers the sun, in fact almost the whole sky. A huge sand storm arrives the next moment and blows and whistles around the car. Due to lack of visibility we take refuge in a "cafe-guest house". The wind is blowing with such force that it is difficult to extricate ourselves from the vehicle. We push against the wind and eventually enter the very dismal, dark room. Kemal and Tuya order tea; we join them and relax until the storm subsides.

* * *

The Checkpoint:
"He will / He will not come!"

We head for Ashgabat once again with one hundred ninety miles to go. After a couple hours, we arrive at a check point. These are common in countries governed by dictators and supported by large militias. The soldiers check all permits and work papers, hoping they will find someone whose papers are not in order that they can punish, even put in jail. This leaves drivers cringing at the wheel, hoping they'll get through yet one more time. Sometimes the guards are willing to take bribes, but other times not.

This time is not to be an occasion for slipping through. The guard informs us that the dictator, Turkmenbashi, "Father of all Turk-men" as he has named himself, determined arbitrarily this morning that no foreigners will be allowed to enter the capital this weekend or, indeed, for the weeks following which precede Ramadan. He wants no one to enter who might disturb the peace in HIS capital. This is impossible for Kemal or Tuya to comprehend. How can this order be implemented? Our visa says we must enter the country at one point, Urgench, and leave by another point much farther to the east. So we cannot solve the problem by turning around and going back to Uzbekistan. There are also many air flights daily from other capitals to Ashgabat. We all wonder what the authorities will do when these people disembark the planes!

Kemal offers a large bribe but the head guard refuses it. Kemal and Tuya confer about what to do. At last they say they will drive into the city to the police station to inquire about what to do with us. We will remain at the check point's hut with the military police and they will come back eventually to get us.

We agree -- nothing else to do. There are two chairs in the hut. We read our Lonely Planet guidebooks to keep occupied. The guards don't know what to do with us. At one point they make a huge pot of plov (rice pilaf) on a gas burner outside on the ground. They

247

stick a big spoon in it, and, every once in a while, walk by the table and help themselves to a spoonful. They invite us to do the same. People everywhere are very hospitable and want to feed their guests. Well, we decline, bad manners probably. Then one guard cuts open a large melon, leaves a knife in it so everyone including us can help himself to a wedge at any time.

A very big problem at this time of year is that hundreds of flies alight on any food. They arrive quickly and enjoy the plov and melon! This makes the food totally unpalatable for us.

During all this period, the chief guard keeps walking by us saying, "He will NOT come!" ("He", of course, is Kemal). We answer, "He WILL come!" This banter goes on hour after hour.

Now and then we have to cross the road and descend into the ditch to go to the bathroom. It is obviously the place of choice as shown by all the bits of paper. Hundreds of busses and trucks ply the road daily; passengers continue to add to the mess. The problem is to climb down deep enough in the sparse bushes so the drivers at their wheels cannot peer down on us.

After six hours of waiting it starts to get dark. A guard turns on a generator and pulls a string to turn on the one light bulb hanging from the ceiling. Observing the "record-keeping" phenomenon is a fascinating pastime. There is no typewriter or computer, but there is a book with lined pages and carbon paper between the pages. A vehicle driver and all passengers must come inside and write their names and their identification number or passport number. I don't think anyone ever will look at these records. It is all busy work.

It is dawning on us that this might be an all-night affair and we are beginning to rue the fact that Kemal had not left our luggage and sleeping bags with us. We continue to be quite disgusted with the chief guard's comment over and over: "He will NOT come". Each time we answer: "He WILL come". At one point the guard offers to drive us to the police station in the city, saying the police will HELP us! We know better than that!

Seven hours after leaving us, Kemal and the driver return. We jump in the car and head for the city, shooting looks of triumph toward the guard. Kemal explains that we cannot enter the boundaries of the city. But they have arranged with a family outside the city to let us stay in an apartment above their own. And that's where they take us now.

The owner is a kind but very concerned man. Concern for both his family and us. The apartment is obviously ordinarily occupied. There are indoor and outdoor clothes hanging on a hook and dishes in the cupboard. Beautiful Persian rugs cover all the floors, and there are two nice sofas and a television. However the water is not turned on, nor the gas for cooking, There are a sink and bathtub, but no toilet!. Obviously people in that apartment complex share an outdoor toilet. But we have been told not to leave the apartment. Both the owner and Kemal instruct us not to open the door to anyone but the owner. Kemal says just use the tub to go to the bathroom!

The owner comes up with a huge pot of boiling water. We can make our dry soup and take a sponge bath standing in the tub. And there is television. Best of all, it works. We can now see what has been going on in the world --The US is bombing nearby Afghanistan! And there is anthrax in the mail in America! What a mess the world is in, but we are snug and "safe" on the Persian rugs in our sleeping bags in a country whose dictator decided this morning that he didn't want us in his country.

In the morning we are off to the Ashgabat Sunday market. We planned the entire itinerary around a visit to this market. Every time we made some little change with Salom Travel, we had to adjust everything so we would still be at the market on a Sunday! It is "legal" for us to go since the market is outside the boundaries of the city. Such an immense market, and an extremely colorful one!

249

Women wear flowered dresses down to just below the knee and small but brightly colored scarves. Red is the favorite color in fabrics. A huge array of handicrafts is for sale. The most colorful area of all is the extraordinary carpet market. People travel from far away to visit the market, even those desert villagers we visited. Such an exciting place!

Carpets for sale at Ashgabat Sunday Market

250

A Riot of Color -- Any Central Asian City

Mosques, madressahs, minarets, mausoleums
Stunning turquoise domes and blue tiled walls.

Women in long floral-patterned dresses
And brightly colored scarves.
Reds, blues, yellows, greens, and purples.
Crafts spread out everywhere:
Flawless soutani, embroidered purses,
Gorgeous vests, irresistible tablecloths,
Even brooms made lovingly with perfection.

Beautiful luscious tomatoes,
Delicate constructions of pumpkins and melons,
Yogurt balls, boiled yellow sugar sweets,
Complete with satiated wasps.

Pyramids of nuts -- vari-colored, every kind imaginable.
Scents of multi-hued spices swirl and beckon.
Fast food on offer wherever one turns --
Samsas, mantys, shashlik
No need to stop for lunch -- it's all here for the tasting.

Carpets, carpets on the left, on the right, behind,
In front, on the ground, hanging up.
All reds, all blues confront the eyes.

People, people bumping, jostling,
Carrying every object imaginable.
A wonderland of sounds, of bargaining, of money,
of real life.

Finally we have our fill of this amazing scene. Kemal tells us he went to the five-star hotel where we were to have stayed last night and had a long, productive discussion with the manager. Kemal gave him a huge bribe in return for our not having to list our names in the guest book. We are acceptable patrons for tonight. So off we go to the apartment where we stayed last night to gather up our sleeping bags and back packs. But first we visit a liquor shop and pick out a nice bottle of vodka for our host. When we arrive, the host, his wife, and five-year-old daughter come out to greet us. The daughter goes back inside and returns dressed in her national costume, looking like a little Turkman doll. They are pleased with the vodka, then give us embroidered purses. How generous.

A short "illegal" drive in the city to see the public gardens, the parliament house and president's office building ends at the hotel. We spend a delightful time here. Our baths last a long while, the first since Khiva. We order room service because we are "to stay under wraps".

Driving west the next morning, we turn south on a narrow road which leads up into the mountains that separate Turkmenistan from Iran. At one village square a UN truck unloads huge bags of rice. People wait to take them home on bicycles, on mules; some even carry them on their shoulder. A sight like that brings home how poor the country is.

Climbing and climbing, we stop at a cemetery where local men are buried, each grave marked by a set of bighorn sheep horns on a pole. This identifies the men as members of a certain clan and also as successful hunters.

*　*　*

We Find bin Laden - Sort Of

Finally we reach a tiny village. Well beyond the far end stands the house where we will stay tonight. The owner is here with many children and a set of grandparents. His wife went to take care of a sick friend. The man is very friendly and, for quite a while, is the only person from the family that we see. Eventually, thanks to my stickers, a couple of young children dare to come near us. Next we meet a young man about twelve years old. But it takes an hour before the teenage girls peek out at us. We say we would love to see them in their national dresses if they have them. Finally they appear complete with the usual jewelry and we duly admire them.

In this remote area, surrounded by kind people, we are not connected with the "post 9/11" concerns of our families back home (who may be worried that we are staying with Muslim families, in Muslim villages, while our country drops bombs on nearby Afghanistan).

Marilyn and I whisper to each other that the father looks like Osama bin Laden. We tell Kemal who then tells the driver. They laugh. Finally he tells the father. We say there is a huge reward for turning in the criminal. Just think how rich his family would be! He enjoys the joke. He enters the house and returns wearing his Russian army jacket. He had to fight in the Russian army as did the all other Turkmen against the Afghanis for ten long years. The jacket looks brand new. It is his souvenir of that time in his life.

We have been given the second of the two rooms comprising the house. The whole family will squeeze into the other room. We eat on the floor of our room. Kemal, Tuya, and the father sit around one piece of oil cloth; Marilyn and I another. Kemal says we are eating a famous holiday dish which is simply a mutton stew with chunks of bread broken into it. The mutton seems very rancid; perhaps it is just that the animal was very old. It takes quite a bit of willpower to swallow it.

Water here is at a premium, as it is everywhere else in desert lands. The girls have to walk downhill about an eighth of a mile to the river to carry up pitchers of water for drinking, washing one's hands and face, and also washing the clothing which is hanging on the fence.

We hate to leave the next day, but are excited when we stop at a riding stable about thirty miles outside of Ashgabat. The horses are the famous Akhal Teke breed which Turkmen claim is the oldest in the world, older than the Arabians. These horses even appeared in Egypt at a very early date. On cuneiform texts found in Assyria, Herodotus tells of ten sacred horses in Xerxes' army. Images of the horse have been found dated to 2000 B.C.

What magnificent horses they are. Very tall and slender, bred to not need much food or water as they cross the desert for days with their riders. At night their owners give them a small quantity of barley; the next day they run for hours and hours again.

Kemal and driver with our host in his Russian military jacket

Alexander the Great, Cyrus, Darius the Great, Ghinghiz Khan were all known to have used the "godly, heavenly horses" in their military campaigns.

The owner of the stable expects us to ride without a guide. But we say we need one and it is a good decision. The landscape is all dry brown hills with trails in every direction. Alexander the Great was said to have used these trails! It seems as though it would be rather easy to get lost.

The horses are very sensitive, they are even able to respond to mental suggestions of humans; their intelligence is far greater than any other breed. I speak to my horse in a low voice. His ears turn half way around to hear me better. He seems so interested in what I am saying. If I barely touch his ribs with my boot, he starts to trot. He is truly magnificent, the most marvelous horse I have ever ridden.

We return to the forbidden hotel for another wonderful bath and room service dinner. From here the next day we travel east, visiting the site of Anau, one of Turkmenistan's vanished cities, but inhabited from Neolithic times. The mosque was once a marvel, but was demolished by the earthquake of 1948 as was the entire city.
We come at last to Merv, one of Central Asia's greatest cities on the Silk Road. It was once known as "Queen of the World". There are few monuments left standing, but, like other Turkman ancient cities, most is left to the imagination.

Riding the Akhal Teke horse

Kemal knows a wealth of legends. He tells us that the top of the high crenelated wall, all that is left of the castle, is where ten maidens jumped to their death rather than be captured by a marauding king. These stories make every monument come to life for us.

One day we ask Kemal and Tuya if they are Shiite or Sunni Muslims. The two of them confer and arrive at the conclusion that they are just Muslims! They have never heard of any other kind. Whenever we pass a mosque, Kemal wipes his cheeks downward to his chin with both hands and ends with a posture of praying hands. But both men say they rarely visit a mosque nor do they pray daily. Of course, this is the result of seventy-five years of Russian domination when religion was officially abolished.

The next day we drive north to the border of Uzbekistan, and by evening cross over and meet our new guide, Erkin. In effect, we are in the middle of making a large circle from Tashkent. We trav-

256

eled to the western part of Uzbekistan, south through Turkmenistan and now will cover the middle of Uzbekistan before arriving once again in Tashkent.

*　　*　　*

Uzbekistan Again And Dinara

Bukhara, the location of Erkin's company, Salom Travel, is an incredible ancient city on the Silk Road. It, too, is feeling the lack of tourists.

One crisp morning as we walk through the city, the golden leaves are falling. I always think of Chekhov's stories as happening in fall and winter. I am struck by this similarity and blurt out, "This is a Chekhov kind of day!"

Erkin answers, "It is. But more than Chekhov, my favorite author is Aitmatov." I have heard of Aitmotov and even read one of his books, "The Day Lasts More than A Hundred Years", one of the best books I have ever read. Erkin proceedes to tell me about this marvelous Kyrgyz author who is considered the greatest modern author of Central Asia. He walked the line between Communism and something more akin to democracy between the 1950's and 1980's. He was a Communist party member, but somehow escaped any censure during this period of his writing.

Erkin tells me other books to read by Aitmatov such as "The Place of the Skull" and "The White Steamship". What a marvelous time we have discussing literature.

The most memorable event of the entire day occurs while I am walking along with Dinara behind Erkin and Marilyn. Dinara is learning to be a guide. To begin the conversation she says, "I imagine you have met many wonderful people on your trip and been in-

257

vited to their homes."

I say, "No, no one has invited us."

Dinara answers, "Well I am inviting you to my family's house for dinner on Sunday!" Needless to say, Marilyn and I are thrilled.

Bukhara was a key city on the Silk Road. It is a fascinating place which we visit one entire day in detail. It is full of madressahs, mosques, minarets, and several covered markets. We climb the 141 foot high Kalan minaret. The Ark was the royal palace and fortress. The main square in front of it, the Registran, is where executions took place.

The next day we drive south to visit a World Wildlife Fund reserve for wild Persian gazelle, wild Asian ass and Przhevalsky's horse (the most ancient wild breed in the world). A devoted woman has been caring for them alone for twenty-seven years!

Sunday arrives and in the afternoon we walk to Dinara's house. It is lovely, with some fine antique furniture. We meet her mother, father and teenage brother. Nellie, the mother, and Dinara spent all day Saturday and early Sunday preparing the meal.

They serve us plov, which is rice pilaf, carrot salad, chick pea salad, cabbage salad and raisin wine that Nellie made. The father brings out a bottle of vodka between the main meal and dessert. We have several toasts. Then comes a fantastic white cake. All in all, the meal couldn't have been more delicious. How fortunate we are to have met such a nice family. It is the sort of experience that is impossible to have if one is traveling with a group or even more than two people, and is the reason Marilyn and I travel as a pair.

We are very sorry to leave Dinara and her family, but we must drive to Samarkand the next day. On the way we visit Nurata Fort, where Alexander the Great stayed while he was preparing to sack

Samarkand. At the fort are two holy wells which are thought to bring good health. The best part of the day is stopping at a little known site containing hundreds and hundreds of petroglyphs. Even Erkin had never heard of it. But I had seen it in Lonely Planet and knew I had to visit it. It is wonderfully interesting to climb up and down a high shale hill, spotting more and more glyphs.

Sunday dinner with Dinara's family

Samarkand is really the jewel of the Silk Road. The Registran buildings and courtyard remains are complete and breathtaking. The gorgeous buildings with all the ornamentation preserved are unbelievable. There is a street of tombs called Shahi-Zinda, which contains the grave of a cousin of Muhammad. The Guri Amir Mausoleum holds the tombs of Timur, two sons and two grandsons, including Ulughbek. Timur (Tamerlane) claimed kinship with Chinghiz Khan. When the Mongol empire fell apart in Central Asia, Timur, following in Chinghiz' footsteps, razed the same glorious buildings and cities a second time, killing hundreds of people. But his grandson, Ulughbek, was a different kind of horse. He

259

was intensely involved with mathematics, science and astronomy. He built a large observatory in Samarkand and another in Rajasthan, India, both of which lured scientists from all over Asia.

Before we leave this area of Uzbekistan, we drive south to Shakhrisabz, Timur's hometown. The architectural remains are numerous, including the burial complex of Timur's forbears.

Erkin tells us a legend about Timur and his wife. Timur went out on one of his long rampages. His wife decided to have a mosque built in his honor while he was gone. She hired a builder and told him he must work quickly and have the building ready when Timur returned. The builder worked for several months, but the wife could see little progress. She was agitated and told the builder that he must increase the speed of his work. He told her that he could work faster if she would let him give her a tiny kiss on her cheek. She said she could not do that. This continued for some time, but finally the wife said he could give her a tiny peck on the cheek. Once the favor was granted, the builder worked at a great rate and the building was ready and waiting for Timur upon his return. His wife proudly showed him the mosque, but Timur noticed a red blotch on her cheek and realized she had been untrue to him. He had her carried to the top of the building and thrown down to her death!

We return to Tashkent by car and even take a small detour into Kazakhstan where there is a wine and spirits shopping area on a sandy place beside the main road. I buy a bottle of vodka for Jim named The White Swan.

This has been an epic trip during which we learned so much basic information about the history and present-day situation in Central Asia. It will require a second trip to Kyrgystan and Tajikistan, the mountainous countries, to round out our impressions. One memory, though, that will always stay with us, the kindness shown to us by so many people, even though our country is at war with the country next door.

260

Kyrgystan and Tajikstan

Kyrgystan and Tajikistan are mountainous countries in Central Asia which should be visited in summer. So in the summer of 2002 I was flying to Istanbul and then Almaty, Kazakstan, to meet a woman I had never set eyes on in a hotel room at 5 a.m. Her name was Shiriin Baraksai. She had answered an ad I placed in the British travel magazine, Wanderlust. Actually I had just about given up on anyone's answering the ad six weeks earlier. But then her e-mail arrived. She was twenty-eight; I requested a woman forty or somewhat older. She certainly had not traveled much; I was hoping that someone with travel expertise would answer. She had enough money to only visit Kyrgystan. We decided to go for it and made our plans.

I worked out the itinerary on the internet with a tour company in Bishkek, Kyrgystan called Top Asia. They did a great job putting together a variety of adventures.

* * *

Kyrgystan

Shiriin's trip from England through Frankfort to Almaty is much shorter than mine. She arrives at 2:30 a.m. I travel Denver to Newark, Newark through Istanbul to Almaty arriving 4:30 a.m. Our guide Alex and driver Sasha meet us both at the airport and take us one by one to the hotel two hours apart during the night. When I arrive in the hotel room, Shiriin is asleep in her bed. So I don't really meet her until late morning when we finally wake up.

I am my usual exhausted self after such a journey. I also am dehydrated; I didn't drink enough water on the flight. Alex meets us after a late breakfast and we do a quick sightseeing tour of the city. Our first stop is an antique musical instrument museum during which I FAINT! Alex and Shiriin are, of course, very concerned. I tell them I will be fine, I am just dehydrated. But what a beginning!

We finish the tour, have an early dinner, and are in bed by 9:00 p.m.

Early the next morning we are on our way (Alex our guide, Sasha our driver, and Shiriin and I), driving east along a plain just north of the mountains that divide Kazakhstan from Kyrgystan. We head south over a pass into Kyrgystan and soon have a flat tire. Because Sasha had a flat on their way from Bishkek to Almaty, it is now imperative that someone be found who can patch the two tires. We stop for lunch in a tiny market town and enjoy the sight of a live goat in the open trunk of an old sedan. It was purchased at the market and is on its way to its new home!

Sasha finds a man who can patch tires. It looks as though we are doing fine now. We reach the border where Sasha and the border guard have quite an argument over where Sasha temporarily parks the car. To punish Sasha, the officials say we won't be able to pass through until they finish counting the money in the till at the end of the day. That exercise takes one and one half hours!

Finally we proceed to a large tented tourist camp. Kyrgyz people come here primarily for trekking. There are a large dining hall and bathroom buildings plus about fifty permanent tents. Our tent has a five by three foot area covered with straw just inside the tent for our backpacks. The rest of the tent has space only for two sleeping bags.

The following day we hike along a brook and find many, many wild flowers, some of which I am familiar with and others that are completely new to me. We meet some men camping in a tent and harvesting mushrooms. They are Kyrgyz and wearing typical white pointed felt hats.

Not all the people in the country are Kyrgyz. Alex and Sasha are of Russian descent. Russians were moved to this country many years before by the Russian government. Because they were better educated, they received the better jobs. This creates a two-tiered population in the country. The Kyrgyz are the shepherds and farmers.

On the way back to camp, we stop to visit a family. There are two children, three grown sisters, and a grandmother about ninety years old. The family men are with the sheep up in the mountains. The women invite us in. One of them has very tiny twin baby girls! We have fun holding them and taking pictures of the group. The women wear colorful calf-length dresses typical of the entire Central Asian region. They offer us homemade yogurt with blueberries on it, newly-baked bread just out of the outdoor oven, and newly-churned butter. Such hospitality! All we have are stickers for the children's hands but the children are delighted. Soon children arrive from other houses all wanting their stickers.

In the morning we take a sightseeing flight in a small plane (parked at the camp) to view the very high Tien Shan Mountains which separate China and Kyrgystan. We land at a base camp area to watch various climbing parties as they start out on their treks. The highest peak in Kyrgystan, Pik Pobedy, at 22,300, is visible. On the way back to camp, our plane ferries hitchhikers from remote spots to others in the valley below.

The following morning we drive south to a very remote area. Sasha is adept at repeatedly crossing the rushing river in his Toyota Land Rover, driving nonchalantly through the three to four-foot deep water. We briefly visit with a nomad family and their cute little girl and stop frequently for photos on the way to the top of the mountain pass. At one point Sasha decides he must get out to reconnoiter the best place to cross the river. Two horsemen appear wearing dells such as those worn by Mongolian horsemen and typical Kyrgyz white felt hats. Sasha hands each a cigarette and each rider removes a cigarette perched behind his ear to reciprocate the gift. They smoke while showing Sasha the best place and angle to cross. So off we go once again, into the deep rushing water, dodging some rocks and smashing into submerged ones repeatedly. To me it seems highly doubtful that we will be successful. But eventually, fifty feet later, we pull out onto the far bank, dripping but undaunted.

After less than a quarter mile I see we must recross. A few men on the other side wave and point out where we must "land" and this time, unaided, Sasha negotiates the rocks. Now we drive uphill over grass-covered banks following a cow path, pulling up over the top of the pass onto a flat area dotted profusely with blooming edelweiss. It starts to rain; the car careens wildly in slippery mud as we advance to the other side of the pass where we look down into a seemingly untouched valley. A river runs down this side of the mountain and ends up following the bottom of the valley. It is a breathlessly beautiful sight.

Kyrghiz horsemen advising us where to cross the river

As we head down this south side of the pass, rain starts to pour down heavily. Sasha slowly works his way down a long series of switchbacks through the treacherous mud. The "road" becomes more and more slippery. Finally we are down to a dirt road following along the river to the west. Sasha has a topographical map which indicates the site of a cave apparently large enough to have a printed name on the map. It will be on the steep uphill side from the river. We all strain to see through the streaming water on the side windows. Suddenly far up a hillside, we see a "hole" in the mountain. Sasha stays with the car while Alex, Shiriin, and I investigate the cave on the wet, steep, slippery hill. It proves to be simply a large open chamber, so we are soon ready to start down.

*   *   *

Shiriin Loses Her Passport and Visa

I developed a case of the "runs" back in Almaty, but am more or less over it. Now it overtakes Shiriin. She suggests that Alex and I work our way down the slick grass to the car and she will follow us momentarily. Once she arrives we continue on the extremely slippery, dangerous track, arriving at last at our camping area. We put up our tents in the pouring rain. It is then that Shiriin realizes that she is missing her wallet and her passport with her Kyrgyz visa! I am shocked because I always have my money and documents in my money belt around my waist. I ask her incredulously if she has a money belt. She says, "Yes, but this was going to be such an isolated area that I figured I wouldn't have to worry about their being stolen, so I just put them in my pants pocket."

To compound the issue, we are crossing and therefore camping on land that belongs to a military reservation! Our papers may likely be checked tonight or certainly tomorrow morning before we can proceed.

Alex decides he will prepare our evening meal while Sasha, Shiriin and I drive (or slide) back to the cave area. We carry flash lights because night is almost upon us. We each climb slightly different routes in the rain up to the cave since it is impossible to know just where Shiriin had stopped on the way down. She does find her yellow wallet but not her passport which is a dark blood-red color, very hard to see in the deep grass and in the dusk. We have to give up. We slip and slide back to camp in our car, eat our freezing cold pasta and fall asleep immediately. It is after midnight.

266

Alex is preparing breakfast in the morning when two soldiers arrive. They demand to see our documents and are not pleased to see Shiriin is missing her passport and visa. Alex tries to bribe them with money and a good breakfast but to no avail. They eat the breakfast but then tell us we cannot cross the narrow bit of military land and go though the gate to pick up the road on the other side. They do take "baksheesh" for agreeing not to tell authorities that the passport was lost on this south side of the pass!

Had we been able to continue on the military property it would have taken us probably an hour from here to Karakol, our next destination. But we turn around and retrace our steps, not only to the tourist camp of two nights ago but further back where a road turns west and leads us another way to Karasol, taking at least five hours.

Retracing does allow us to make another climb to the cave and provides opportunities to stop at places that were photo-op spots yesterday where the passport might have slipped out of Shiriin's pocket.

The river on the north side of the pass is very high today, really raging down through the valley. It is almost three feet deep and sixty yards wide. Sasha's expertise is repeatedly tested as we cross and recross the torrent. I am used to this experience now and simply hold my breath a mere instant at the moment of greatest doubt each time.

A tea stop at our old camp relieves the tedium a bit. Then we are on our way once more. Finally we reach a better dirt road which eventually turns west onto a paved road. It is pouring rain and early night descends. Now it is time for car troubles again. One bolt of four had fallen out of a part from the bottom of the car. Sasha does not have an extra bolt. We must wait for a car to come along going back in the direction of the camp. While we are waiting, two men stop. All have to share cigarettes with each other according to protocol.

An hour later a car heading in the correct direction stops and Alex rides with the driver back to the camp. Apparently somewhere at the camp there is a cache of nuts and bolts. Alex finds what we need and waits for a car coming back in our direction. Sasha fixes the problem with the new bolt. We are on our way again, finally arriving at our destination, Karakol, after midnight.

We stay at an interesting "bed and breakfast" run by a Russian woman. Our room has two twin beds pushed together and a giant flouncy bedspread over the top. The curtains are frilled and flounced also. Such a nice place. Better even than this is the presence of a bathtub downstairs in the only bathroom in the house. A fine place to wash out our muddy, rain-soaked clothes in the morning. There is a clothes line in the yard and it has stopped raining! I surmise that Shiriin's clothes have more appeal than mine when she discovers several pieces missing from the line the next day!

The police department is our first stop. This takes at least a couple hours. Top Asia's director in Bishkek says we can continue the itinerary until we get closer to Bishkek where Shiriin will have to take a bus to the city and spend at least a couple days working on paper work.

We drive about the town admiring the old Russian Christian churches and their unique architecture with many carved wooden decorations and white paint. We visit a museum and memorial to the noted explorer who originally discovered the ancient breed of small horses which were named in his honor--Przhevalsky!

The next day we drive up into the mountains to a building that serves as a hostel for trekkers and campers. On the way up the car radiator runs out of water! But Sasha and Alex have small containers that they use to carry water cupful by cupful from the nearby river. One more little problem solved!

We spend three days here trekking and riding horses, a delightful experience.

Profuse mountain wild flowers of various hues bloom everywhere. We hike for several hours. Then we take horses and ride up into the hills. Such responsive horses. They love to canter. We cross wide deep streams. Rain starts falling but we are prepared with our rain-suits, and the horses don't mind a bit. These horses are normal size, not small like Mongolian ponies.

Our mattresses are on the second floor of the lodge. Other groups are in larger rooms and guides in yet another.

There are hot springs in the area. About a quarter mile away the locals have "captured" a hot spring in a large concrete building with a pool on each side, one for men and one for women. However, because the rooms have no windows, it is like soaking in a prison cell with water.

As I am walking to the springs a man is in the process of slaughtering a goat. I have seen this done often enough that it no longer upsets me which indicates that I am now at home in cultures where raising and slaughtering sheep and goats are vital parts of life.

On the way back down to Karakol, more car troubles await us. As we drive along the edge of a grassy trail the car stops. Sasha finds long grass caught in the entrance to the fuel pump. He pulls it out and sticks a screwdriver in the hole to stop it up!

Back once more at the guest house in Karakol, we find that the owner has arranged a performance of "Manas" for that evening. Manas is a legendary super hero. His deeds are recited from memory by itinerant minstrels (called manaschi) dressed in the costume of Manas as he would have appeared in ancient times. The minstrels use exaggerated hand, face, and body movements to get the story across to the listeners. A very few performers have memorized the entire cycle of oral legends which is twenty times longer than the Odyssey! I feel so very fortunate to witness a short performance of this art.

The next day we drive west toward Bishkek along Lake Issyk-Kul, the largest lake in the country. At one point Sasha pulls a bit off the road and tell us we can take a swim in the lake! We change to our swim suits between two car doors. The "dip" is memorable only because it "is the thing to do". One must swim in this lake for good luck! But the bottom is rocky with slippery seaweed and the water very cold.

A few hours later we drop Shiriin off at a bus terminal so she can continue to Bishkek to work on getting a new passport. She has been a great travel mate and I hate for us to part. I offer her money for her journey, but she has a few travelers' checks and is sure she will have enough. It turns out she is right, but an experienced traveler would probably not have turned down the offer.

Our crew: Sasha (driver), myself, Alex (guide), and Shiriin

As Shiriin boards the small bus, a French girl, Elsa, whom we met at the hostel, appears out of the crowd and calls to me. She has been hitching west and hopes that we will take her to our next destination, Song-Kol lake. We invite her to come with us and drive for a couple hours up switchback after switchback to the high mountain lake where we stop at a site with two gers (round tents), a cooking tent, and an outhouse.

This is the home of a lovely nomad family who lives high in the mountains during the summer and retreats to a town in the lowlands for the winter. The father works in Bishkek while the mother manages the "summer home". There are four boys in the family; they help with all the chores such as sheep herding and milking the cow. I have fun playing jump rope with the younger ones.Elsa and I sleep in one ger, while Alex and Sasha set up a tent for themselves.

In the morning Alex and I hike several miles along the dirt road and through marshes. He explains the social structure of this country which was Russian but now is an autonomous nation. The indigenous Kyrgyz are second-class citizens while those Russians who stayed when the USSR collapsed have the good paying jobs, and as such, feel superior to the true Kyrgyz. To me it seems a sad situation. Alex grew up in the affluent Russian society in the country. He admits there are various inequalities but he is content with his status. He has a girlfriend in Bishkek. His brother in Moscow has offered to have Alex come and live with him and will pay for his college education. Lucky boy! We also discuss Putin and Bush. He believes that Putin's ideas are superior, including how Putin treats the Chechens. I disagree so we have some good-natured arguments.

Next morning I tell Alex I want to ride horses. However, the family only has one horse. But the oldest boy, sixteen years old, says he can borrow another horse from a neighbor. Alex says it won't work for the boy and I to go alone because we won't be able to communicate. I tell him I can communicate with anyone using sign language. He says, "it's not possible". I tell him the boy and I can handle it, so finally Alex gives in. I mount the family's horse and ride him around a bit. The boy rides to a neighboring camp and returns with a second horse. Off we go, even cantering a bit.

The boy understands about ten simple English words. Yet we are able to communicate extremely well with just hand signs. I point at beautiful profuse wild flowers just to show my delight. But each time I do, he dismounts and picks the flower and sweetly hands it to me. We ride through lush meadows, along the river, and past interesting rock formations for about two hours and really have a nice time together. It is the one-on-one relationship that I value so much in my travels.

We start for Bishkek the next day leaving Elsa behind, and, true to form, we have yet another car problem! The car stops because we are suddenly, mysteriously, out of gas. The fuel pump tube is broken. But Sasha, the ingenious soul that he is, splices the tube together. We hobble off to a gas station not far away (because we are entering a more populated area as we draw nearer to Bishkek). Sasha's optimistic outlook assures us that we can safely leave the main road and drive a few miles on a dirt path to ruins of an ancient fortress. This was once a walled city, but nothing is left except a bit of the fort. A small museum displays ancient pieces of pottery, horse tack and old coins, all found at the site.

The car quits two more times after we leave the museum, but Sasha figures out new clever repairs each time.

Finally we reach Bishkek. My friends deliver me to an air-conditioned hotel (except the aircon doesn't work). It's nice to have my first shower since Karakol.

Alex and Sasha will pick me up in the morning to take me to the airport.

*　*　*

272

Tajikistan
Our guide, Michael, has no guiding
or cooking experience

I fly in a prop plane the next morning over high mountains south to the capital of Tajikistan, Dushanbe. An Englishman named Michael meets me. He represents one part of a two-man team running a brand new British company called Great Game Travel. His partner, John, lives in England and handles the paperwork.

Michael drives me to an area far from the center of town. He assures me I can use a bus to get back downtown where I will be able to find food to prepare at the apartment where I am to stay! Once at the apartment building, we climb up two long flights of steps in a dark stairwell and arrive at an apartment door he opens with two keys. The apartment is obviously inhabited, though not at this particular moment. In each of the two bedrooms all clothes and bedclothes have been shoved into large plastic bags. The beds have been remade with clean linen.

About thirty one-liter soft drink bottles sit on the counter filled with tap water. I inquire about them and Michael says they are there in case there is no tap water from time to time. It never runs the whole time I stay here! The rusty toilet has no water nor can it flush. The bathtub is also rusty with no water in the tap.

This is not exactly the kind of accommodation I expected when I arrived in the city. I don't dare use the water in the bottles to drink or wash because I have no idea how old it is. Microbes may have grown in them which could possibly give me a rash or worse. It is so hot that I do use a tiny bit of water from my own water bottle to wipe off my face. And I add some purification tablets to one soft drink bottle so I can use it to wash out a shirt. It certainly seems to me that the owner of a tour company would feel obligated to put a client in a better place than this!

I am learning that this isn't an ordinary tour company. When I had difficulty finding a tour group in Tajikistan on the web, I wrote to Salom Travel (Uzbekistan) and Top Asia (Kyrgystan). They knew of no one operating a tour company in Tajikistan. But one of them had heard of a British group possibly starting up operations. That is when I wrote to Great Game Travel. Their description of the one trip they were offering was a road trip on the Pamir Mountain Highway. They described how the area was extremely isolated and not set up for tourist travel. The one dirt road ran along beneath the stunning Pamir Mountain range, the one I had failed to see because of fog when I had been on the Silk Road trip. We would be camping and cooking our own meals. Much of the time we would be at 12,000 feet!

Well, it sounded like quite a challenge, probably a "bare-bones" operation, possibly because the company was new and had no cash. But it would afford me the opportunity to see the Tajik people in the remote area of the country. So I signed up. A few weeks before I left home I received an e-mail from Michael telling me that only one other person would be going on the trip; his name was Karim Jivraj.

I was amazed; I felt sure it was the same person I had met on the Silk Road trip several years before. And indeed it was. I was happy to know I would be traveling with Karim, one of my favorite people. However, I had a sneaking suspicion that we would be on the "maiden" Pamir Highway trip. I had to bring my own sleeping bag and wasn't at all sure that I would be warm enough at that altitude. But I insisted I would not bring a tent; Michael would have to provide one!

Returning now to my first night in Dushanbe, suffice it to say that I won't attempt to cook in that apartment. I take the bus to the city center, find a restaurant, eat a pizza and return by bus to the apartment building. At least I think I have! I wander all over a quarter of a square mile for an hour looking for the building and finally enlist the help of a teenage boy who speaks a little English. We finally find the building. He accompanies me up the stairs in the dark and successfully uses the strange keys to open the door.

I am more than a little nervous. I don't dare keep the windows open as hot as it is because the room is only one floor up from the ground. I just lie naked on the sheet and finally fall asleep.

In the morning Michael arranges for a driver to show me the sights in the city. Karim arrives but won't be able to get his permit to travel on the Pamir Highway until Monday. So on Saturday, Karim remains with his host while I embark on a two-day trip to the northwest to see an ancient city, Penjikent, founded in the fifth century by a group called the Sogdians. For a long time I have wanted to see this ancient archeological site. It is located in the extreme northwest of the country. There are three of us; my driver Yunice, a second man (Escondar) who works for Michael, and myself.

Tajikistan is divided into small areas separated by mountains. So, although there are road passes from one district to another in the summer, in winter the areas are totally isolated. This doesn't make for a very united country and, indeed, it isn't.

We have to drive over a very high pass on a very rocky dirt road. Michael had said the entire trip would take seven hours. We reach about a third of the way to the top when my driver explains with hand signals and a few words of English that we have a car problem. He has struck a rock and severely bent an axle. The men try hard to hammer it straight with a rock, but it is impossible to do this while the axle is fastened to the car.

Somehow I now understand that we must return down the pass to find someone to fix the car. At the bottom, on the road back to Dushanbe, they leave me at a rock-crushing operation indicating that they will return to get me once the axle is fixed! The head man at the operation invites me to sit down at a table under a piece of cloth with holes that serves as an awning. He pours tea into a cracked and dirty cup, offers bread covered with flies, and melon which he cuts with a filthy knife. He is being the good host and I feel compelled to drink the tea. However, I don't eat any of the melon which is also covered with flies.

The men return within the hour and we start back up the mountain road. Vehicles race up and down the bumpy, rocky road. The drivers are accustomed to it because it is their only way to the next valley. But there are also cars strewn all over the road that seemed to have balked at the challenge of going uphill. A few feet from the top our car ceases to respond to Yunice's efforts. Both men leap out and literally push the car the last few feet to the top! They immediately have the tire and wheel off and are examining the brakes. They say something to me about "torsion" which perhaps is linked to the fact that they can push the car easily from side to side (not a good sign, I take it). They put the wheel back on, Escondar pushes, and off we go down the other side of the pass in low gear. More abandoned cars lie strewn everywhere in the road. It seems to take forever to come down in low gear but there is no alternative because the brakes don't work! Eunice tells me in very broken English that he has had this Lada for twenty-nine years. He says he drives it every day and has never had a day like this one!

About an hour later we stop at a restaurant, of all things, in this isolated area. It is a round building extending out over the river and rotating while we sit on the floor eating at a low table. It is a bit like an amusement park ride.

On we go. At one point I lean over the front seat to show Yunice that my mineral water bottle is empty. Escondar jumps out and, in a second, produces a full bottle. When I take a sip, however, it tastes very strange which I tell Yunice with sign language. He indicates that Escondar filled the bottle with river water! But now he produces a new sealed one!

After another hour we are stopped by soldiers at a checkpoint. They don't like the photocopy of my passport. Michael had retained the official one to get my permit for the Pamir Highway. The guards decide they will not accept baksheesh, and will have to go inside their building to check their computer. Yunice says the men have no computer and are probably playing cards. We sit in the car in the broiling sun for two hours. While we are sitting here, a British woman and her two young children come walking along the road. They are "Born Again Christians" and want desperately to visit the "wonderful church organization in Colorado Springs, Colorado"! Is this amazing, or what! The woman and her husband have lived in this hamlet for eight years trying to develop a dried apricot that will be juicy. They have finally succeeded and now will move to some place in Russia where they can cheaply package their product!

The soldiers finally return and give me my passport. But now they decide that Yunice's papers have some discrepancy; the way he signed his name doesn't match the printed name on his passport. Back inside they go for another half hour, when at last we are dismissed! Such a lot of nonsense!

We've lost a great deal of time with all our problems. Night arrives and now the dark road is cluttered with loose animals, people on donkeys or just walking along the road. By the time we finally reach Penjikent, it has long been dark. I am to have a home stay with a woman and her little girl. Of course no one explained this in the morning. My hostess is very nice. She has a maid fix us some plov. I lie down to sleep on the carpets on the floor of the living room while my "helpers" sleep on a rope bed in the courtyard. The toilet is next to their bed; when I feel the need, it seems as though I am practically jumping in bed with them.

After a difficult night trying to fend off flies, I am glad to see morning come. We have tea and bread, then drive to the excavation site. A person who speaks some English takes charge of me, leading me through the area and explaining it. Russian archeologists from the Hermitage Museum in St. Petersburg are busy digging, chipping, and brushing hour after hour in the broiling sun. I can see the excavated ruins of some two-story houses probably owned by wealthy people long ago. A large ancient temple in excellent condition stands uncovered. I've always wanted to be an archeologist and now "pretend" to be part of the crew.

After a walk through the market and lunch at my hostess's house we start back over the pass. Three hours later, we turn off on a side road. Again I am completely in the dark as to what is happening. We arrive at a tourist camp with stone bungalows beside a mountain lake where we unload the car at a two-room cabin.

As Yunice and I walk along the lakeshore, Escondar begins to cook our meal in a kitchen building! Finally I understand. This is HIS designated job and is the reason he is along on this trip!

Yunice somehow conveys to me that a yeti (abominable snowman) lives up in the mountains and that there is a mountain hiking route from here to Dushanbe. If I care to hike the distance (probably about sixty miles), I probably will encounter him!

We sleep tonight in the cabin. For water we use an outdoor hose. The men suggest a sauna for me. They build a fire, heat rocks, and cover the floor of the sauna building with firey hot rocks. They keep pouring water on the rocks, creating steam. What an event this is all turning out to be!

We arrive in Dushanbe the next afternoon and go to Michael's house. I inform him that I want to take a shower in his house since I have not had one since Bishkek and that also I refuse to be quartered in that same apartment as when I arrived in the city the first time. Michael isn't too pleased; but it helps when Escondar says I can stay with his family!

I spend a delightful evening with the family. Four teenaged girls wait on me hand and foot. I stand in the bathtub with a board across it and a bucket of hot water on it. My "bath" is heavenly. The girls fix me fried eggs, chips and sausage which I eat on the oriental-carpeted floor of the living room with a piece of oil cloth for a table cloth. One of the girls offers to wash out my dirty clothes. Another tries very hard to speak English with me. There is a sweet four-year-old boy playing with a toy car. The parents are utterly gracious.

I think the trip to Penjikent was a crazy adventure. Little do I know how much crazier this trip will get!

* * *

The Pamir Highway
The adventure gets a lot worse

In the morning I fly in a tiny prop plane to the village of Khorog in the very southeastern most part of the country. It is an incredibly beautiful forty-five minute flight. We actually fly between peaks and low along river valleys with no indication of habitation or roads. It is clear that there are not many hamlets anywhere in the Pamir Mountain area.

A young Tajik man named Ruslan who speaks fairly good English meets my plane. He is an assistant to Michael. In fact, the reason he is here is because he must find a place for Karim, Michael, me and himself to stay while we are in the town. But just as important a mission is that he must find and bargain for a vehicle we will use to drive the Highway! It is now painfully obvious that this "tour company" has no vehicle to use for the trip!

He bargained with two women living in an apartment to move out for a few days. So the first part of his responsibility has been carried out. After I take "ownership" of the place by putting my backpack in one of the bedrooms, we take off for some sightseeing.

279

People in the high-altitude valleys do not even speak languages related to each other, so they can't understand each other. But the thing that binds them together is their faith, Ishmailism, which is a breakaway sect of Shia Islam. This group has "cousins" in the Northern Provinces of Pakistan. Ishmailis also live wherever there are many Indians and Pakistanis in cities anywhere in the world. In fact, Karim is an Ishmaili Muslim. The sect has no mosques, no clerics and no weekly holy day. Their spiritual leader worldwide is the Aga Khan, a very rich businessman and horsebreeder. He is extremely charitable, building and supporting schools and hospitals. The Pamiris look upon him as "Our God who sends us food ". Because the unemployment rate is almost 100%, it is easy to understand the importance of this remarkable man.

Ruslan and I visit an interesting history museum and stroll through the grounds of the local university which is connected in some way with Oxford and, of course, the Aga Khan. Some classes are taught during the day, entirely in English. There are night school classes taught in Tajik which are basically concerned with improving farming techniques.

The reason Ruslan couldn't find accommodation for us in a local hotel is because the only two establishments are disgracefully dirty, but more importantly, completely booked! It is ironic that the precise time that we are here looking for a place to stay is the moment that a dam has broken in the back country. Water is flooding towns and creating disaster zones all the way down through the river valley. In fact, the situation is so desperate that influential government people from surrounding countries including China and Russia have flown to Khorog to view the damage and offer aid. All available accommodation and transport have been appropriated by these dignitaries.

Ruslan's huge cousin joins Ruslan and me for dinner. He hired a taxi to drive us to the local Marco Polo disco! He also seems to me to be a "strongman" who could protect us from unpleasant people

280

and situations.

When we sit down at a table for dinner, I notice a group of perhaps thirty men and women, people who are friends and apparently celebrating an occasion together. The disc jockey provides the Tajik music and the people dance in Tajik style. I enjoy watching them so much that I go over and ask them with hand language if I can take some pictures. They acquiesce with the provision that I will join the group and dance. I indicate that I don't know the dances, but the men assure me they will help me.

I remember a bit of the hand motions from dances I saw in Uzbekistan. The dances are executed with the man and woman dancing side by side in a large circle with other couples. I find I can watch and copy the foot steps of my partner and others. Also I notice that the hand motions are "not fixed" but used by the women as they are inclined to express themselves. I can't believe I am dancing with people in a tiny mountain village in Tajikistan!

In the morning Ruslan hires an ancient taxi to take us out in the country to visit his relatives. As we drive along the Amu-Darya River which separates Afghanistan and Tajikistan., I look across the river and see an Afghan peasant plowing his land.

Ruslan repeatedly asks me if I think the small jeep is acceptable for our long journey. This is certainly wishful thinking as there will be the four of us plus the driver plus all our gear. This jeep has absolutely no storage room. Ruslan starts to cry because he has been unsuccessful and knows Michael will not be happy. I try to reassure him that he has done the best he can.

We come upon a small community of adobe houses resembling those in Santa Fe, New Mexico. People come out to meet us and the children either want stickers on their hand or their picture taken. We are invited into one house for tea. It belongs to Ruslan's aunt and uncle. The main room has a raised platform where we sit on an upholstered couch. The entire neighborhood crowds in to watch this American lady. They smile warmly at us. After tea, the aunt invites me to go to the local hot springs and Ruslan invites his uncle. Men and women always have separate bathing facilities in Central Asia. Ruslan's aunt and I strip down at the end of our pool. She picks up a pumice stone and starts to rub me all over. Obviously this is her way of selflessly ministering to me and is reminiscent of other experiences I have had in Central Asia. What a beautiful gesture! I reciprocate by cleansing her with the stone!

Our next stop is the home of another aunt and uncle who prepare scrambled eggs for us for lunch. I'm sure eggs are a luxury. More relatives crowd into the room to see Ruslan's friend. Before we leave, the aunt presents me with very thick colorful high wool socks, the type women wear in winter in their unheated houses where shoes are not worn. Such a lovely gift! The cost of the wool and the time it took to knit them makes me realize how generous this woman is.

We return to our apartment to find Michael and Karim unloading Michael's car. The two of them drove a very long way around the mountains from Dushanbe to Khorog, bringing all the supplies for our expedition.

Michael cooks the dinner that night on the apartment stove. It is in no way a successful endeavor because the vegetables he brought from Dushanbe never get really cooked. My new discovery is that Michael has never cooked anything in his life, yet he will be our cook on this probably ill-fated high altitude expedition!

Michael spends the next morning searching for a cheap vehicle to rent, but, of course, finds none. Ruslan introduced me yesterday to the Minister of Transportation. It seems logical that one would begin with that man in trying to locate a vehicle. I suggest that to Michael and finally, many hours later after searching through the entire town, he takes my suggestion, realizing that no vehicle will appear until he is willing to pay the price!

Recalling that Michael was so stingy in not providing me with a hotel room in Dushanbe or money for food, it's now obvious what the problem is! He and his partner do not have sufficient money necessary to pull off this expedition in a reasonable manner. However, it seems there is nothing to do but forge ahead!

The Minister has a nice vehicle and driver for us. I am sure it almost bankrupts Michael to pay the money. He won't get the van until the next morning because he doesn't want to pay another day's rent!

That evening we visit Ruslan's grandmother's house. Ruslan says that she invited us for dinner. Michael, remembering his manners temporarily, takes along a large melon for dessert.

We arrive at the grandmother's house. She suggests that we sit in the gazebo. Ruslan translates for us. He tells us that the grandmother's husband died two months before and she is very lonely. I sit next to her at the table. She searches for my hand under the table and holds it the entire time we sit there. Such a tiny, sweet, dear person.

It finally is apparent there will be nothing to eat for dinner. She has no money. So we eat an apple apiece from her tree and all enjoy the melon. Just as we are leaving, the grandmother goes inside and comes out with a beautiful pair of thick wool socks, just like the socks from Ruslan's aunt! These are very small. I think she made them for herself. But her generosity is incredible! Now I have met two generous endearing women in this family. I can not believe my good fortune, and I will remember them the rest of my life.

In the morning, once packed up, the expedition departs. We have 728 kilometers to travel before we reach the other end of the Pamir Highway. This doesn't sound like much, but road conditions are extremely poor. The road is mostly dirt. If there is pavement, it is full of pot holes. Often there are only deeply rutted tracks. But our nice official-looking van has good suspension, so we will have the best ride possible.

The scenery is stunning as we look back down the valley. Switchbacks climb sharply mile after mile!

After two hours we arrive at a tiny village named Jelandy and stop in the "tea house" to visit with a man from the community. He says the only food they ever have is tea and sugar except rarely when a truck comes through with some wheat so they can have bread! These are indeed extremely poor people.

We hike a short way up the mountain admiring the wild flowers, many of which I saw in Kyrgystan. Here is a peat field where people dig up fuel and carry it down the mountain on a flat board with handles at two ends. A few sheep graze on the hill. I think they are saved for very special occasions. Our four men go to the local hot springs building. I decline because the stark room in these places leaves much to be desired for a pleasant experience. However, the truck drivers on the road look forward to a hot bath because not even Khorog has any hot water facilities.

Now so much time has elapsed that Michael feels it is time to cook a meal. He has recipes from his wife and brought carrots, potatoes and onions from his garden at home. He also brought grapes, but they all spoiled in the heat of the sun. He had purchased a two-burner gas "stove". Everyone except the driver feels compelled to pitch in and peel the vegetables which we put in a pot with water and cover.

We wait and wait for the water to boil. But we are at about 9,000 feet and have a very small, inadequate stove. The water won't boil, so after two hours we eat the hard vegetables along with one sausage apiece from a can! We start driving again at 3:30 and have five hours left to go.

We lost so much time cooking that we can't stop to see a huge area of petroglyphs along the road as we cross the Koitezek Pass at 12,800 feet. As we descend, the mountains which earlier were so close to the road until now seem to pull farther away. So the new scenery is a very wide plain. This is the Pamir Plateau, the "Roof of the World" as the locals call it. The road is raised above the plain and very narrow.

Just as dusk is falling, we arrive at the tiny town of Murgab, 310 kilometers from Khorog. There is one truck-stop cum guest-house and no place to eat. We arrive before any truck drivers show up to quibble with us. The two-room guest house is ours! What good fortune! I have one whole room to myself; the four men share the other. I even have a metal twin bed while the men sleep on the floor. Luck is with us: we have electric light bulbs hanging from the ceiling.

The first and only activity of the evening is peeling onions, potatoes, and carrots and trying to boil them again. I explain to Michael again that it is almost impossible to cook the vegetables at this high altitude with this small stove, and that people all over Asia use a wok and oil to cook. Of course, we have no wok and Michael doesn't believe me, a woman. I ask the lady of the guest-house for a very small amount of boiling water so I can make one of my dried packets of soup in my room, leaving the cooking attempt to the men. And then I go to bed contemplating this disorganized man and disorganized day. Hard to imagine that this new travel company will last. I begin counting the hours till the trip is over.

We have a free day in Murgab. After breakfast of bread and jam Michael and I visit a very tiny local museum which is quite interesting. We find a small market with practically nothing for sale except a few root vegetables. But I find a new flashlight which I desperately need, having left mine behind in Khorog. Amazingly, there is a small handicraft center for products made by the women of the village. A French aide group has an office in Murgab. The French encourage the women to do the unusual embroidery which is part of their culture. The agency takes the products to Dushanbe to sell in a shop there. But we can buy the products right here. They are the nicest souvenirs of my trip and will make lovely Christmas gifts.

The aide group is primarily here to teach the farmers to grow a new kind of potato which does well at high altitude in a short growing season. The group also teaches the men better animal husbandry. It surprises me to find the aide group in this isolated spot along the highway.

I spend several hours wandering about watching village women at the well and boys playing in the dirt making "roads" with sticks.

Late in the afternoon Michael takes us to the home of a husband and wife for tea. They have tea and sugar but nothing else and tell us, as had the man at Jelandy, that all they ever have to eat is tea and sugar unless a truck comes along the highway carrying flour. It is a wretchedly poor existence. Maybe the new kind of potatoes will make a difference for them.

At one point the man tells his wife to bring out the rug she has just completed. It is a gilam made of several nine-inch wide horizontal woven strips sewn together to make the rug. I ask her the price of the rug. At first she and her husband say they want $125. Knowing one must always bargain, I offer $100. They are so happy. The money will support them for two years! It is nice to know I have helped this couple. The rug will always be important to me because I know the woman who made it, and, when I look at it, I see her and her husband in the room where we had tea.

I ask Michael if it is possible to have a little bit of hot water to take a "sponge bath". The woman of the family where we are staying brings in a large pitcher of hot water along with a dish pan. She enters my room with me and indicates that I should take off all my clothes and then step into the dishpan. I have a "handy wipe" to wash with. She pours a tiny bit of water on the wipe and with my soap I wash my face, neck and arms. Then she pours a bit of water to rinse these washed parts. We continue this down to my feet. At the end she pours some on my head. I wash my hair with this bit of water. And finally she pours more small quantities of water all over my head and down my whole body. A pitcher of water has sufficed for a bath. I feel gloriously clean; the last "standing in the tub" bath I had was at my home stay in Dushanbe almost a week earlier.

Here is another kind woman who ministered to me without a word, using hand signs. I feel real love and appreciation for her. I will never forget her. And she is certainly one of the people who make this trip so very special for me.

A high, frigid plateau where practically nothing grows,
A winding dirt track 500 miles long
Often traversing passes 12,000 feet high,
Encircled on every side by stark towering grey peaks,
Punctuated only four times by tiny clusters of houses.

A forbidding environment where the poorest Tajiks
eke out a living;
Eating nothing but tea, sugar and bread from flour
Transported on this, the Pamir Mountain Highway,
From Kyrgystan hundreds of miles away.

Sometimes a lamb is killed
in honor of an important family occasion.
Otherwise life goes on the same, day after day.
The women collect the water from the village well.
The samovar boils outside heated by chunks of dry peat.

Huddling in freezing rooms, sipping tea,
Wearing brightly colored high thick socks.
The women weave a gilam or sew embroidery.
Village men gather to gossip and sip their tea
Through a square of sugar held between their teeth.

287

Perhaps three times a day in summer
And only a few times during the interminable winter
A lorry is heard lumbering through the pot holes in the road
And, who knows, possibly delivering flour to this hamlet.
Soon the smell of baking permeates the rooms.
The daily events end as each family breaks their bread

During the day two Irish men in their forties stop by and chat. They've been backpacking about a year. We start talking about all manner of subjects. At one point we are on the subject of foreign films. They actually have seen the Mongolian film, "Close to Eden". Incredible!

Michael has made some contact with the head of the aide group. He (not us, unfortunately) has been invited to dinner at their house that evening. He is quite interested in promoting affairs which might improve his tours.

Michael leaves Karim in charge of fixing the evening meal. First Karim tries cooking a sauce for pasta. Of course, it never gets done. By this time the second burner of the portable stove is not working. So we have to wait till the sauce is "finished" and then start cooking the pasta. During this time, Karim and I discuss how the women of Asia never use a pot. They always use a wok and oil to cook. We lament that we have no wok. An hour later the pasta is pronounced finished even though it is still hard. I'm sure Michael is happy not to be here as we crunch our dinner!

We are off early the next morning after our breakfast of tea, dry cereal with powdered milk (reconstituted with water), bread with jam. I wonder how long the bread will last before becoming moldy.

The road today runs for hours within 60 feet of the barbed-wire fenced border with China. We are so high that the scenery is simply bare mountains and no vegetation. Everything is brown. Close to noontime we reach the top of White Horse Pass, the highest pass on

the highway at 13,965 feet. We arrive at a checkpoint which is re-
puted to be "difficult to maneuver" successfully. The guards make
us empty the vehicle totally. Our driver must drive the van over a
hole in the ground so the soldiers can go underneath the vehicle to
check for any illegal "cargo" fastened underneath. The soldiers pick
through our cooking apparatus, our meager food supply, the tent
which I insisted that Michael bring on the trip plus our sleeping
bags. Then slowly we have to open all our personal luggage. I offer
my day pack first. Since I am the last person, they hardly glance into
my back pack which is very fortunate. I have been nervous that they
will not like the "pharmacy" I always take on trips; I think they
might make me leave the group. Where I will go instead is a mystery, but I imagine there is a cell in a compound where I might stay
for months.

So after an hour and a half of unpacking the van, standing around in
the bitter cold wind waiting for "inspection", and repacking luggage
and the van, we are released into the new area we will traverse on
the other side of the pass.

We drive downhill forty-five miles to Lake Karakol, the highest lake
in Central Asia. There is another check point which goes smoothly.
Also there is a miniscule village. We drive out by the lake. This is to
be our camping place for the night! As we look back at the check
point, we see the soldiers watching us with binoculars the whole
time we are here. The village people are also very interested in us.
They gather about 75 yards away to stare for hours.

The area in front of the lake is disgusting. Cruddy slime has come
onshore. There are broken bottles and bones of roasted sheep. The
locals apparently use the area for slaughtering and roasting their
animals.

Michael decides we will camp in this god-forsaken, desolate garbage dump and fix a meal that will serve as lunch and dinner. So
the inevitable begins once more. We peel and cut up the vegetables
and put them in the pot. I'm not particularly interested in the ac-

tivities. I'm freezing cold because of the strong wind blowing off the lake and I also want to catch up on my journal. I go inside the van. Ruslan comes in after me. He is very upset. He says that he only has the short sleeve tee-shirt, a thin jacket and thin pants with him. Michael did not tell him what to bring! He has no sleeping bag! He is convinced that he will freeze to death that night and he starts to cry.

Very concerned now, I go out to tell Michael of Ruslan's dilemma. But first I realize there is water in the cooking pot. I ask Michael where the water came from. He says from the lake and, no, it hasn't been treated. I am suddenly very, very angry. I tell Michael that the water in the pot will never reach a temperature hot enough to kill organisms that could make us sick. He looks at me in disbelief. I reiterate that water at high altitude boils at a lower point than at sea level and is harder to disinfect. Then I also tell him that the vegetables will never cook, that what we need and do not have is a wok and cooking oil. I go on to say it will be unbearably cold tonight and Ruslan, for certain, will get sick. Also that I for one will be sick from the untreated water.

One of many "ill fated" attempts at cooking

Michael looks suddenly crestfallen and dismayed. He asks ME what to do! I say to ask the driver if there is a truck stop along the road. The driver says, "Yes, four miles ahead!" So I tell Michael that we must go there for the night. I think he is so relieved to have someone take over the responsibility. But I'm sure he is extremely worried about his finances since he will have to pay for the guest house and food.

We arrive before other drivers plying the road decide to stop for the night. There is one room with tables and chairs. The family uses a second room and will have two women, one man and two children in there. The women are busy at the moment fixing dinner for travelers and themselves. They are using a WOK and cooking oil! They have already fried pieces of Marco Polo sheep. This is an endangered animal listed in the books of the World Wildlife Organization. But people as poor as these we have come across on the highway kill the sheep for food, and I certainly can't fault them.

Now the women fry vegetables in the oil. Dinner is ready in a matter of minutes. We are five very hungry people. One wonders how inadequate Michael feels once he sees how quickly the vegetables cook.

Now we pile most of the tables and chairs on top of each other and settle down in our sleeping bags on the floor. I am asleep immediately. In the morning I awake surprised to have twelve men sleeping around me! I never heard them come in.

We are on our way by 5:30 a.m. the next morning. It will be a very long driving day over many passes. We stop for lunch in a tiny hamlet. Michael buys some new bread and we have jelly sandwiches. I have diarrhea. Well, there are many places where I can have picked it up. Michael accidentally leaves his precious decoder (calculator) there.

Things seem to be falling apart.

We come upon a wedding celebration! People are dancing in the road. The bride, groom and the concertina player want their photos taken together. Michael says he will bring the photos on his next trip. It is nice to see these people so happy in such a miserable harsh climate.

Wedding celebration in the middle of the road

Finally we reach Osh, the end of the highway! Michael has arranged a home stay for me (at my behest). He asks about twenty different people how to get to the house. We drive about eight kilometers out of town. I am feeling very ill. When we finally reach the house, a man tells Michael that there is no one here who can speak English, but someone will come later. I do not want to be left alone in such a situation, feeling as miserable as I do. So we return to the city. Michael begins driving to various guest-houses and checking prices. He obviously wants the very cheapest one available. He finds one at last and I am soon resting in my private room. I suppose it bankrupts Michael to pay for it. I tell my companions, however, that I will accompany them to a bar for a beer so we can toast The Pamir Highway!

Unfortunately, my friend Karim must return all the way back on the Pamir Highway to Khorog and then around the mountains in Michael's car to Dushanbe from where he will fly to Istanbul.

The toast completed and a bowl of rice consumed, I go back to the hotel to sleep.

The next morning is my last day in Tajikistan. I contract over the phone for a guide to show me the museum and bazaar. He appears a couple hours later. The natural history museum is interesting in that there are vignettes off to the side of the circular steps as we climb slowly to the top. They depict "early man" and how he progressed. At the top is a tree with narrow strips of fabric tied on the branches. I query the guide, knowing full well that it is a "holy tree." He is incensed because it shows that the people worship the Great Goddess, and, of course, we are only to think of Islam.

Someone is hired to take me to the airport. Soon I am in the sky, leaving all traces of Tajikistan behind.

When I arrive in Bishkek, Sasha and Alex are waiting for me with smiles and hugs. They are so happy that all "went well" and I arrived back safely. They put me in a beautiful wooden building, a kind of hostel for travelers and trekkers. There is rustic furniture and a nice bathroom.

We spend the next day visiting Bishkek city sights, including numerous statues of Manas and the central market. They take me to a unique dress shop which exists, I am sure, for tourists and rich Russians. I find some nice souvenirs.

The next morning I have to leave these two wonderful friends and return to Istanbul and my country. I am so exhausted that in the Istanbul airport, I find a wooden bench which I lie on holding my day pack with two hands. Luckily no one tries to steal it.

*   *   *

I have certainly learned a great deal about two young countries ruled by dictators. One seems to be doing alright, but the second seems to be in a more precarious position. Hopefully both will be ultimately successful.

Teaching in Afghanistan - 2002

A Love-Based Decision

I n early November 2001 just after I returned from my trip to Uzbekistan and Turkmenistan, my husband and I were watching BBC News. Thousands of Afghan women and their children and babies were fleeing hundreds of miles to escape the bombings by the United States. They were hoping to reach Pakistan or Iran. It was a pathetic sight. I said to my husband, "Our country is just going to turn its back on those women when this is over. I have to go there to show them that I love them and care about them."

Suddenly I had a self-proclaimed mission that would prove difficult to fulfill. It was barely two months since the terrorist attack of September 11 on the World Trade Towers. Al Quaida headquartes in Afghanistan claimed responsibility for the bombing. The U.S. declared war on the terrorists and retaliated by bombing Afghanistan. When "mission accomplished" was declared, America and British troops were stationed in the country to "keep the peace". The refugees streamed back to their homes.

As I began my search to find a way to get to Afghanistan, I had no idea how I could help women in that country. At first I even envisioned such "far-out" possibilities as helping a woman make an adobe hut by hand or baby sitting children while a woman learned to read and write. I was willing to do anything to help.

I started working on the Internet reaching individuals and a whole list of organizations that work globally. I was an unacceptable candidate for aide agencies because I only wanted to be gone a month and also I was an American. It was considered too dangerous for Americans to be in Afghanistan.

After months of fruitless effort I found a small organization in Boulder, Colorado called Afghans for Tomorrow. It was now 2002. I learned that I could go to Afghanistan to teach for however long I wished, but, of course, would have to pay my own way. It was as simple as that.

In March, Wahid, the leader of the organization, was leaving for Kabul with several geologists to dig wells in rural areas north of Kabul. While there he agreed to search for a family with whom I could stay in the fall. I wanted the cultural experience of living with Afghans for three weeks instead of staying at a guest house with other foreigners. It was very difficult for Wahid to find a family willing to take me because they all worried about my being kidnapped or hurt by remnants of the Taliban while I was in the their care. This could also lead to brutal repercussions for any family with whom I might be staying.

Wahid found a woman named Suroya, who was working for a different school system other than the one owned and run by Afghans for Tomorrow. It was called Aide for Afghanistan and was run by a young Afghan woman, Hassina, who spoke perfect English. Her organization was running three girls' schools. Suroya was an assistant administrator for these girls' schools. She and her husband, Omar, said I could stay with them and teach in the schools for three weeks starting in September 2003.

When Wahid returned from his trip, he helped me obtain a visa under the auspices of Afghans for Tomorrow and explained how to travel from Denver to Kabul. From then on, it was entirely up to me - - so I made my final plans. I had an email address for Suroya so I could communicate with her; one of her sons could read and write English. She told me to arrive in my shalwar qamiz which I had owned since I visited an Indian ashram some years before. She would help me buy clothes once I arrived. I knew that the outfit I had would not be suitable because the sleeves didn't reach my wrists and the top was too revealing because of the V-neck.

I would be teaching six hours each day, six days a week. I would spend two hours daily in each of the three schools whose female students would range in age in each class from nine to seventeen years of age (their education having been interrupted during the years of Taliban control). During this period when education for girls was banned, women were secretly teaching them in base-ments and back rooms. When the war ended, Hassina brought these women and girls together to form three schools with a total of about 500 girls. She miraculously obtained buildings suitable for schools and was in the process of readying a fourth building. An organization on the east coast of the U.S. organized by Hassina was helping to fund the schools.

Finally September 4th arrived and I departed Denver for Newark. After staying overnight at a Day's Inn I left the next morning on Malaysian Airlines for the twelve hour trip to Dubai, arriving at the Dubai Ramada Inn at 8 a.m. only to find the lobby full of people waiting for rooms that would not be ready until noon. Most of the people were from Muslim countries. The women had happily re-moved their veils because Dubai has no dress code. Women can dress and act like Westerners including wearing swim suits in pools!! Many were here for an exciting "Western" vacation. Out-side the hotel it was "desert hot" while inside with air conditioning it was 60 degrees F.

Once I received a room, I turned the thermostat up to 80 degrees, showered, and slept until 6:30 p.m., ate in the hotel coffee shop, and was back in bed by 8 p.m. I was up at 4 a.m. and sitting in the waiting room of a section of the airport reserved for domestic flights. I amused myself by watching an amazing assortment of apparel. Men wore shalwar qamiz and pill boxes, rolled berets, turbans, or scarves for headgear. Women wore traditional Afghan tunic tops and trousers. Some wore shawls, some had not yet donned theirs. Some wore burqas. Most of the travelers were men. Some people were en route to visit relatives, and there were members of aide groups returning to Kabul.

My flight on Afghan Air lasted four hours and landed in mid-morning in Kabul. Now the real adventure was about to begin! I had no idea what my hosts would look like or how to recognize them.

* * *

Kabul and my Host Family –
plus Dust and Flies

A woman with brightly hennaed hair waves to me as I step off the plane and walk inside the tiny airport building. Suroya, Omar and I meet at last. We speak in sign language. It is Sunday, a work and school day in Afghanistan. Suroya's children are not here to translate.

A relatively new-looking conveyor belt brings in the luggage. Because state electricity does not run during the day, a kerosene-run generator powers the belt. It keeps sputtering, stopping and starting so there is plenty of time to view what is haltingly making its way along the belt. There are ancient suitcases of all sizes and huge boxes containing who knows what. A giant overstuffed sofa has been moved to the center area which the belt encircles. Men leap on

298

the conveyor trying to sort out the piles of containers inching along.

Eventually most of the travelers recover their possessions and leave. The conveyor continues to rattle round and round with a few unclaimed items. My two suitcases are not on it. Two hours after my arrival my suitcases are delivered from some mysterious hidden area. Omar piles them in our "family" vehicle which really belongs to the school organization. As he drives us to their home, I am wondering what to expect. We drive through the bustling city with paved, pot-holed streets crowded with mostly taxis and aide agency-owned vehicles, as well as horse-pulled carts and men on foot carrying heavy loads. Now we're on dirt roads and enter a residential area of houses with high surrounding walls, and turn into a short driveway in front of a gate.

As we enter the yard, I meet an eight year old girl named Sadaf and her fourteen year old sister Hoosbu who have been waiting for us. The house in front of us is a two story white cement building in an L-shape with a large raised cement patio in front of the door. We take off our shoes as we step on the patio, then kneel down around a piece of blue printed oilcloth to eat breakfast: a large flat bread for each of us, some jam, and a large thermos of tea. Each of us pours our own tea and then adds several spoon fulls of powdered milk plus a couple spoons of sugar. The two girls can speak English. Suroya tries to understand and speak a few words. Omar simply smiles.

We tour the house. The main floor has a large dining and sitting room reaching from front to back. There is an alcove on the right with a double bed and a cloth hanging for a door. The entire living space floor is covered by patterned Persian carpets with deep red backgrounds. At the front end there are continuous flat cushions in front of windows which reach from floor to ceiling. The cushions are covered with fabric of the same deep red as the carpets. There is a white entertainment center at one end of the room which houses a television set and VCR plus some shelves holding knick knacks. The only other piece of furniture is a large china cabinet against a side wall in the back part of the room.

A large chandelier hangs from the ceiling of each room.

Breakfast on the patio - Suraya, Omar, Sadaf, Sagia, Samia

Outside to the right another door leads inside to two rooms, each with two double bunk beds. It is the boys' area. In the L-shaped part of the main floor, which is to the left of the front entranceway Suroya and Omar have their bedroom and small sitting room. It is furnished with a large double bed which Suroya indicates is "hers" and a cot on legs with a mattress which is Omar's. She smiles conspiratorially, evidently wanting me to appreciate her "coup" which ended the former yearly appearance of babies eight years ago. There is a dressing table, chair, and small sofa. The room has lacy curtains and a pretty bedspread. A Persian rug partially covers the cement floor.

We go upstairs where a large room to the left of the stairwell sits

300

above Suroya's room. This is "my" room, lined with many floor to ceiling windows covered with lacy curtains. "Sitting" cushions lie in front of the windows and also on the opposite wall. At the far end an L-shaped upholstered "Western" sofa and a very large round wooden coffee-table complete the decorating except for an ornate chandelier over the table. It is a mystery to me why this "Western" style furniture is hidden up here unless it provides a room for an infrequent guest and quite likely is the only furniture brought back from Pakistan where the family spent eight years in exile.

On the other side of the stairwell Suroya has provided two connecting rooms for her 21-year-old married daughter Samia and new bridegroom Rahi. One room is a sitting room with the cushions on the floor and the other room a bedroom holding a double bed. A small room behind my room serves as a small kitchen for Samia where she can squat and cook on a single burner stove.

A long porch extends out to the front of the house on the second floor. It is a perfect place to hang washed clothes to dry.

Suroya leads me outside to the right of the garden where a small white cement building houses the family kitchen containing another one burner stove and cupboards with cooking utensils, some pots and condiments. Behind this building another tiny building houses the family Asian toilet (hole in the floor). The room is hidden from view of those in the yard by a hanging curtain. I can see it's going to be quite a hike in the middle of the night from my room down the stairs, out on the patio, down a long walk to the toilet. I notice flies everywhere. Windows and doors are screened but the screens have holes.

A huge metal water container stands on a table close to the patio, supplying the family's water for the day. Omar replenishes it every day with water from a neighborhood well. I sense that every drop is precious; it is not for washing our hands or faces. (But each day I surreptitiously use a corner of a handy-wipe to wash the grime from my face and forearms with a few drops of water.)

Now we are off to the bazaar for a quick shopping trip for fabric. We find two cotton fabrics, one a brown and black tiny pattern and the other a rather flamboyant bright orange and green large pattern which is Suroya's choice. Omar made his living as a tailor for many years but now his eyesight is bad and he is instead the driver for the schools' passenger cars. However, he has his own foot pedal sewing machine at home so he will make my outfits. There is no time to look around the bazaar and we make a mad dash for home. I notice several men on the curb of a large square changing money. We arrive to find it is time for the midday meal.

When all are assembled, we eat our meal sitting on the floor of the big room around a large solid color piece of oilcloth which serves as the table. Now I meet all of the children: Sadaf (6), Gizu (8), Je-bran (17), Khaim (18), Sagia (15), Hoosbu (14),Samia (21); one other brother lives with an aunt in Iran and another apparently died at some time. All the girls wear their hair in a pony-tail. They don't wear their headscarves indoors, nor does their mother.

Sagia brings in pans of food from the kitchen house. Sadaf comes to each of us with a small pitcher of water and a catch plate and towel so we each can wash our hands before eating. We eat with our hands. Each person has traditional flatbread and a small plate. A huge mountain of rice is in the center of the serving dish and a tomato sauce surrounds it. Each person reaches to the center dish, grabs a handful of rice into a ball, squeezes it, rubs it through the sauce and brings it to his mouth without spilling anything on the table. When you've done this all your life, it is of course second nature. Not so to me. What a mess I make, fistful after fistful! How embarrassing to spill most of my rice on the table or plate before it reaches my mouth every single time. Everyone watches me criti-cally. I am thinking, "Certainly I will master this in a few days?"

There is no beverage on the table nor is there dessert. Tea is avail-able after the meal with the powdered milk and sugar. Flies are omnipresent on our hands and on our food but no one seems to notice. The children all speak English but not Omar. Suroya understands quite a bit but speaks little. During this, my first meal, the children speak English in deference to me.

After our meal I go upstairs to my room for a nap and to unpack my suitcases. I have very few clothes with me, basically only underwear and socks. The rest of the space in the two suitcases is taken up with the supplies I brought for teaching. I know that many of the girls I will meet will know very little English. I decided back home that I would use my class time with these students doing action songs such as pre-school children sing in my culture: "Head, Shoulders, Knees and Toes", "I'm a Little Teapot", and the Brownie Girl Scout "Hello" song. I do have twenty copied sheets of two Dr. Seuss books for girls whose English might be advanced enough to handle them. The suitcases primarily contain craft supplies because my thought early on in my planning was that the most important thing I could do for these girls would be to enable them to make "something pretty"; I have scissors, paints, brushes, and Styrofoam cups cut down to low size for water to wash out brushes, plus stacks of paper.

In addition to the five reams of computer paper for artwork, there are elastic thread and beads, pipe cleaners, tissue paper, colored construction paper, and crayons. I lay out my supplies in neat piles on the upholstered sofa and am well satisfied with what I have managed to bring with me. It is time for a nap, but all the girls including Samia (who had cooked upstairs for her husband) burst in on me and begin to rifle through the half-unpacked suitcases grabbing everything. I keep saying, "no, no" but to little avail. There is much discussion about all of the items. They are like a bunch of third graders in America. This is a get-acquainted time so it is definitely worth all the mess and "mix up" of supplies. I can see the different personalities of each girl immediately and fall in love with Sadaf (six) and Gizu (eight), so sweet and innocent. Hoosbu is fourteen and quite pushy. I know she will be harder to like. Sagia at fifteen is really a very different sort of person. She is serious, quite boyish in her dress and appearance, rather hard to fathom. She is the next in line to be married and so assumes the role of "slave girl". She does go to school and seems quite bright but practically all of the rest of her waking hours she is preparing meals in the kitchen and cleaning up afterwards. She must do all the family laundry once a week with the help of a hired woman. I have the feeling that she wants to be appreciated for the person she is, not for performing her slave duties.

Hours later I manage to close my eyes briefly, then go downstairs because I have no idea what the schedule is or what time the evening meal will be served. As we sit around relaxing before dinner the boys ask me what kind of music I like, a question which takes me a bit by surprise. I reply slowly saying I like some classical and name some famous composers. But there is no sign of recognition. So I add I like "rock" and receive a questioning look. I ask them what music they like. Their response is music in Indian movies and they claim excitedly that they have rented a CD for tonight's viewing - an Indian film. I am thinking I'll never be able to stay up that late!

Eventually Suroya and Omar come home and it is dinner time. We have basically a repeat of the midday meal. However, I see there is a fork on my plate and Suroya explains that I might be happier to use a fork rather than my hand. I hate the thought of giving up so quickly. But the thought crosses my mind: I am left-handed and used that hand to reach into the common dish earlier in the day. The left hand in much of Asia, even much of the world, is considered the dirty hand, the one a person uses to clean his private parts. It should not be used to touch food. Be that as it may, I feel that all worries have been handled now by my having a plate and fork.

As we finish our meal Sagia cleans up the dishes and Gizu wipes the tablecloth and folds it. It is time for the two hours of electricity per day to come on. People in this country have had to learn to live without electricity during the day. Public power comes on in the evening for two hours. But if citizens want the power to last longer, the remedy is to own a family generator that runs on kerosene. The shops all have generators to use during the day to light their rooms and Internet cafes use generators all day until the public power comes on in the evening.

The family turns to the news on TV which is the only programming there is. It is spoken in Dari.

Before coming to Afghanistan I spent one morning a week with an Afghan woman living across Denver. She is Wahid's mother and she helped me with vocabulary and some conjugation of basic verbs. We did this for 10 weeks and I reviewed it all several times a week at home. I believe that if my family had not spoken English and I were forced into using Dari, I might improve quickly, but, unexpectedly, the children in my family speak English and the teachers in the schools where I will teach will speak English. So I can envision losing what little I have learned so far.

I am glad when the news is over since I can't understand any of it. The boys' rented film is a violent Indian movie starring Van Damme as the star. So I excuse myself to go to bed. First I spend at least an hour racing around my room (which has a high ceiling) with a sweater in hand swatting flies. At long last most are dead. There are still some live ones between the curtains and the windows; I hope they will stay there while it is dark and I will be able to sleep. I am in bed by 8 p.m. It has been an extraordinarily long, busy, exhausting day with many new experiences.

I am up at 6 a.m. Monday dressed in one of my new outfits made by Omar and am down on the patio to have breakfast of bread and milk tea. Suroya announces that we women and girls will go to the amman (public bathhouse) before school and work. This is quite a production. The older girls, including Samia, gather up dish pans, buckets, stools, pumice stones, shampoo and soap. Everyone takes clean clothes wrapped in a towel. This morning however I don't take extra clothes since I am already dressed for the day. We pile in the car so Omar can take us to the bathhouse which is about two miles away. We pay our ten cent entry fee and enter a large steamy room where about 25 naked women and children are standing around pouring hot water from a faucet into dish pans and then on themselves and their children. Pumice stones are the tool for scrubbing. Often adults scrub each other. I watch the procedure and try to follow suit. Once I have some water on myself, I start scrubbing. Suroya picks up the stone and scrubs my arms and back. I realize this is actually a way of ministering to me as I had experienced on the Pamir Highway in a guesthouse in Tajikistan. So I scrub her in return. The girls pour water on their long hair and wash it. It is very hot and steamy in the room which makes it hard to see since I wear glasses. Once we are all soaped, we begin rinsing each other with the dish pans and buckets. Finally, satisfied that we are clean, we walk out into the first room where we left our towels and clean and soiled clothes in a pile, dry off, get dressed, grab all our bath equipment and dash out to the car where Omar is waiting.

He takes Sadaf and Gizu to their school for younger girls, then returns for Suroya, Hoosbu, Sagia, Samia (who teaches in one of the schools) and me to go to our schools. Suroya, Omar and the princpals of the three schools I will visit each day have worked out a complicated schedule for me. I will spend two hours at one school; then Omar will pick me up and deliver me about twenty minutes later to a second school where I will teach more classes and have lunch. He will then pick me up again to go the third school for afternoon classes. The schedule is never the same and most days I see entirely different classes. I don't know the schedule but fortunately Omar does. I am dependent on him to transport me from school to school, while at the same time he is doing other driving for the schools.

Before the beginning of morning and afternoon sessions, students gather in the courtyard of their school. They sing a religious song in unison followed by two patriotic songs. Then they remove their shoes at the school entrance and go to their classrooms. Classes seem to last 45 minutes. The girls study math, Dari, English, reading and writing, and Islamic history.

Teaching 500 girls at three schools –
six days a week

Suroya accompanies me into the first school halfway through their morning session. The principal and teachers are awaiting our arrival. I am introduced to all of the adults who shake my hand and smile in a very friendly manner. I feel very welcome. A class of girls is sitting on the floor in the lobby. They all wear black tunics and any trousers they wish. All wear white scarves. They stare at me wondering what this woman will be like who has come to teach English. I walk over to them and introduce myself as Joyce. Classes vary extremely in English ability. Some classes are learning the English alphabet while some have studied English for two, three, or four years. The girls regard me quizzically. They are nervous and pull their scarves across their faces and hold hands.

Since I have no idea what these girls know or understand in English, I decide to sing action songs with them as a beginning. I start with the Girl Scout Brownie "Hello" song. They soon understand they are to sing the four "hellos" after me.

This seems to go reasonably well after several repetitions. So we move on to "Head, Shoulders, Knees, and Toes". I point out the names of body parts with their locations on my body. Slowly we go through the song. They begin to get the idea that they are to touch the places I name. Possibly a tiny flicker of a smile flashes on some faces. Then we switch to "I'm a Little Teapot". One of the teachers explains the meaning of the words and actions. We do this one like we know what we are doing. I say the words and they do the actions and seem quite pleased. I decide to count in English and I find that quite a few know some of the numbers.

The bell rings. A teacher guides me to my next class. I spot girls much older than others and remember there are girls whose education was disrupted probably not once but many times during the ten-year war to force out the Russians, then again when the Taliban decreed that girls could not attend school, and again when the Americans bombed their country to evict the Taliban. It is a wonder that any girl would have a cohesive idea about any subject. Some girls went to school in Pakistan while their families were refugees there. Others attended classes taught by women in basements or hidden back rooms. The present teachers really have done an amazing job of pulling groups into classes and sorting out girls' abilities. One or two girls smile at me on their way out. Omar and Suroya have waited and now take me to another school about twenty minutes away.

The girls learn by rote. The teacher says the sentence and it is repeated in unison, a method used in most parts of the world. Girls and teachers are comfortable with it. Girls write important facts in their notebooks and complete assignments at home. Their books were written and published in Pakistan. There are very few drawings to spark up the pages. Teachers work only half a day. At least this spreads out the pay among many women.

The bell rings signifying the end of morning school. Suroya and Omar transport me to a third school where I have lunch of rice and bread. Students arrive for the afternoon session, some with a friend, others accompanied by an adult who in some instances wear a burqa. After the singing in the courtyard, there is a loud clatter of girls leaving their shoes by the door as they enter the building.

I meet my first class and am welcomed warmly by the teacher. Just as in the morning, there are girls of all ages and knowledge. I repeat what I did in the morning in each of three classes. When I arrive tomorrow I will meet all new girls. If I were in this school during a morning the first time, I would spend the afternoon at that school next time and meet new classes.

There are a total of five hundred girls in the three schools and I am supposed to teach them all!

By the time I arrive home I am exhausted, seeing only a sea of swimming faces in my mind. I remove my dress and lay it out on a cushion to keep it looking as nice as possible. The fabric is cotton and wrinkles badly. The episode this morning at the amman with my dress wrapped in my towel certainly messed it up to start with. I put on a shalwar qamiz which I brought with me from a previous trip to India. It is a tunic with matching trousers. The reason I can't wear it in public here is that has a V-shaped neckline and only three-quarter length sleeves.

I lie down to rest. But after a half hour the family girls burst into my room to play with my craft supplies and mess up my neat piles. I teach them to play "Go Fish", a card game I brought with me. They are delighted and we play endlessly.

When Omar arrives home with Suroya, I ask to go to an Internet cafe to email Jim. I see consternation on their faces. They tell Khaim he must go with me and sit and wait. The agreement is that I will be on the Internet for one hour. It seems pretty silly to me that Khaim must be with me at all times. The shop manager is pleasant to me, gets me situated at a station, and helps me find Yahoo. The shop has a generator which runs during all shop hours, so electricity is no problem. The patrons are the usual males that I see everywhere in the world at such places. But there are some Western women from aide groups and I wonder what Khaim is thinking as he watches them come and go freely and independently. Omar is back waiting in the car after exactly one hour to take us home.

After dinner Suroya, Omar, their eldest son and I discuss what I will be paying them during my stay. Omar says he needs $100 a week for gas and his time taxiing me around. Suroya says she needs $50 a week for room and board. It sounds like a good arrangement especially when I would have paid much more to a guesthouse had I stayed at one.

I excuse myself to go to bed. Of course that is postponed by my incessantly chasing after flies again. But at last I fall exhausted into bed.

Tuesday is a national holiday in honor of the assassination of a military hero. I don my shalwar qamiz (my play dress). Suroya and Omar go off for the day to the office. When the boys get up, they soon leave because they have free range of the city while we women must stay behind the walls of the "compound" as I call the yard and buildings on our property. The boys ride bicycles, play pickup soccer here and there, explore the bazaar and other shops. We don't see them again until dinner time. But the girls cling to me all day just like flies.

BEHIND THE WALL

Far from home I'm behind the wall
With my new-found friends.
Girls who chatter constantly
Who want to search through my suitcases
For treasures they cannot even imagine.

Who clamor for me to sing with them
Action singing games for American young children,
But for these girls new ways to express their exuberance.
Who beg for us to play "Go Fish" yet another time
And dance the Hokey Pokey again and again.

The city does not exist beyond the wall;
Only this unique room is real,
Hidden from all but these girls and me.

Their hands shuffle through all the craft supplies in my suitcase and laid out on the furniture. I have to caution them repeatedly to try to maintain my neat piles. They immediately set up a clamor to play "Go Fish". I relent and we play this simple game over and over for at least an hour. We have brief conversations now and then between hands. I learn that Samia's husband, Rahi, is a university graduate from Islamabad. He studied law which includes religious Shiite law and is now working with a committee to rewrite the Shiite law more clearly. But I suspect that no statutes will really change. He wishes that Samia would read and study the Koran. I slowly understand that the only history she teaches is about Islam. She is ignorant of any world history from classical times to the present. This means she really knows nothing about the countries and continents of the world, nor any of the famous scientists or explorers that all people in western schools are so familiar with. I vow secretly to buy her a history book to enlighten her.

I sense that she is very lazy. But I have to consider that when she married a couple of months ago, her life changed forever from being a "schoolgirl and slave girl" to being a wife. Suroya gave Samia the two rooms on the other side of the stairwell for her married quarters. When a girl marries in Afghanistan, she and her husband become part of the girl's family and live with them. I wonder what will happen when Sagia marries; where will Suroya contrive to put them?

The day drags on. Our cook and cleaning woman, Daljan, fixes a delicious lunch for us - rice and eggplant in a red sauce. The boys stop by briefly for lunch. The oldest one is discontent with his life; he feels there are no parks or places to play soccer. Of course there are no video games. He has a terrible teacher in school and is learning nothing.

He asks me about dating in the States. It intrigues him but he can't imagine doing it. After lunch I tell the girls that I must sleep. Hoosbu demands to know for how long!

After an hour they bound back in again. I only have a cloth hanging over the door opening, so I really have no privacy. I think that the day will never end.

For tonight the boys have rented another film, not violent. It is a melodramatic Bollywood romance - sort of an operetta. A boy actor sings lying on the grass. A girl hears him from far away where she is hiding behind a rock. She sings back briefly. They work their way from one hiding place to another, always closer and closer. Finally they face each other and sing and sing. They lie down together on the grass and eventually he puts his arm over her. I can't imagine what Suroya and Omar think of this. But perhaps they regard it as a harmless fairy tale and dismiss it.

Wednesday - I couldn't sleep all last night and diarrhea struck. When I was at the bazaar on Sunday, I mentioned to Khaim that I would like to find some sort of pot which I could use in the middle of the night. It was so embarrassing to discuss such a thing, but it was essential that I do so. He found a child's potty dish, not exactly what I was looking for but it will have to do. Last night it certainly got a workout. I was afraid it would overflow - it certainly isn't big enough for all this use!

At 6:00 a.m. the girls call me. We are going to the bath house. Suroya always decides when we will have a bath. I am "OK" at the bath house, but when I get home I am sick again. So back to bed. No way I can go to school. I use Cipro all morning to no avail. Our lovely cook and cleaning lady Daljan decides to be my nurse. She empties the potty. I mix up rehydration salts and drink them. Then Daljan brings me plain tea. I eat a protein bar that I brought with me on the trip. Daljan brings me homemade yogurt.

Gizu and Sadaf implored their mother before she left this morning to let them stay home to help me. They have been so attentive, so much so that I haven't been able to sleep. But I do love them. Gizu reminds me of my granddaughter, Brianne, when she was this age.

By late afternoon I am well enough to play games!!

This evening Samia and her husband Rahi invite me for dinner in their apartment. I am their first guest! Rahi is intelligent but he "puts Samia down" continually and calls her lazy. Sounds like this marriage is heading for trouble. Samia shows signs of depression; perhaps she is worried about not being pregnant yet? Well, they are married for life. So they will have to figure something out.

Thursday - After breakfast on the patio accompanied by hundreds of flies, I wait and wait for Omar to come to take me to my first school. It seems that Suroya constantly has school business which requires her visiting the schools each day. Omar is busy driving her around. After I finally arrive at one school today and teach classes, I find myself waiting an hour to be picked up to go to the next school where Samia teaches. When the morning session is over, Samia and I wait yet another hour for Omar to show up. Finally we take a cab to get home for lunch. Then I wait and wait for Omar to arrive to deliver me to the afternoon sessions at another school. Finally Omar with Suroya in the car arrives to take me. But I wait over an hour to be picked up at the end of these classes. This is not how it is supposed to be. This time Suroya arrives in another vehicle driven by a second employee of Aide to Afghanistan. We race to the airline agency across the city to get my return ticket to the U.S. But the office is closed already!

Now Suroya, the driver, and I stop at the bazaar. I just sit and watch while she has three tops made by a tailor! It is obvious now that Suroya conducts much personal business during the day while on the payroll of Aide to Afghanistan! The driver delivers the two of us to the house at 5:30. Omar is there but says he is too busy to take me to the Internet Cafe. I say I will take a cab. The answer is "no"! I will have to wait for one of the boys to accompany me in the cab. Finally Khaim shows up; we go to the Internet shop and he waits 45 minutes while I retrieve and send emails. We return just in time for dinner and the TV news which appears to have much discussion about terrorism. Remembrance of September 11.

Friday - Hard to imagine no school again but it is Friday prayer day, which is a holiday just as Sunday is in the United States. It is the only non-work day of each week. At least I was forewarned and sleep in to 7 a.m.

After breakfast Omar, Suroya, and I go back to the airline ticket office to get my return ticket.

On the way home they take me on a bit of a sight-seeing ride through bombed-out areas of the city. People live among rubble of destroyed buildings. Families huddle under single tarpaulins with "UN Aide" printed on them. They are refugees who returned to Afghanistan after the American bombing stopped. The government will not allow them to return to their original villages until housing has been rebuilt for them. It seems obvious that this could take years. I envision it never happening. These people have no access to public services such as health care. Adults are not allowed to work in Kabul. Children cannot attend school. And, of course, no electricity ever reaches them in this labyrinth of rocks. Adults must go to busy city streets and beg for money for their families. An unsolvable problem in the midst of this war-torn city.

We stop at the bombed-out mosque of the Shah's father's family. Below it a cemetery containing remains of thousands of casualties of the many years of war extends as far as the eye can see. It is just brown dirt with a brown haze over it.

Omar drives along roads with signs everywhere warning of unexploded ordnance. Large two-story buildings pierced by huge gaping bomb holes sit everywhere on this land along with bombed and broken planes and trucks. Bombed tram cars have been piled two high and two deep in a row that extends for blocks. How desolate. I wonder where the present city transportation came from and eventually put two and two together. I have been seeing quite a few Austrian tour buses driving around and wondering why so many Austrians would want to tour Kabul at this moment in time. Now I realize these busses are welcome gifts from the government of Austria.

When we arrive home I go upstairs to rest and come down an hour later to find the "tablecloth" laid out on the floor of the large room. Suroya's cousin and her nine year old daughter are here and they sit around the cloth with Suroya and all of her girls. A picture flashes through my mind of the book "The Red Tent" about the nomads of the Old Testament. The red tent was erected at each sojourn to be used by women and teenage girls with menses. The women welcomed this respite from daily duties and reveled in each other's company, often singing and dancing together. This scene in front of me now reminds me of that ancient time, especially with all the women and girls in their traditional clothing and barefoot as usual in the house.

Wonderful womens' event –
making samosas with cilantro and scallions

Immediately I somehow sense I should take a place in the circle. I learn from Sagia and Gizu exactly what to do. Suroya rolls out the dough on a huge round wooden board. Her cousin cuts it out into circles about two and a half inches in diameter. The rest of us place about a tablespoon of filling on each circle. It contains onion, chopped spinach, herbs such as cilantro, and salt. What a tantalizing smell. We press one side of the circle against the other and crimp the edges like a pie.

Suroya brings out a large steamer with several levels. She places as many "pies" as possible on all of the levels. They will steam for one hour, then other batches will be cooked until all are done. We have produced huge numbers.

While we wait for the steaming process to be finished, the young girls play school with their cousin. I brought small blackboards and chalk with me because I had no idea whether there would be blackboards in the schools. I give the girls three of the boards and some chalk and they are delighted.

Suroya's nephew, about eighteen years old, arrives unexpectedly from Iran. He has been living and working illegally in Dubai, then Iran, but has now been deported. He will live in the boys' quarter.

Finally it is time for the much-anticipated meal. The samosas are served with pieces of dried pepper and smothered with sour cream on top. They are piled in the center of large platters surrounded by red beans in a red sauce. How incredible they are with the bread. Rahi and Samia join us making a total of thirteen around the table.

Suroya's cousin and daughter leave soon. New guests arrive: Omar's brother, his wife, and two small grandchildren. I feel compelled to sit while the adults have tea although I don't understand a word of the conversation. These people live in the same neighborhood as Suroya with their four sons, their wives, and children - all in the same house. Omar's brother and his sons are all butchers.

When everyone leaves, I pay Suroya and Omar for my first week and then go upstairs to get organized for school tomorrow. What a busy, tiring day this has been.

Saturday - As Omar drives me to my first school, I see construction going on everywhere. Rebar stands atop first floors waiting for second floors to begin. Old shipping containers stand next to each building under construction. All unused building materials are locked inside for the night. The landscape is brown dirt with much of the dirt blowing into the air creating a heavy dark haze. There is no grass, no gardens. When the Shah was in power, Kabul's streets were lined with trees and gardens in abundance. Decorative pools of water graced important buildings. But now, as we drive along, we see huge empty spaces which Omar somehow tells me are littered with unexploded bombs and grenades. It is incredibly dismal.

One building we pass appears to be finished. Many colorful signs on the main floor and second level are placed on the floor next to the door of each narrow shop.

Everywhere I see more old containers left by the Russians and Americans, but clever businessmen have shops inside and live in the back. There are no windows, heat, or water, but these people have learned to survive in the worst of conditions. And I think with dismay of the extreme heat inside these windowless boxes in the summer.

It seems to me that with all of the building going on, this should be an excellent time to find work, particularly since everything is done by hand with little or no mechanized equipment. I even see hundreds of men digging holes in the median of a street. Hours later as I return, the men are planting small trees. I don't know who is financing this attempt at beautification and I wonder who will water these trees over the coming months.

Today has gone quite well so far. Omar, Suroya and I have a written plan of when Omar will take me and pick me up. But Omar misses "big time" once again and I miss my entire class. The principal and teachers are unhappy. Omar can see this, so maybe he gets the point. We will see?

The other classes go very well except for the final one where I don't particularly like the girls; they are uncooperative and unwilling to try. But I make progress in the earlier classes. Maybe with some continuum in my attendance, I will see even more progress.

On the way home, Omar stops at a meat stall on wheels. The stall is run by a nephew. A huge chunk of meat is hanging under an umbrella which is turned periodically to keep the sun off the meat. No one worries about the hundreds of flies seemingly attached to the meat. Once the nephew cuts off a chunk of meat, Omar asks him to grind it with an ancient hand grinder such as my mother and grandmother used. I wonder how one cleans out a grinder sufficiently?

I get Omar to drop me off at the Internet alone on the way home and then come and retrieve me! So I finally briefly break free of Khaim and the harem.

I feel good today; perhaps I am finally over jet-lag.

Suroya's nephew from Dubai is sick, and we all use the same dishes, simply rinsed over and over. Suroya arrives with a new tunic for each of the girls and herself, purchased at the bazaar, probably with money I paid her last night. She loves shopping and buying. I noticed that the girls wear the same outfits every day for however much time elapses between laundry days. I believe they sleep in their clothes as I have never seen any evidence that they have night clothes.

Suroya and Sagia do the laundry tonight after dinner. There are two weeks of laundry. So much! So it takes hours and hours.

Sunday - Omar is on time all day! A big improvement. I have several classes with no English teacher present -- a real waste of time. In other classes there are some bright students, but many who are not or simply don't care. And I never have the same class twice.

318

Frustrating! All the teachers at each school are so nice and friendly. At the last school today there is a big commotion outside the window. About fifty girls are scrubbing chairs and any cement areas outside. The noise is incredible! But no one tells them to stop nor can we move to another room.

It is so so hot and the flies are unbearable in every room. They perch on the girls shawls and arms, sit on the desks, and cluster at the windows.

All the clothes got washed last night, but the dry ones including my purple "play" outfit are in Suroya's locked room. So I am stranded in my room since I've removed my good "school" dress to keep it nice for tomorrow. I rest but can't sleep, drink a lot of water, and eat part of a powerbar. Now I have more energy.

It is hard to figure out the economics of this family. They have TV and DVD, a generator, but no inside toilet or running water. When I first arrived, Omar went to the neighborhood well and filled large containers which he carries in the back of his car. He filled the huge metal container in the back yard. This supplies all of our household water including that used for the laundry. Now, however, the well is not working, and he must buy water at a store.

Suroya finally comes home and brings out my purple outfit from her room and Omar agrees to take me to the Internet. Very nice.

One of the girls told me recently that Omar had denied Hoosbu's wish to go to computer school. What an opportunity it would have been for her to get a well-paying job. I guess Omar thinks girls are good for nothing but arranged marriages.

Monday - After school, relatives visit in a never-ending stream. The nearby bath house which has been closed since I arrived is open once more and we will be able to walk to our baths. About seven o'clock tonight it is obvious that no food is being prepared.

Dinner and Hidden Vodka at Relatives

One of the girls says that we are going to relatives for dinner. Omar drives us to an apartment where one of Suroya's brothers and his family live. We walk up five floors with Suroya huffing and puffing all the way. She had told me that she is not entirely well. This is a nice apartment - Suroya's brother, Asiz, wife and four children live here. Immediately all the women and girls go to the kitchen to help. I remain in the living room with Omar, Asiz (who speaks excellent English), and two small sons. Much to my amazement Asiz reaches behind a large red drapery and pulls out a couple of bottles of warm bootleg beer! He holds out a bottle and asks me if I would like some. He is not surprised when I accept because his wife drinks a bottle of beer every night to help her sleep. I am totally shocked because alcohol is forbidden in this Islamic country.

We have a delicious dinner sitting on the floor. As at Suroya's house everyone reaches in the common dish, grabbing a handful of rice and sauce. I, however, have a small dish with a fork; Suroya no doubt has seen to that. We have delicious melon because this is the melon season in Afghanistan. Dinner lasts very late and I am almost falling asleep. Finally we leave and I thankfully fall into bed at 11 p.m.

Tuesday - Omar is somewhat screwed up today, but I believe that it has to do with Suroya's needing to go to three schools and pay teachers. The students and I do a craft by glueing foam pieces of different shapes and colors onto colored construction paper -- the girls love it. One class seems to have trouble moving ahead with "Go Dog Go"; another moves so fast -- amazing. This afternoon after school many relatives call on the family: another cousin of Suroya's, then the aunt and uncle from the other day, plus several others.

Now the brother of the deported cousin has arrived also from Iran.

People are beginning to get respiratory problems. How can I avoid all of this?

This morning the huge pile of garbage is gone from the street, but a new pile is starting, just like in India.

Tonight we have a real electrical problem. First, Omar can't keep his generator going and finally it just quits (Kabul electricity is only on for an hour instead of the normal two hours). We eat by candlelight. Nice. We have a delicious dinner of meatball soup (called shurwa). I am in bed by 9:30 totally exhausted.

Wednesday - Classes have gone well in general, making tissue paper flowers which the girls love. The family has been invited to a wedding party Friday night. So tomorrow I must go with Suroya to buy more fabric that Omar will make into a proper dress. I have no jewelry or decent shoes with me. Somehow it will all work out I guess.

Thursday - I am on a different schedule every other day. Today it seems as though more girls appear than I have ever met. How can this be? There is real confusion trying to figure out where each class is in the book "Go Dog Go". It seems the class before lunch hasn't gotten very far at all. I have enough tissue paper left to make flowers with two classes today. Tomorrow it will be on to stringing beads.

Seems like we are going backwards with the reading. Guess it was too good to be true. My last two classes are thoroughly confused with all of the words. It means starting over again and going ever so slowly. But my teacher partner is very good, and gets all of the vocabulary on the board.

Off to the bazaar after classes to buy an entire wedding outfit for about $50 -- shoes, hose, jewelry, and a grey two-piece outfit. Grey bead patterns decorate the top. It is really quite lovely. Suroya says that I should get another two-piece suit made because it will be getting colder - - price unknown. Arrive back home to discover we won't be going to the wedding after all because it would mean a two-hour drive through the hills and it is not safe to drive in the dark! We would have to stay overnight and I guess they think that I can't make the grade. I am just as happy, but rue having spent the $50.

Friday (Prayer Day) - There is much work going on in the yard. The boys are building a rabbit house of bricks, one story with many openings. I sense this is a new financial venture for the family -- to raise and sell rabbits. Certainly it is Suroya's idea and not Omar's (as he probably would never have a new or creative thought).

The girls are excited to show me the new prized family acquisition: a modern four- burner gas stove with oven below in the outdoor kitchen building replacing the old two burner stove which sat on the floor (requiring the cook to squat on the ground the entire time). This reminds me of a stove I saw in a yurt in the desert in Turkmenistan where the owners used the burners but stored all manner of kitchen equipment in the oven. I am sure in this household it will be the same, because they have never used an oven. Sagia has rearranged the kitchen and dish-washing area. I realize that this is the first large expenditure made with money I paid the family. The girls tell me that the stove cost $160.

For the past two weeks two employed workers have been digging a well in the backyard. I inquire as to whether there has been a test for the presence of water. And the answer is "no". The well has not produced water, but the digging continues and the men assure me that one day there WILL be water. I believe that the hoped-for water will be used to water the vegetable garden in the summer.

There seems to have been a great push to clean up the yard. The boys and even the girls have been busy picking up stalks, old plants, and loose sticks. The boys even rake the area and the final result is a much improved appearance.

The "Pik-nik" and Purduh

Suddenly, out of the blue, the girls announce that we will go on a "pik-nik". They tell me to rush and get ready. The girls fold up the carpet we use on the patio and stuff it in the trunk of the car, along with the old two-burner stove plus all the food necessary to prepare a meal "out in the green". Two huge bags of spare clothes for the boys and the two small girls must be included plus a large blanket.

Thirteen people pile into the car, the women sometimes sitting three deep in the back seat and the boys of course with no one on their laps. It is so very hot but Omar only runs the air conditioner intermittently. We have to keep the windows rolled up because of the inconceivably thick cloud of brown dust surrounding us. We drive one and a half hours in terrible traffic; everyone else in the city is going to the "green" today also. The road winds up and up. Finally Omar stops the car and we begin extricating ourselves. The girls tell me this is a national park. All I see are a few trees and further along the path to a narrow creek. Everyone carries some of the gear. We go down to the creek, cross and go up the other side to a slightly flatter area which Suroya pronounces is the "spot" for the picnic. The boys lay out the carpet, then hang up the blanket by two corners next to our site. When I inquire the reason for this, the girls tell me it is "purduh" - - the practice of protecting women and girls from the view of non-family men. Because we seem to be in a secluded area, I exclaim in astonishment, "Why"? The girls point way up the creek bed to a couple sheep herders eating their lunch. They are the possible culprits.

Blanket tied up for "Purduh"

Sadaf and Gizu run off eagerly to play in the creek wearing their long sleeves and long trousers. They are thrilled to lie down and roll over in what to them is a huge amount of water. I realize that they have never experienced water that isn't poured on them in a bathhouse. This is such a wonderful treat for them. The big boys get into their own water act, throwing and splashing it at each other. They are so excited to see small fish and a frog! The water fun goes on for at least an hour. Suroya seems to have the executive privilege of rolling up her trousers and wading in the stream, but the older girls remain quietly on the carpet. The boys climb into dry clothes behind the blanket and go off to play volleyball along the path. Omar immerses several melons in the creek to cool off. The young girls continue to play in the creek while the others start to prepare dinner. We peel the scallions and wash them in the creek along with the grapes -- giardia waiting to happen if I ever saw it. Sagia has been preparing the rice and sauce.

Cleaning scallions and washing them in the creek

Sadaf and Gizu emerge from the creek and change their clothes behind the blanket. We all gather around the carpet for this most unusual event. After dinner Omar retrieves the melons (kharbusa), slices them, and we all savor this traditional seasonal treat. The dishes are washed in the river. When all is cleaned up, Suroya, the older girls, and I sit on the carpet and Suroya unexpectedly produces my Go Fish cards from my bedroom! She says she has been hearing about this game for days from the girls and she wants to see what it is all about. She learns the game quickly and we enjoy several hands. In the meantime the older boys take the two younger girls to a cleared area with a swing set.

Now the older girls decide to try their hand at volleyball on the path and are actually very good. While they continue, I wander over to the playground and realize that my "minder" is right there behind me!

We pack everything in the car to go home. Another suffocating packed journey and seemingly more traffic, probably due to the end of the holiday.

Soon after we arrive home, Suroya gives a command that we are going to a relative's house for dinner and that I should wear my "wedding outfit" which I do. The boys and Omar never get dressed up for anything. But Samia does even though Suroya wears every-day clothes. Our hosts are Omar's brother and his wife. Their four grown sons all live with them, along with their wives and children. One has a five year boy and a two year girl, both of whom I met when they came for tea last week. The other couple has a one year old daughter. Everyone, particularly the men, cannot get enough of holding, fondling and kissing these babies.

I have noticed that all Afghan women, including the schoolgirls, have a fetish about their shawls, adjusting them constantly.

Now dinner is ready. All the children are banished to eat in another room, leaving only adults. This is truly an Afghan banquet -- so many dishes and all delicious. There is even yogurt and a wonder-ful custard which I have not seen before. There are thirteen of us sitting on cushions around the cloth which is piled high with food.

Saturday - Last night was really late and I am exhausted as I get up at 5:00 a.m. to go the bath house. I ask Omar to find a photocopier to make more copies of the "Go Dog Go" book. He gets the fin-ished product back about 6:00 p.m. What a total disaster! At 10:30 I am still trying to make sense out of it. It is stapled with back page first, Arabic style. Impossible. But I wasted only six dollars. Rahi says he will get them done at the Italian embassy where he is working with the Italians to create a judicial code, "law of the land", for Afghanistan. He shows me some of the draft work they have completed. Italians! Their English is not correct, but they claim they have a right to have their own English! It should not be only the domain of America and England. We will see if the Italians can do the copying job properly.

Sunday - One class makes tissue paper flowers and loves it. I am doing traditional memory games, laying out several items on a tray. Then I remove one while the girls close their eyes. They have to guess which one was removed. The girls are enthralled.

One of my teeth crumbled a few days ago. Today I mix epoxy from a kit I carry, but it doesn't set up the way it should. I rub on a thick layer over the hole hoping it will do the job?

I never seem to know the what the "scoop" is in this house. Where is my towel? Will we go to the bath house tomorrow? Will my washed outfit ever get ironed? It is the eight-year-old Sadaf's job to do the ironing for the whole family. She does it in the evening when the city power is on. Power failures are frequent and the other night it took Omar two hours to get the generator started. Sadaf was still ironing at midnight.

Today I see a Czech aide group driving around on my way to school. Our teachers tell me that a fourth Aide for Afghanistan school has opened. It was built by Denmark. Italy talks a lot about building a school, but won't part with their aide money. Where are the Americans?

I have now figured out that Suroya's girls will never go to the bazaar alone, even as adults. Husbands will always buy the food for the family as Omar does. However I see many women in the small markets as we drive along. Maybe it is a "class" thing? Why can Suroya go anywhere she wants? Our family girls know only school, their compound, and riding in the car!

Tonight we watch the entire video of Samia's wedding. I feel like I am there. The dancing is amazing. The men and women were in the same room but dance in separate areas.

Monday - The car is "broken", but later I discover that it was needed by the office. Suroya and her driver have books to deliver to the schools. I am a passenger, but of course, never on time because Suroya talks so long to everyone. Consequently, I miss the first ten minutes at each school. At my last school the principal gives me three classes (sixty children) who hardly know their alphabet. So I just do songs with them. We sing, "I'm a Little Teapot", and I teach "This Is the Way We Sweep the Floors, Cook the Pilau (rice), Iron the Clothes" and so on. I sing and we all do the actions together. I teach the Hokie Pokie in one class; it thrills them.

Suroya says she will be home at 5:00 pm to take me shopping, but she arrives at 6:15 and complains that she is too tired to go. However, one of her many brothers who has a taxi shows up and drives me, and of course my "minder", Khaim, to Chicken Street, the famous Kabul shopping area. We find a book store that sells books in English. The shop owner produces a two-volume set of Afghan history as a gift for Samia. We walk through the rest of the stores along the street which offer nothing but western food products - worthless. I hope I can find some handicrafts somewhere? It is impossible to shop other times because I can only go with Suroya's permission.

The ugly head of domestic violence has arisen. The older kids always hit the younger ones, usually for little reason. While we are all sitting around before dinner tonight, Khaim really socks Gizu for no apparent reason and no seems to see it or say a word. Finally later Suroya tells him not to do it again after she sees my disapproving look - but, of course, he will. This behavior is learned from others and never stops. I am certain he will do it to his children.

After dinner we watch a video of Samia's henna ceremony the night before her wedding. This is the day the bride has her hands painted with henna designs. The men and womens' dancing once again is fabulous.

328

Tuesday - The promised bath does not materialize because Suroya is sleeping. Omar and the car again are missing. So I have to take a taxi and Roki, one of the deported cousins, has to go along as my "minder" and sit all day at all three schools. He does get free lunch.

School is so frustrating. I never get the same class two times, and, if I do, it is a beginning class. Where is that class that only had eight pages to go to finish "Go Dog Go"? Today I do more songs to cut down my frustration. We do the Hokie Pokie in several classes. In the last class today I finally do the bead necklace project and IT WORKS! Our daughter, Jenny, who gave me the elastic thread and beads, explained that the thread would stretch and go over the girls heads, but I've always been skeptical that it wouldn't work. The girls are skeptical also. I use pre-cut elastic lengths and then explain how to tie a knot at one end, thread the beads on, and then tie a very secure knot attaching the two ends. Using hand signs I show them that if the knot is not secure the beads will go all over; this elicits a few small smiles. Then I show them how we will pull a necklace over a girl's head, but they look extremely doubtful.

Stringing bead necklaces

It is gratifying to see how intent they are on their stringing. Finally one finishes and ties her knot. I ask her in sign language if it is a very good knot and she says yes. Because every Afghan girl has a thick ponytail, I show the girl next to her how to lift the ponytail up and pull the necklace over her friend's head. The entire circle stops threading and looks with trepidation at this procedure as does the girl who made the necklace. But the necklace slides down over her hair and head, and a lovely delighted smile spreads over her face as the other girls exhale in relief. Another girl fails to tie her knot securely; the beads spill all over the floor. Everyone looks mortified. Then they all help retrieve the beads and the girl begins her project again. When all the girls are proudly wearing their necklaces I snap a picture. This is a true success story.

The principal in one school tells me that the class schedule has been changed. Now classes will only last thirty minutes instead of forty-five minutes (what can a child learn in one-half hour?). The principal's explanation is that the days are getting shorter! Come on! Well it wrecks my time schedule. I spend needless time waiting for Omar's brother because he doesn't know the new schedule. When I get home the Minister of Education announces on TV the new shorter schedule. But it won't hold true for Suroya's schools! Interesting to see who shows up and when tomorrow. Suroya says she will call at 6:00 p.m. to see if the Internet is working, but, of course, her phone battery is dead because she talked all day!

I am catching cold. At 6:30 pm I take two Vitamin C pills and three Ibuprofin. Samia has been coughing all over everything and everyone for three days. She complains of terrible pains in her stomach yesterday and today. Either she will miscarry or it is a tubal pregnancy. I tell her to inform Suroya, but Suroya is so "busy", Samia can't find a chance to get through to her!

Where is Omar if Samia needs to go to the hospital? Rumor has it that he went to visit his mother.

The two young women whose house we visited for dinner last night show up for tea with their children. They are all dressed in beautiful clothes. All our children leave the room except Sadaf and Gizu who love to carry the babies around. So I conclude that I can leave and go upstairs.

In the evening we all sit after dinner waiting for the electricity to come on. Sadaf teases Gizu; Gizu drags Sadaf by a leg. Sadaf carries on - -unhurt I feel. But Gizu is in trouble and right there Samia slaps Gizu hard on the cheek while Suroya cuddles Sadaf. I am so glad that I will only be here three weeks instead of four!

Wednesday - While I am waiting for Omar this morning on the patio, Suroya and Sagia are in the living room alone - no one else around. Suddenly Sagia comes running out to the patio sobbing uncontrollably, throwing up over the edge of the patio. I think it is a symptom of shock. I believe Suroya beat Sagia on the head unmercifully. When Suroya comes out, I ask, "What is wrong with Sagia?" and she answers that she is sick. I DON'T THINK SO! This afternoon when I get home Sagia sports a layer of gauze wrapped around her head and bruise marks on her face! So I was wrong in my thinking last night; parents abuse the children too.

Turns out Suroya didn't go to work today. Khaim tells me she had a bad headache. I don't believe it. She spends the day having the boys rearrange the living room! Once more they are also in my room while I am gone. Lies again. Suroya tells me to come down at 5:00 p.m. for melon, but there is no melon cut. Promises, promises.

We make bead necklaces in two classes in two schools. Great success. However, I feel I am going backwards with the classes learning English. I am given more and more level one groups who only know the alphabet. Since they only learn by rote, the girls know nothing of phonics; making the letter sounds means nothing to them. I simply can't cope with this since there is no way to help them move along.

The wind blows all day like a sandstorm. Tonight the temperature drops; it's the end of September. After school I make bead necklaces with Suroya's girls, but Suroya doesn't like to allow any child to sit for more than five minutes without an assigned task, so the project is disrupted time after time.

Khaim goes with me to the Internet by taxi but it is closed. We try a couple other Internet shops but they are all closed. Apparently something about a lost connection.

It is unbelievably dusty in the city, so much dirt just hanging in the air.

Thursday - Last night I slept with long underwear plus my old Hong Kong tee shirt so the weather is definitely changing.

At Qali-Wasir School after reading we sing some songs and dance the Hokie Pokie. The male principal observes and is extremely pleased. For once he doesn't give me sixty girls at one time. A second class looks like they will finish Go Dogs Go.

At Perwan School the girls present me with a hand-made cloth doll. So sweet. Four girls sing loudly and beautifully to me. A girl gives me a pen she decorated and my favorite teaching partner gives me a bracelet she made with the necklace beads. I can't believe the love they are showing me, and here I came to bring love to them! How touching. I must hurry now to finish the Go Dog Go book in two different classes because time is running out.

Jebran, Khaim's brother, takes me to a new photocopy store to re-copy the book. $50 for twenty books! Really, really expensive. But I feel compelled to leave the teachers with some new unworn copies so they can continue to teach from the book. Afterward Jebran takes me to a handicraft store where I purchase some wooden boxes of terrible quality. But at least they are from Afghanistan, which is what counts. Also I find five lapis lazuli hearts on chain necklaces as gifts for the family girls.

Tonight one of Omar's brothers arrives with his four small children for dinner. His wife died suddenly two months ago at the time of Samia's wedding celebration. The eight-year-boy has obvious problems with the loss of his mother; he plays and plays with Sadaf's baby doll-- cuddles and cuddles and loves it. Very sad. There are no workshops here to help children work through grief.

* * *

Slaughtering a goat in my honor, Parties, Goodbyes, and the Sound of Music "Goodbye" song

Friday - Very early this morning, before I am up, ten mullahs arrive to read the Koran with the men in our family, while all the females are secluded in Suroya's room. Then Suroya serves the men breakfast. Last evening Suroya bought a live goat to be sacrificed today, and then, like in Uzbekistan, they will cut it up, give some to neighbors and relatives and we will have goat meat for dinner today, a rare treat for a family that seems to never have meat. I suspect that today is a special occasion in my honor but I am not sure.

The children turn the goat loose in the yard and are chasing it with hilarity. Sickening. This is certainly a different world view.

Once this morning Khaim jumps at Gizu to beat her and she cowers down. I point at him and say, "Don't do it". When Jebran later reports this to Suroya in private (as the children report everything I say and do), she says she will tell Khaim not to do it after today! Not likely.

Now they have a hat on the goat and are leading it to slaughter. The excitement is mounting! I suppose I should join the family, but cannot bring myself to do it and go upstairs to my room and pull the draperies.

In two hours the girls come to get me. By this time the butcher (one of Omar's nephews) has cut all of the goat up and put some in ten small packages to give to the poor. I explain to Rahi why I could not attend the event. He agrees that people should not laugh and torment an animal, but should show respect.

Now we have the celebratory meal in my honor. I sit next to Omar who gives me special desirable cuts such as the stomach and some of the intestines. He encourages me to eat more and more. Eventually I am happy to go to my room. I realize that I am exhausted and stressed. It has been a good thing to have this "rest" day. I am sort of at the end of my rope. I put so much effort into each class session. It is so tiring to do this easy work over and over six days a week, with the girls never "getting" it.. I also feel such pressure moving from one school to the next and starting in again. There are six hours of teaching each day and often as much as forty minutes driving from one school to the next.

Jebran has been great today. He has gone three times to get the books from the printer and each time the shop is closed (just like Italy). I need the books for tomorrow - but I won't have them. We were to have gone for a bath at 1:00 p.m. but true to form, Suroya "misspoke" - who knows when we will go?

Saturday - I feel so rested today because I didn't have to work yesterday; I really needed that break. Today two classes have finished Go Dog Go. "Hooray!" I expect the girls to smile at the last page where the dogs are having a party on top of a tree, but there is never a snicker. I finally realize that the entire concept of such a silly adventure with talking dogs simply never registers in their minds - such an absolutely foreign idea to them.

But at least they learned the words. At home I teach the family girls the Hokie Pokie and they absolutely love it.

At the Internet this afternoon I write for an hour and am ready to send it but suddenly it is "lost". Certainly not a new experience for me. After dinner this evening Suroya says, "what is this Hokie Pokie - I want to learn it". I arrange them all in a circle including the brothers and cousins. Omar declines to participate. Everyone has a marvelous time.

Sunday - I ask Suroya to make reservations for dinner for Thursday night so I can take everyone out to eat. I imagine she won't get it done. Also I have asked her several times to order a cake that I can share with the teachers at the three schools during breaks. I ask Rahi what to buy Suroya and Omar as a goodbye gift, but he has no ideas. I ask him to order a decorated cake for the Thursday night dinner and he agrees.

Omar's car is still on the blink. He must be losing a great deal of money by paying taxis to do his work!

Monday - I receive close to fifty gifts from the girls at the schools as they had heard this is my last week. Lovely embroidery. Why doesn't my family embroider? I have spent every moment this afternoon writing thank you notes.

Tonight at long last, we attend a wedding party; not one but two. They take place in two different rooms in the same large building. I am wearing my "weeding" outfit (Suroya's pronounciation) in all its glory. Amazingly, Suroya is dressed up, as is Sadaf. But Gizu is in a sports outfit. Having seen Samia's wedding video I know what to expect tonight. At the first wedding the men and women are separated by a curtain. Both groups dance unseen by the other. The women dance beautifully. The food tables are set for twelve women and children with many, many platters of delicious food. At the second wedding we watch the bride and groom walk in together while a woman walks behind holding some type of religious object over their head. They walk first through the mens' area and then the womens', ending up on a stage for photos. Gizu dances in the womens' area and is absolutely amazing. Suroya asks me to dance, so I do, using all that I remember from dancing in Tajiki-stan. The women clap to the music while I dance so I guess I perform alright. We get home at 11:30. Will I be able to hang on until Friday?

Tuesday - We do lots of songs and games at the schools. Today I only teach in the advance English classes and we play two different memory games in most classes. However, three advanced classes have now finished "Go Dog Go", a real accomplishment. We go to Suroya's brother's house again for dinner. Asiz has his stash of bottles behind the curtain. This time it is bootleg vodka with Pepsi. I drink my vodka straight - very nice. I probably have two or three shots!

Wednesday - This is my last day at school. A couple of my favorite teachers are not here. I wanted to give the copies of the books and staplers to them. At Perwan school the principal keeps appropriating the staplers for the school and I keep reiterating that they are for the teacher. Probably all my work has been in vain: finding and buying the extra-strong staplers for the teachers, leaving small blackboards for the absent teachers, but I have done all I could.

Also, at the Perwan School one class is making good progress through "Ten Apples Up on Top".

I tell the girls that I am leaving tomorrow. I say goodbye and they start to weep uncontrollably. It seems that the only thing I can do is to kiss and hug each girl; so I do so while we all cry including the teacher. It is so emotional.

At the next two schools the girls give me hundreds of gifts and notes. At Qwal-i-wasir School I tell them goodby and they also start to cry. Again I kiss and hug each one. They cling to me in seeming despair. Maybe I am the best friend any of them has ever had. They sob and then turn to the wall still sobbing. This is extremely emotional. I will never forget them and this love we have shared.

336

When I get back to the house I am exhausted. I start getting supplies organized that I want to leave for each school and writing thank-you notes.

Diarrhea strikes. I don't go to dinner. Terrible chills are overcoming me and every muscle aches.

Thursday - I was sick all night. Kabul Electric was off since early last evening and my flashlight batteries are very low - perhaps having been left on one time. I am so weak that when I get up at night I keep falling on the floor in the dark. Finally I find my rehydration salts, mix and start drinking them, and feeling better. I told Suroya last night that I couldn't go to the zoo today, but by 8:00 a.m. I eat some bread and milk and decide to go.

Suroya has outdone herself. She arranged to have the zoo closed except for her schools. She rented buses for all the children. I ride in a car with her. As we enter I see a sign saying that an international organization is supervising the zoo! We visit the animals: six huge bears, two vultures, a gazelle, a tortoise, a lion, several wolves and a couple monkeys. Each class in each school has brought their own lunch and tablecloth. Every group clamors for me to come and sit with them, but, of course, I can't show partiality. Finally the headmaster of Perwan School with the other principals and teachers from each school stand up. He says the teachers have all worked together to make a traditional Afghan costume for me as well as for my granddaughter, Kayla. What an overwhelming surprise! I just cannot believe it! All the stitching has been done by hand. The two dresses are amazing pieces of work.

As the picnics are gathered up, I attempt to reach every teacher and hug her and thank her. Again, what an emotional time. As we head out the gates of the zoo, children are crying. They line up outside of the gate. As I walk farther and farther away, I feel a sudden impulse to turn, lift one arm, and sing the Sound of Music "Goodbye" song. I know I will never see these girls again.

Tonight I take the family and Suroya's brother, Asiz, and his family to dinner at a restaurant. Rahi made the reservations for me and also brings the cake decorated with "Thank You Mrs. Suroya and Mr. Omar". Even though no else is at the restaurant we sit tightly squeezed in a hot, breathless room because of purduh - it must be certain that no man will see the women in our group. The whole group of twenty is served for $100.

The meal includes the usual food plus individual kabobs. Everyone falls ravenously on the meal and finishes it in less than ten minutes. Now it is time for the cake. Suroya and Omar hold the knife together and cut large pieces to be shared by several people eating with their hands.

Last night I wrapped the lapis lazuli gifts for the girls in small pieces of gift paper and put $20 in an envelope for the boys. Just before leaving for the restaurant tonight I realize that I did not put the gift packets in my purse, so I went back upstairs to find two of the necklace gifts opened -- paper on the floor and necklaces missing! I am really disappointed in whoever did this. I report it to Rahi and he says it couldn't have happened because the children are taught otherwise! One of the boys goes back upstairs to look and finds the two unwrapped necklaces on the steps. So when I give the gifts at dinner I just hand the unwrapped necklaces to Hoosbu and Sagia and the wrapped ones to Gizu and Sadaf. After we return home I find that the culprit also ate most of the energy bars I had laid out for my trip. In general, however, the evening went very well. The cake was beautiful. Everyone loved it and had a good time.

Friday - I have been resting most of the day trying to wind down from last night. For tonight Suroya has arranged a party for me with Asiz and his family joining us. She has asked a small musical group to come. It includes two of her brothers. The band arrives and sets up; they have two drums and a self air inflating keyboard (sort of like a concertina). One band member starts the festivities by dancing. One by one the other men take their turn including the brothers and Asiz. Omar and Khaim dance facing each other. Omar is so swarthy that I feel I am watching them dance around a fire out in the desert, Bedouin-style. I take my turn as well as the two younger girls. Gizu is an incredible dancer, as though she is in another world. I say goodnight and goodbye at 10:30 p.m. It was very nice for Suroya to arrange this for me, but I suspect that they have family parties fairly often.

Saturday - We arrive at the airport at 7:30 a.m. Suroya allows my favorite Gizu to join us. It is hard to part with her even now. She is very controlled at first but then goes to a seat and begins to cry uncontrollably. Everything is chaotic and Suroya is pushing and pulling me from line to line. Finally I climb the steps to the plane and give a final wave to Suroya, Omar, and Gizu.

*   *   *

I was told yesterday by Ariana Airline that I would get a dayroom in Dubai for $50, but once we land, there is confusion all day long. I wait in one line, then another, receiving different information at each place. This is Terminal 2 - no day rooms. Passengers with luggage are bussed to Terminal 1. I need special permission to go through my backpack to get the things I am going to need tonight; then it is relocked while the officials watch.

Terminal 1 seems to be a maze; I cannot find the hotel section. I go up elevators, here and there. Finally I find it with rooms at $130 per night. So I take the room, have a wonderful bath, go down to the bar for a Manhattan, a draft beer, and lasagna (made with lamb that looks raw to me) which I only eat in part. To bed by 6:00 p.m. I set my alarm clock to be up at 1:00 a.m. to walk downstairs to get my boarding pass, then back up to my room to sleep fitfully until 4:00. Finally I enter the gate waiting room.

I board the plane. Incredibly I get a whole back seat. Yeah! Hope my bags are there when I get to Newark!

La Ruta Maya

Maya Ruins and the Corn God

I n January 2003 Jim and I meet our Explore tour group in Merida, Mexico for a trip to the Mayan ruins of southern Mexico and Guatemala. A large festival, Dia de los Reyes (Day of the Three Wise Men), is in progress. There are mariachi bands, colorful folk dance shows, and snack food stands everywhere.

We travel south to Uxmal, best preserved of the ancient sites, and climb our first Mayan pyramid. I discover an un-restored area overgrown with bushes and trees growing out of the roofs of temples and am surprised to see a stone phallic symbol where fertility prayers were offered by the people. We see many beautiful birds singing songs we have never heard before.

We reach the jungle-covered complex at Palenque in the Chiapas province of southern Mexico. This is the finest surviving example of Mayan architecture, dating from 600 to 800 AD. Pakal was a club-footed king, represented by the heiroglyphic signs of sun and shield, which appear on many bas-reliefs. The sculptured wall panels and roofs remind me of buildings at Angkor Wat in Cambodia.

We climb down inside one of the pyramids to see King Pakal's tomb --and this reminds me of Egypt!

Crossing the border with Guatemala we drive through gorgeous highlands scenery where corn grows on every hillside and at every angle like patchwork quilts. The waterfalls at Agua Azul provide a refreshing change from ruins. We climb a long way to the top and even walk behind one of the falls. When we return, we find the bus bogged in sand in the parking lot which requires some real "road building" with stones and planks and some of our men pushing the bus to get it out.

To Lake Atitlan the next morning. With its stunning blue water, it is considered to be one of the most beautiful mountain lakes in the world. Three tall volcanoes overlook the lake, their slopes purple near the top and olive green near the bottom. I learned about this famous lake in my first-year high school Spanish class and am thrilled to see it at last. The lake lies in a collapsed caldera 980 feet deep.

A boat takes us to a quiet lagoon to swim off the boat. The water is not cold and is truly beautiful. Then the boat motors slowly across the lake (about two hours) to Santiago Atitlan. We walk up a long set of stairs from the dock to the village at the top of the hill.

At the end of the one street stands a centuries-old church. Inside along both sides of the walls of the church, stand wooden statues of the saints. Local women make clothes of fabric for them and change the garments each year. On the carved wooden pulpit there are three sets of carvings: a Quetzal bird, a Mayan god, and a lion and a deer with wings. The corn motif reaches all around the outside of the carvings and a row of carved beaded work frames the outside. I actually meet the young man who was employed by the church to do the carved beaded frame.

The corn god is God here. The Spanish call him "San Simon", the mestizos "Maximon", and the Mayans "Ry Laj Man". He is the revered deity found all throughout the Guatemalan Highlands. In the center of the altar stands a large glass-enclosed case containing a draped effigy of this god. He has a large cigar protruding from his lips. Jesus never has the place of honor in churches in this area but is always off to the right side. People bring the god cigarettes and bottles of the local firewater; they request his blessings. A local elder, a "cofradia member", cares for him. This welcome responsibility switches to a different cofradia each year. It is fascinating to encounter this ancient religion. I feel privileged to have the chance to enter into a previously unknown world for me. This is what I like so much about traveling, the chance to experience local religions and customs. .

In the morning we drive to a small Indian town high in the hills, Chichicastenango. It is an important center for the pagan rites of "Mayan Catholicism" with shamanistic undertones, those of the Corn God. Our bus turns on a dirt road, drives only a short way until the driver tells us he can go no further. We begin walking along the path, passing a cemetery where the crosses all face east to the rising sun. Ears of corn are tied on top of the crosses.

At a small town square, there is a cross decorated with painted images of corn on each of the four corners. Corn ears are tied on top of each one. There is a "Catholic" church indicated by the cross on top. However, it is not really "Catholic". The only Catholic sacrament that the Indians observe is baptism. Long ago the Indians turned out the priests and shamans took over the building. Shamans squat in various places on the floor of the building, surrounding their clients with lighted candles and shaking dried herbal branches over them while chanting continuously. Never before have I seen so many shamans practicing their healings in one place! There is a mysterious feeling about the place because of all the candles and chanting.

Corn god in place of honor. Jesus to the side

We continue down the path to a small thatched building. We enter and sit on chairs in a narrow area at the front of the building. There are dried corn plants and leaves hanging down vertically like a curtain between us and the secret rear of the building where the figure of the Corn God resides. I can peep through between the leaves and see the dressed figure.

The cofradia in charge of the effigy at present explains that each guardian has the job for two years. He is in charge of parading the god around the village during festival days. He has to buy new clothes for him and "throw" parties in his honor. These events cost him a great deal of money, but he welcomes the debt he accumulates. Sometimes he presides over the sacrificing of goats and chickens.

Several other cofradias enter the room and pour Quetzalteca Especial for us in honor of the god. We toast the god several times! I wish we could be here at the time of a religious festival in his honor.

On to Antigua, the original capital of Guatemala, an attractive, charming city with great views of two volcanoes. There are over 30 Spanish language schools. The streets are cobblestoned and twisted. We visit an original villa complete with garden, a monastery, churches, markets. I want to climb a volcano but our pre-trip information from Explore never mentioned that we should bring hiking boots. So I settle for horseback riding which proves very unsatisfactory because I am with two beginners. We only ride through corn fields!

We drive on to Guatemala City, the present capital, and fly out to Flores in the north, then proceed to Tikal, the most famous and impressive of all the Mayan sites. The Maya settled in this area 700 B.C., and probably built this huge site on top of a hill to avoid swampy ground.

The very steep-sided pyramids rise up to 130 feet. The site is within the jungle. The plazas and pyramids have all been cleared of rainforest; but when you walk from one place of interest to another, you wander through the jungle with branches and vines all around you. There is abundant flint for building stone tools to help in construction of the buildings.

The Mayans devised a new method of warfare. Their army would encircle the enemy and throw spears at them. A brutal system, which allowed the people of Tikal to eliminate competitors for this area and become the dominant kingdom covering 30 square miles with a population of 100,000.

Back into Mexico, to Tulum, which is set on a cliff above white sand beaches. Our hotel is on the beach and this water is warm. We have the next day to swim and visit cenotes (sacred sinkholes).

Our last stop is at famous Chichen Itza, where we see a huge statue of Quetzalcoati and come to the end of our great explorations with sacred overtones.

Bangladesh, Sikkim, Bhutan

I arrived in Dhaka in the fall of 2004 after many exhausting legs of the journey. First Denver to LA, then LA to Taipei (14 hours) to change planes. I felt so sorry for the parents of babies: having to wake them in the middle of the night and drag everything off the plane for a one and one half hour layover. Next I had a four hour flight to Singapore and a nine-hour layover. I got a day room for $58 in Singapore and slept well. Then four hours to Dhaka, Bangladesh, arriving 10:30 p.m. My taxi driver found the hotel where I would be meeting my British tour Explore group in two days. I really needed some good sleep and a little wandering around in the area (R&R, I guess you'd call it).

*   *   *

Bangladesh - Very Liberal Muslims

I have my roommate. Her name is Jo, once a parole officer. A tough cookie who marshaled her husband through five years of life, chemo and all, that he wouldn't have had. They kept taking long trips during all of that time. I like her.

A bus tour takes us down to Old Dhaka for a boat tour on the Dhaleshwari River. Everywhere on both sides of the river there are brick kilns and people breaking up bricks with hammers (all day long). The powder that results provides the grainy stuff for making cement. Bricks and hammers create cement which is the main industry of this river area.

Now we're walking through the noisiest, most confusing bazaar I have ever been in. We must keep our eye on the person ahead of us. Still people tend to get lost because they stop momentarily to look at something. This means Jason, our guide, has been running back and forth looking for them. Finally, he puts us back on our bus to be safe while he does another complete trip around the market looking for our missing tour member. We sit on the bus about half an hour in unbearable heat; finally the missing woman shows up. She happened to take a wrong turn while following the group. Easy to do.

We are on our way early the next morning at 7:30 for a day filled with lots of driving. We stop at an ancient village named Puthia to see old buildings. The locals stare at us, always a good sign that we are off the traditional tourist path. We have a box lunch from the hotel to get us through the day. In our hotel room for the night, the electric wiring is truly a mess. Cords dangle everywhere, bathroom pipes are fastened all over the walls including the bedroom, and it's our first example on this trip of the Asian ceiling shower heads which invariably drench the entire room. Jason has us change roommates because we have an uneven number of women. How this helps the situation I don't understand. Now instead of Jo, I have "know-it-all Kate".

We're off the next morning at 7:30 because we again have a great distance to cover. Mahasthangarh, from the 3rd century B.C., is the

348

oldest city in Bangladesh, and today it is a huge archeological site of foundations and hillocks. There are remains of the world's largest Buddhist monastery where one can still discern cells for 211 monks. There is also a tall structure in the middle of the site, but there is no way to enter it and maybe there never was.

We have lunch at a Thai restaurant with good food. The ruins and the restaurant prove to be the only stops of the day. It is 8:15 p.m. as we pull into our hotel. I have no roommate tonight because I am the extra person. We drove on "B" roads today to get to the archeological site. They were just dirt tracks. But it was a great way to see the lush, green countryside and the people who farm it and swim in the Jumuna River. It is really part of the Bramaputra River which has its origins in Tibet at Mt. Kailesh. Bangladesh countryside is so peaceful and so green. The rice paddies go to the river's edge. There are few trees and buildings.

Our hotel is in Rangput, a tiny town that forms a crossroad for intersecting traffic. The bus drives us on narrow dirt paths the next morning to the edge of a river, where two men in a dug-out canoe take us over to the other side. And there, at the water's edge, is a tiny village of thatched houses. Jason takes us inside one of them where there is a wooden bed frame and mattress with a baby sleeping in the middle of it. We see large containers for storing rice and water. Extra saris and men's clothes hang on hooks on the wall. The cooking equipment and fireplace are outside in the courtyard. These are very primitive living conditions, typical of those in the rural areas of the country.

We walk west on a dirt path to an amazing Hindu temple which is considered one of the most spectacular monuments in Bangladesh. It is the country's finest example of the ancient brick and terracotta style. All of its surfaces, inside and out, all available spaces, are covered with superb decorations. Terracotta panels depict thousands of tiny flowers and figures. These are not the large bas-reliefs of Angkor Wat, but somehow they feel a bit similar, only smaller in size.

Lunch is in a tiny hamlet in a working man's restaurant. Noisy, but a nice combination of dishes. Nothing really spicy. We eat with our hands after using antibiotic cleanser.

Today on the bus I am sitting next to our local guide and I learn tremendous amounts of information about Bangladesh. He explains that Bangladeshi Muslims are very liberal; they don't follow their clerics' teachings. Young people can choose their own husband or wife; rarely is there an arranged marriage. Family planning has been in existence since about 1976 and our guide's mother worked in that first office. Families now have only two to three children due to the availability of condoms, birth control pills and tubal ligation. However, as in all Third World countries, rural families still have many children because parents need help with the crops.

There is a primary school in each village so children only need to walk one to two kilometers. The government pays for the books, and gives 500 taka to the family each quarter to encourage them to keep the children in school.

Bangladesh is a constitutional republic with a multiparty parliamentary democracy and universal suffrage. 70% of the people are Muslims and 29% are Hindus. In addition, tribal people still exist and animism continues to influence their beliefs.

We read at home about the terrible flooding along the rivers every year, but it is a necessary evil because the flooding brings the fertile silt up onto the fields. While inhabitants expect the flood, that doesn't mean that many people won't be affected since they have no where else to go.

The farmers grow three crops of rice each year. They also raise jute, tumeric and goats.

The vistas as we drive along are idyllic. Water everywhere. Rice being planted. Everything is green and gorgeous.

My guide also talks about the Grameen Bank which was the prototype of microcredit experiments all over the world. Poor women have benefited tremendously with this credit system; women are entitled to borrow small sums of money from the bank and repay it from their business profits.

The last three hours of driving have been on very curvy roads constantly going uphill. We arrive at our dirty hotel very late. The carpets are as filthy as in Chinese hotels, and of course, the shower sprays all over the bathroom.

We go through customs this morning in order to enter the West Bengal State of India. It takes us two hours, but we are lucky, since it usually takes three. We fill out the same forms three times at three different locations. The clerks have no computers. Everything is done in ledgers; three different people copy the same information into three different ledgers!

We have a new guide, Mr. Ali, and a bigger, noisier bus. The seats are tight and narrow and there is no air conditioning! We drive up, up, up to a very interesting monastery, then down to the river, and then up and down again all day long. Finally we are on the long road paralleling the railroad tracks that lead up to Darjeeling, the famous hill town where British ex-pats escaped from the oppressive heat of lower parts of India. It is a charming town and our hotel is posh -- obviously it catered to the rich from the time it was built by the British. The employees are so very courteous.

In the morning we drive to a sunrise viewing site which overlooks the huge mountains of the Himalaya. Then we visit the Everest Museum, a Tibetan handicraft building, and finally the zoo where we see two magnificent snow leopards, one male and one female. They have successfully bred here -- slowly the numbers are increasing.

We take a ride on the Toy Train, a narrow gauge steam train. The track actually turns around on itself at a place along the route. At

Ghoom we visit a huge Buddhist monastery. Mr. Ali and Jason both talk to us at length about Buddhism.

The lights in the hotel switch alternately off and on all afternoon, perhaps due to a faulty generator. It is even too dark to take a shower. During an "on" time I write a forty-five minute long email to Jim, but when I push "Send" nothing happens. Guess the connection was broken for a second at some moment, so all is lost. My roommate's laundry (two tee shirts) is still quite damp even though we had an electric heater on in our room for both the last two nights. I wonder how women in this area of the world ever get their laundry dry before it gets moldy.

*   *   *

Sikkim
Visiting a poor woman in a very poor hut

In the morning we drive back down the long, long road to the plain. It is subtropical rainforest on the way down with many gorgeous wildflowers and orchids. We cross the border into Sikkim very easily since it is another state of India located just west of Nepal. We begin climbing a huge mountain after crossing the Tintse River. We follow the river all the way to the top, the rainforest keeping up with us. Many gorgeous waterfalls splash down on the road. After a picnic lunch we arrive at the second oldest monastery in Sikkim--Pymangantze. Beautiful. Stunning butter sculptures take me back mentally to Tibet. I feel the peace that Buddhism always brings to me even though I can't accept all the dogma and miracles. But each religion is complicated by dogma, certainly not what the founders intended.

We drive back down the mountain a short way to a lovely lodge. The rooms are in delightful separate chalets all facing the third-highest mountain in the world (Kanchenjunga). It reminds me of stopping for lunch on the Silk Road in Pakistan with the snowy mountains just above us.

The hotel beds are very damp. It's as though the monsoons left everything wet. We take our beds apart each night and remake them with as little of the wet part under us as possible.

We continue down the mountain on tight, continuous switchbacks in the morning. Sub-tropical foliage covers the two sides of the roads. Waterfalls pour down at the side. At long last we cross the river, start up the other side, drive across the top of the mountain, then down the other side, switchbacks all the way. Such slow going for hours. The rainforest is all around us. Monkeys are running along the cement guard rail. I open the window to get a close up shot of one. I have to admit I am afraid he will just leap through the window. I know that this is really a possibility since I had a pet monkey one time. I slam the window shut, perhaps just in time, for he looks as though he is truly now ready to jump.

We go north exclusively from this point aiming for the Tibet border. The capital of Sikkim, Gangtok, is the goal for today. It's not as big as Darjeeling. There are buildings all along the main road and other roads above and below. Diarrhea has struck so I stay in the hotel for dinner and eat solely rice.

Jeeps arrive in the morning to take us farther north, always uphill. Glorious waterfalls pour onto the road along the way. Much of the road was washed out during the monsoon season and hundreds of workers are trying to repair it. We have to stop and start frequently as we move along trying to get through the wash-outs. Very slow going. Lunch is at a tiny cafe. Delicious food with the usual Indian custom of many small variety dishes.

After a long slow drive in the afternoon, we reach the small town of Lachang. Our hotel is a rustic lodge with a fireplace in the front room. It is a building with many small floors and hundreds of steps. The kitchen is on the second floor. Kathy's and my room is

353

on the fourth floor.

We gather in the dining room to sample a local alcoholic beverage made from millet and boiling water, drunk from tall wooden cups with straws. As one sips a little, it is customary to keep adding more boiling water to make it last longer. It is really good and very potent. There is a good buffet for dinner but no hot water in our room. It's very cold outside and inside because we are at such high altitude. We have no heater tonight. I'm wearing long underwear, a turtleneck, a sweater, and my rain jacket and rain pants to bed!

In the morning we slowly ply our way north to an area called Yachung, twenty miles south of the Tibetan border. The road ends here, while a footpath continues over the Himalayans. We get out of the jeeps and wander about. The Brits all go down to the braided river which is white from the silt carried down from the glacier. While still in the jeep I noticed a woman up high on the hill on the other side of the road. I saw her walk out of a very poor hut. I climb up and look in her door with my hands outspread in a question. She motions me to enter, bids me sit on an upside down crate, and offers me milk tea in a cracked cup plus some fried treats. The inside of the hut is constructed of wooden boards with cracks between them. The dwelling is tiny with only two shelves and very few utensils plus a table made from a board across a couple crates.

A few quilts lie folded in a corner. I think this is a temporary summer residence and that the people take their horses and yaks down to lower pastures in winter. She indicates her husband is working in the area, perhaps farming but more likely repairing the road.

The woman's horses are very small like Mongolian horses. Two of them, indeed, have the dark line from the mane down the back to the tail which proves them to be true Mongolian. Her husband arrives momentarily in the doorway and we nod our heads in greeting.
When I take leave, I offer to shake hands with her. She responds

by holding her right elbow with her left hand (this means "Thank you" in Mongolian). I do the same. A gratifying, unexpected, thrilling encounter with a woman who is in some way related to Mongolians in far away Mongolia. This experience could not have occurred if I had not been by myself. It shows the benefits of being alone on the hillside. These are the moments that I cherish while I am traveling.

Lady in shack up on mountainside who gave me milk tea

After a long ride down the same muddy, almost impassable road, we arrive back at the lodge. I decide to go out along the road exploring and getting some photos. As I am walking, I hear footsteps

355

behind me. It is a monk in sandals walking fast. But he slows down to walk with me. His English is quite good. He tells me his life story. He and his father and mother lived in Tibet in the small town of Gyantze until he was twelve. His parents decided to attempt to escape from the Chinese. They had one horse to carry their belongings; the family walked all the way across the Himalayas. It took them a week to reach the border. He is fifty-eight now and his parents are dead. He has been a monk since he reached manhood. What a special connection! Again one that would never have happened if I had not been alone! I feel so privileged to have met these people today.

We are on our way at 4 a.m. because we have a very long way to drive on bad roads to the border of Bhutan. Returning to Gangtok we have lunch and exchange our jeeps for our bus with a long ride yet to come along the south shore of the Testse River to Phuenthaling, just over the Bhutanese border.

* * *

Bhutan

The entire next day we drive on slow twisty roads. The king decreed that all buildings built in modern times must adhere to the age-old architecture of the past. As we drive along we see hundreds of houses in the countryside built of stucco with lovely wood- carved details. Often there are painted details on the walls; sometimes these paintings depict penises which apparently confer good fortune on the houses. They are similar to carved stone phalluses seen in other cultures. The beautiful buildings seem to me to be the most obvious and important part of this culture and they are what makes Bhutan a special place to visit.

When we reach Thimpu, Jason says we should purchase a national costume because all citizens must wear them every day and especially to festivals. It takes a while to choose the outfits. Once dressed, our group looks magnificent. Unfortunately, we arrive at the dance festival in the courtyard of the dzong (monastery) only in time to see one long dance. The performers wear huge papier-mache masks over their heads depicting Buddhist spirits. Their dance is similar to those I have seen at festivals in Mongolia. The steps are large and clumsy and extremely repetitive.

Up at 4 a.m. to witness the thangka dropping down on one wall of the dzong courtyard. It is a huge brightly painted piece of silk and is shown only one day a year. People of the city flock to see it and file past slowly, some of them prostrating themselves.

We drive on to the town of Punaka and the gorgeous dzong there, built picturesquely beside the river. The architecture inside and out is of wood with incredible carvings on all the walls. Visiting it is a very special treat.

Now we drive back to the Thimpu dance festival, but arrive there too late for the dances! Frustrating to say the least! So we visit a factory making hand-made paper, then the zoo where we get to see the national animal called a takin. Religious history and mythology describe how the takin came to be. A great lama visited the country in the fifteenth century and the people gathered to witness his magical powers. He first ate an entire goat, then a cow, then stuck the goat's head onto the bones of the cow and created a new animal, a takin, which is very odd and clumsy. Takins migrate to upland pastures in the summer and down to the lowlands in the winter. Hunting them is forbidden. I am so pleased that we get to view one of these unusual animals.

We stay in Paro tonight, having seen the one and only festival dance yesterday! I have a feeling that something may have gone wrong in the planning of this visit to Bhutan causing us to drive back and forth slowly from town to town, thereby missing other dance performances we expected to see.

In the morning some of the group climb a high trail to a tea house. Three of us go with a young guide to see ancient ruins of a castle. We walk up many rustic stone steps, then through a doorway into the roofless courtyard. It is an overcast day and the mist is floating around the area. I am overcome by the "Arthurian" feeling of this castle with its holes for archers to shoot arrows toward enemies. I exclaim to the guide, "This is Arthur!" And he smiles and says, "Yes, it is!" I tell him, "Arthur is my hero" and he says Arthur is his hero as well! He had to memorize an epic poem about Arthur when he was in school. The guides, and presumably many of the young men in Bhutan, go to schools run in the British tradition using British teachers. I feel a great kinship with this guide in a country far from Britain who knows the legends of my hero.

On our way back to town I notice activity in front of a building and ask our guide to stop. We observe three adults working by a fire. They have soaked oat kernels overnight in water. Now one person is frying the kernels in oil in a wok. The other two people take turns pounding the fried kernels with a heavy mallet. The final product looks and tastes like real oat flakes! The people are very friendly. I put stickers on the children's hands and find that the adults want them also!

After lunch we walk up to the Paro Museum built in the shape of a conch shell. It depicts archeological information about ancient peoples who lived here and also displays modern day life. Excellent! We walk down many steps to the Paro dzong which is, of course, built in traditional architecture and extremely beautiful. As we walk down to the road afterwards, we see several homes with painted objects on the walls including a number of penises that resemble plump sausages!

Early in the morning we fly to Kolkata (Calcutta) from the only airport in the country. It was built in the traditional architecture. We are met at the Calcutta airport by a bus for a tour of the city. We drive past Mother Teresa's compound. I remember that my roommate, Sue, from my Tibet trip, spent six weeks working here with extremely ill, indigent people of the city. What an experience that must have been!

People pounding fried oat kernels into oat meal flakes

The bus has no air conditioning and it is unbearably hot. We are turned loose in the city to eat where we want. Then back on the non-air conditioned bus to the airport to catch our plane to Dhaka.

A very special and informative tour! Now I have the long, long flights to the States to endure.

Mongolia Again

Two More Trips

There were several other magnificent trips with Jim: an entire month exploring Australia; another month driving and camping on the North and South Islands of New Zealand; a very soggy week of an Icelandic road trip. But these trips didn't provide exceptional glimpses into peoples' lives or cultures. However, I did return to Mongolia two times, once in 2003 with granddaughter Megan when she turned 16, and again in 2006 (with her sister Brianne, then turning 17, and cousin Cody, then 17). The purpose of these trips was to introduce the teens to the nomadic culture of the country. I wanted them to see this vanishing way of life as it had been lived for thousands of years on the Gobi Desert and the steppes. Therefore I made a pact with the young people to join in the chores of the families we would visit, to "live" the experience, not just "watch" it, so they could tell their children and grandchildren about this ancient culture that will have vanished probably before they are old enough to visit themselves.

Megan's Trip - 2003

When Megan and I disembarked the plane from Ulaan Baater to Dalanzadgad, we were met by a woman guide, Saraa and a driver, Bat, with an ancient Russian jeep. Saraa was about 40 and the mother of two teenage girls. Bat and his wife had a small baby boy. She managed their shop while he was gone. These people quickly became wonderful friends.

I was shocked to see everything green on the desert - due to a very rainy spring, as explained by Saraa and Bat.

In the afternoon of the second day Bat "found" our nomad family because nomads move frequently to provide sufficient pasture for their horses, goats, and sheep. Bat just kept stopping and inquiring of other nomads where the family might be. Once we found them, we were welcomed with the customary airaq drink, which Megan instantly disliked. We gave them our gifts.

The grandfather ground up some juniper root, arranged it in a special dish, and lit it to produce incense. Each of us passed the incense around ourselves three times - sort of a "welcome" ceremony - and then passed it on to the next person.

The family consisted of two grandparents, their grown daughter and her husband and their two year-old son, their grown son, plus a hired hand about 15 years old. They were living in a large ger with a small dairy ger next door.

We helped separate the sheep from the goats. Meg and I learned to milk the mother goats and watched the daughter milk the mares. The grandmother readied the goats' milk for soup by adding water to it and simmering it on the stove in the middle of the room. Meg began grinding dried goats' meat with a mortar and pestle while Saraa and I broke up larger pieces of meat with our fingers. The meat was eventually added to the soup to soften it enough to chew.

Grandfather lighting juniper as incense

Megan began churning the mares' milk which has to be stirred 200 times every hour while it is fermenting to turn into airaq.

The daughter mixed flour and water to make pastry which she eventually rolled out and cut into narrow strips for noodles for the soup. Then she pulled out a well-used Chinese Checkers board and made it clear that she expected Megan to be her opponent. Meg actually played rather well against her formidable opponent who was obviously extremely pleased to have someone new to challenge. Eventually the girl executed some unconventional maneuvers which Meg, Saraa, and I declared unfair; she was not above cheating if she could get away with it. Then she produced an ancient chess board, set up the pieces, and motioned Meg to play against her. Megan played alright but the other girl was a "pro". She played expertly and bested Meg very quickly three times running. But the fourth time Megan pulled herself together and actually won to the great dismay of the girl.

Megan churning airaq

Finally about 8 p.m. the grandfather declared it cool enough to ride horses. Saraa, Meg, and I received saddled horses. Their saddles were western style. Mine was a wooden Mongolian saddle. I had to tie my heavy jacket between my legs to avoid bruising my thighs. We set out across the desert with the grandfather. The desert was green with grass and many wildflowers. It wasn't long before we had ridden so far out that we could no longer see the gers. It was just wide open space in every direction.

We returned from our ride about 10 p.m. The sun was still up. A rug had been pulled outside so everyone could enjoy the coolness of the evening while enjoying goat's milk soup.

The daughter set up her dishwashing bowl on a low "mongolian" table. She washed with cold water and no soap while Meg dried.

Darkness fell about 11 p.m. and we all gathered inside the ger. We sat in a rough circle and played the game known world-wide which we call "rock, paper, scissors". Two people sitting next to each other played; when one missed he or she had to drink a bowl of airaq and then sing the first verse of a song. When the Mongolians sang a verse, all the rest would join in for the remainder of the song with their beautiful voices and magnificent harmony. Megan and I worked hard to come up with inspiring songs in English. The grandfather ceaselessly teased Megan and the hired boy without mercy, promoting a "fictional" romance. At about 2 a.m. it was time to sleep. Saraa, Bat, Megan and I slept in the large ger; all the others somehow crammed into the kitchen ger.

In the morning there was still much bantering about Meg and the hired boy's supposed romance.

The grandmother showed us how she distilled airaq into vodka.

Bat led us out to the family well where first the horses drank from the wooden trough, followed by the goats and sheep.

The traditional ceremony occured where the hosts dress the guests in traditional costumes for picture-taking. The grandfather brought out his bottle of vodka which we passed around for a farewell drink.

We prepared to leave. The family had plans to drive into Dalanzadgad in their truck to purchase staples.

Once we were in the jeep, Meg declared we should return and continue the "charade", saying she had decided to marry the boy and had called her parents who had agreed to come for the wedding in two months. In the meantime Meg and the boy would buy their supplies to build their own ger which would be completed in time for the wedding! The four of us laughed and laughed and continued to embellish the story. Well, we did turn around and returned to the ger. The "family" had gone, leaving the two oldest sons in charge. They were surprised to see us, obviously; but even more amazed to hear our story. They just didn't know what to say, but enjoyed the joke once they learned the truth. It was great fun to have gotten to know our family "so well" in such a short period.

Later that day we visited a camel breeder's family. They had a tiny "perfect" ger on display, made by the teenage son. Meg bought it - to everyone's delight.

We rode camels on the desert beside high dunes. The twelve year-old daughter rode with us. She often participated in camel-riding" events, somewhat similar to our rodeos.

Two days later, while riding in the jeep, it began to rain hard, and then harder. It was a deluge. We were headed to a remote ger camp near a waterfall much farther west than Bat had ever been. He crossed a swollen stream with the jeep. As we emerged on the other side, it was immediately apparent that we were bogged in the mud. Bat unloaded his shovel from the roof and started to work on the problem. But he could make no headway. Men from a nearby ger came out to help. Soon more neighbors arrived, one with a long board which I thought held some promise. Eventually a neighbor leaped on his horse and rode 10 kilometers to where someone had a tractor. As the rain continued, children from the ger invited us inside. The mother was making soup and offered us each a bowl before we left.

Bogged

In the meantime a large truck arrived and attempted to pull out the jeep. He got stuck, but eventually another truck came by and pulled him out. The tractor arrived at last and soon our jeep was free of the mud.

By this time it was late in the day and still pouring. We drove for a long time beside a river which vehicles were still crossing successfully.

Night fell early because it was such a rainy day. Bat didn't know how to find the path to the camp because there were so many tracks that could be followed. He turned around and around a number of times using the headlights to illuminate the surrounding area. We would stop now and then beside an isolated ger where we could hear the occupants snoring but could not awaken them.

Meg was convinced that we would have to spend the night in the jeep. She reached into the back, managed to pull out her long underwear from her bag. She pulled it on in the dark, so she would be prepared for the long, cold hours ahead. Bat continued swinging the jeep in circles, casting the headlights around, hoping to find a trail. At last the lights fell on three bedraggled figures: a sodden young man on foot, and a second on a horse. They had just dragged themselves out of the now-raging river. A brief conversation between Bat and one man revealed that the men had crossed the river on horseback in the morning to visit a friend who owned the horse that had won the race at Naadam over a week earlier. Custom demands "touching" the winning horse to obtain good luck; then remaining to drink vodka for several hours afterward. In this case, while they were celebrating the good fortune of the horse's owner, the river had continued to rise precipitously. The horsemen started back across very late in the evening. The rushing water carried one horse and rider downstream. The rider lost his "seat" on his horse; the animal was carried away on the current, leaving behind the swimming rider. The two men had spent an unknown amount of time searching for the animal to no avail. They were giving up at the moment Bat's headlights caught them.

Bat talked to the men and found that they knew where the camp was. I suggested to Megan that we would have to find room in the vehicle for one of the drunken, soaking wet men. She had already figured this out, as had Saraa. The man on foot slid into the back seat between Megan and Saraa.

We knew the rider was drunk, but perhaps the horse had also "imbided"? He wobbled from side to side on the path, eventually falling sideways on top of the rider. Both were finally righted and continued to lead us haphazardly to the ger camp where we arrived at 1:30 a.m. This is the "drunken horsemen" episode of our trip which Meg and I delight in telling our friends.

Drunken horsemen on the Gobi Desert

In the morning, after reviewing an "unremarkable" waterfall (the reason for this expedition), we drove back along the river where many vehicles were stranded and partly filled with water. The drivers had not realized how deep the water had become during the night.

At the end of our trip Bat, Saraa, Megan, and I had a farewell dinner at our last ger camp. Saraa ordered shots of vodka for each of us.

Brianne's and Cody's Trip - 2006

Three years later, in 2006, I took Megan's sister Brianne (16) and her cousin Cody (17) to Mongolia in order that they too could learn about nomadic life.

This time Saraa met us as we arrived in Ulaan Baatar and flew with us (after the Naadam ceremonies) to Dalanzadgad. Bat was there waiting for us, this time with an old Russian van just like the one I rode in on my first trip to Mongolia.

As we started out driving to the Yol Valley it was very obvious to me that the desert was exceptionally dry, much drier than on my first trip, and certainly much drier than three years ago. Bat explained that the desert had not gotten spring rains this year, so the plants and grass that were there on my first two trips were totally missing this time. Horses, goats, and sheep that we passed were literally starving; they were nothing but bones. Very pathetic to see.

We walked out toward the end of the Yol Valley and were surprised to see a great amount of ice over the narrow river. It was a marvelous adventure to climb down to lower ice levels where there were countless ice caves and up on narrow ice bridges above them.

The next day we stopped at some ancient rock petroglyphs and rock circles on the ground which indicated ancient simple grave sites. After several more hours of driving across the sand, Bat began asking herders about the "whereabouts" of our family. We found them living in what last time was the kitchen ger. The horses had been recently sent away along with others in the area, entrusted to a herder who would lead them north to the steppes where there would be sufficient grass for them. The family still had large numbers of sheep and goats, but found it necessary to move every three days to ensure sufficient grass for them. Consequently, the family had left their large ger at their wintering area far to the east and were just moving the smaller ger.

We were happily welcomed by the family. The daughter and her husband now had an eighteen-month-old baby girl in addition to their boy who would be attending school in the fall in Dalan-zadgad. They were living in their own new ger close by. The grandmother and the boy would live in an apartment in the city during the school year.

Cody, Brianne, and Saraa in an "ice cave"

After our welcome drink of airaq which Cody enjoyed but Brianne disliked, the grandfather passed his snuff bottle around. Saraa, Brianne and I wiped a small amount off the stopper onto our arm; the grandfather, Cody, and Bat sniffed the stopper. This was instead of the juniper root burning ceremony of the last visit.

It was fun to exchange news with the family. The grandfather inquired about Megan. He got out the photos we had sent them via Bat from the last visit. He laughed again at the humorous story of Megan and the hired boy. It was pleasant to reminisce with them

371

and Saraa and Bat. Now to me, more than ever, we all seemed like "family". Everyone, including Cody, enjoyed passing the little girl around and playing with her. Cody took the boy outside along with Hot Wheels cars we had brought him and showed him how to make "roads" in the sand, including some precipitous "drop-offs". The boy was quite impressed with the possibilities Cody demonstrated.

The grandfather realized as soon as we arrived that there was not enough room for his guests to sleep in the small ger with the family. He was busy almost immediately repairing an ancient two-person tent for Bri, Cody, and I to sleep in. Bat and Saraa decided they would sleep in the van. We spent quite some time picking up small desert stones to make a suitable space for the tent.

The family now owned a small motorcycle. Cody and Brianne eventually drove it themselves. I was not particularly successful, nor was Saraa. Then Bat decided we would all take turns driving the van, since the possibility of an accident was slight in this open desert. It proved a most enjoyable experience for all.

Brianne learned to grind dried goat meat preparatory to making goat milk soup. The daughter prepared the noodle dough and sliced it into strips. It was apparent to me that the grandmother was leaving most of the work to her daughter, because arthritis required her to assume mostly a sedentary position.

Brianne and the daughter played a few games of chess. Brianne happily acquitted herself well.

Cody and the son-in-law drove out on the motorcycle in the gathering dusk to bring in the goats, which we milked when they arrived. The grandfather explained that his goats were of prize-winning stock. He regarded his stud as an extremely valuable animal. He explained that the soft, silky under-fur was what expensive cashmere wool was made of. The owner simply combed the goat with a very fine comb. The cashmere brought in a sizable income to the family as did the sheep wool. The grandfather said he listened to his radio each morning to learn what price wool was selling for. When he deemed the price right, he would take the wool to market.

Bri's, Cody's and my night in the tiny tent was not "the best", nor, I feel sure, was Bat's or Saraa's. But the sunset as we prepared for bed was worth it all.

In the morning, of course, the family dressed us up in the traditional national costumes for photos. As we prepared to leave, the family began to pack up to move to new pasture. What a job!

We drove toward high sand dunes to the west and arrived at our new ger camp for lunch. Then we drove to a camel herder's family. They owned many camels including several babies and had enough pasture for all.

Camel safari

Brianne had requested an overnight camel safari. We mounted our camels and left for our ride along the valley below the dunes. We rode several hours until the herder decided we had reached the point where we would spend the night. Bat had remained behind to locate tents to rent and pick up our evening meal at the ger camp. He arrived soon and we ate dinner and enjoyed a wonderful sunset before setting up the tents.

No one had ever seen tents quite like these. It must have taken at least an hour to set them up after many false starts. By this time darkness had fallen and we were doing the last bit by the flashlight.

Finally it was time to gather on the oilcloth to sing. Our host produced a bottle of vodka from the folds of his dell. Saraa brought out her stash of plastic glasses. She, Bat, and the herder sang beautiful Mongolian songs. The singing continued; the vodka soon was gone.

In the morning we rode back to the herder's ger. His little grandson wore his hair long in pigtails. The herder explained that his son (the boy's father) had been killed when riding his motorcycle at night. The child had been about one year old at the time. The mother departed after this tragedy, leaving the grandparents to raise him. In another week the boy would celebrate his fourth birthday with a ceremony to cut off his long hair.

After lunch at the ger camp, Saraa, Bri, Cody, and I visited the tall dunes. A narrow stream inhabited by frogs ran along the bottom. Bri managed the difficult climb to the top of the dunes with Saraa.

Bat had explored the whereabouts of the young man who had sold Megan the small model of a ger. After much driving back and forth on terrible paths (roads), we caught up with the young man's parents. They explained that he was attending college in Dalanzadgad but would return that evening and have two models ready for purchase in the morning.

374

Brianne said she wanted to buy a dell belonging to the mother. Once the bargain was struck Cody said he also wanted to purchase a dell. The mother found a rust-colored dell belonging to the father who started the bidding at $200! I am a clever bargainer; eventually Cody bought it for $50. the father was very pleased that Cody bought it and now regarded him as his own son.

On our way north the next morning we stopped to observe a ger being assembled at a ger camp. We jumped out and joined in the work. The ger was completed in forty five minutes. Continuing north, we visited the area where dinosaur eggs were partially imbedded in the rock walls along a trail leading down into a canyon. And we investigated Bat's "finds", some of which were fragments of rocks while others were bits of bones. He showed us how to tell the difference between rocks and bones; bone will stick to one's lips.

Mandatory three circles around an ovoe

A bit of car trouble resulted in Bat's spending at least an hour under the vehicle in the desert heat. We listened to music from his tape player and Saraa danced the waltz with each of us.

Several hours later we were entering the area of the steppes where we visited a herder's ger. Soon we were off with him on his horses riding through a delightful rocky area.

Nearby was a large "preserve" for the ancient breed of Przhevalsky's Horse native to Mongolia. I had seen them in Uzbekistan but not up close like we were able to do here.

We celebrated our farewell dinner at the ger camp. It was sad to think of leaving our friends in the morning in Ulaan Baatar just before the three days of the Naadam ceremonies.

Brianne returned home to St. Louis, and Cody and I arrived together at the Denver airport. Cody took a minute to put on his dell and Mongolian hat, then walked to the exit area where people were waiting. I walked far behind him. It took his father several seconds to recognize that it was Cody!

My third trip to Mongolia had been a complete success. Now I am awaiting the moment several years in the future when I hope to take Conor (Megan and Brianne's brother) and their now small cousin Kayla to Mongolia to experience the marvelous culture there.

Afterword

I have tried to share experiences that expanded my way of think-ing, leading to a more spiritual alignment with the world.

I attempted to show how easy it is to simply, "ride your horse in the direction it's going".

But this only works when and if one can "separate" oneself from other people and be essentially "alone", even when traveling with a group. Being separate enables me to be in touch with my inner self and is the key to feeling "the magic of the moment".

In a way, it is akin to meditating: allowing "something to happen" that you otherwise might not be aware of.

If you have the opportunity to travel far afield, I wish for you many magical, beautiful insights as you slowly ride along your trail.

Joyce Rasbach
October 2008

Printed in the United States
145749LV00001B/4/P